To ~~Connie~~ Carolyn

Thank you for helping
me fight against Domestic
violence

**White Room Publishing Company**
Cjohnson406@oh.rr.com

**Distributor: BookMasters.Inc.**
**www.bookmasters.com**
**Sales and Atlas Books**
30 Amberwood Parkway.
P.O. Box 2139
Ashland, OH 44805
Phone: 1-800-537-6727
Fax: 1-419-281-0200
**Manufacturing**
30 Amberwood Parkway.
P.O. Box 2139
Ashland, OH 44805
Phone: 1-800-537-6727
Fax: 1-419-281-0200
**Distribution Center**
30 Amberwood Parkway
Ashland, OH 44805
Phone: 419-281-1802
Fax: 419-281-6883
**Atlas Books**
1-800-247-6553
www.Atlasbooks.com

Front cover painted by **Wayne Reitz**

**NOTE: People, Places, Names and circumstances were changed and created in order to protect the innocent in my book.**

The young lady with professional skills, ingenious capabilities, and her expertise in computer technology that helped me put this book together was **Mrs. Halle Magpoc-Dawson.**

*This Book*
*Is*
*Dedicated*
*To*

# Mrs. Connie Sutter

# TABLE OF CONTENTS

# ACKNOWLEDGEMENTS

"First giving Honor and Glory to God the Father,
To our Lord Jesus Christ, and the Holy Spirit."

A book like The White Room or a life for that matter is difficult to achieve or experience without the consideration, assistance, friendship, and of course the caring love of many people. I want to thank publicly, therefore, the people who have made things bearable and wondrous in my world. Thank you, to my Mother & Father whom I love dearly, Shirley Desso, Ralph Moss, Herman White, Mr. and Mrs. James Adams, Shenetta L. Johnson, Lemeul K. Johnson, Cameale K. Salas, Markell N. Merritt, Carol King, Martha Gomez, Brenda Myles, Joe and Bertha Rogers, Janna Nelson, Valerie and Chris St. James.

Professionally, through my many trials and difficulties there have been those individuals who have made the kind of difference in life that allows one to succeed. I greet you and wish the world to understand the power of your feelings, professionalism, and skills and lastly, the beauty of your mentoring. Thank you; Linda J. Ryan, and most of all Rhonda Armstrong and Antoinette Troy.

And, this sort of autobiography, with the depth of pain and terror I've lived through can be redeemed only, I feel, by reaching out to others in similar circumstances. Thank you for your interest! The greater effort of this book then, the motivation and push from The Lord, has been to help heal all those in pain. May you rise up in Jesus Christ and live!

With deepest gratitude and sincerity,

Cynthia K. Johnson

2002 A.D.

# Untitled

By Lemuel Kyame Johnson

—When I am hurt
I escape
to this room.
No mirrors,
'cause bruises are all
that I see.
No windows,
'cause I don't want
them to see me.
—When I am sad
I escape
to this room.
The bare white
walls are a canvas
as my imagination
pictures a mirror of
happiness.
—When I am afraid
I escape
to this room.
The door is bolted
shut to hold back
the ones who scare me.
<u>protected</u>
There are times
that I wish I
wasn't alone.
But this room is
made for me.
Inside this room
I can picture
a future of happiness.
— Inside my mind
the bruises
<u>on my body</u>
are no longer there.
And away from harm
<u>my soul</u> stays protected

# The White Room
### By
## Cynthia K. Johnson

# Part One

## Chapter One

The earliest memories of my childhood are the best I can remember. I recall standing in front of Mom's Christmas tree and watching her favorite, beautiful bubble lights. Each bulb had water running through it, and glowed in an array of striking colors. An abundance of gifts wrapped in flashy Christmas paper rose high under the tree. Icicles were strung softly over the limbs, one by one, to make each branch perfect. My mother had a knack for putting together the most incredible trees. Only the window displays at Macy's Department Store in New York City during Christmas could compare. Every year she would change or add to our Christmas tree to make it lovelier than the previous season's. The house was always decorated like a fairyland with tinsel, bells, and glowing bulbs.

On Christmas Eve, my sisters, Linda and Farrar, my brother Chuck, and I were allowed to open one gift. Which we knew, was always a pair of brand new pajamas for each of us. Mom always wanted to make sure that we looked like rich kids in the pictures that she took of us tearing open our presents on Christmas morning. I can still smell the aroma from Mom's kitchen on Christmas Day. Fresh-baked ham and turkey complimented by homemade dressing, collard greens, and hot-water cornbread and last but certainly not least, those wondrous homemade pies. Mom even took time to prepare for us home-baked cookies in the shape of Christmas characters; Santa, snowmen, and even iced reindeer! She would spend hours in the kitchen cooking and listening to her Christmas music. Every so often, she would sing a note or two of "Silent Night" or "We Three Kings." I

1

still find myself smiling when I think about how special she made Christmas for all of us.

Mom suffered from Multiple Personality Disorder (MPD), so life was certainly not like a Christmas fantasyland all the time. Her condition was caused by something traumatic happening to her when she was a child. I never learned the exact circumstances involved, but her five distinct personalities individually would appear whenever she wanted to please herself or anyone around her. Only later in life would a psychiatrist diagnose her condition. All of her personalities would play very dominant roles in our lives. I chose distinct names for each of them. They were: Anna, Anna Mae, Mae, Miss White, and the one that I wished never existed, Miss Meany. Each of the five personalities called each of us children by a different name. I thought my mother was being creative calling us by other names, until I realized that this was to be the way I'd identify each individual personality when it appeared.

My Afro-American mother was born when her biological mother was only 12. She was too young to raise her, so she abandoned her in a big-handled wicker basket on the doorstep of a prominent Black Christian couple, landowners during the 1920's. This was a good thing for my mother, since my grandmother treated her cruelly, being very mentally abusive.

Anna Mae's personality developed from her adoptive mother, who was a very loving, Christian woman. She was a gentle and loving mother, but when it came to living righteously, she was extremely stern. She always had to remind her daughter that she was a sinner and needed to get her life together. That affected Anna Mae quite a bit. The personality of Anna Mae became extremely suicidal, with

2

low self-esteem. Anna Mae was very religious and felt that everything she did was sinful. Her stepfather was constantly pushing her to get an education and go to college. She tried very hard to live up to their expectations, but the flaws that all mankind possess kept getting in the way.

The good times were few, but when Mom's "Anna" personality would come out, everything seemed to be the way I thought a family life should be. Anna was the wife of my father, Charlie, and the mother of the four of us. Anna was very kind and motherly to us and a good wife to my father, proving daily that caring for her family was always her utmost concern. Cooking and cleaning were always on her agenda. Anna never gossiped about other people and was always trying to help someone. She was a very good mother. When Anna would see that anyone in her family desperately needed physical or mental nurturing, she would almost magically appear to help them. These are the best memories I have of a life with my real mother. My father was a very gentle and soft-spoken man with a very kind heart. He too was Afro-American. He was very laid-back, loved his children dearly, and was extremely intelligent and wise. Daddy was once a boxer, and during the times described in this book, served as an enlisted man in the U.S. Air Force, proudly defending his country with devotion. Dad was of light-complexion, 5'6", and very strong. He never liked to argue, fight, or fuss. Daddy's love and respect for other human beings was amazing. I love him dearly and consider him my mentor. God gave him the patience of Job.

# Chapter 2

I was born in Texas on March 28, 1954 at 12:13 A.M. weighing 6 lbs. 11 ounces. As a baby, I appeared Caucasian having a very light complexion and blonde hair. My grandmother, along with several other people, didn't think that I was a black baby. My grandmother believed that my mother had been playing around behind my father's back. People on the street stared at my mother thinking she was my nanny. My light complexion and features were passed on from my grandfather, who was of German descent. My parents often commented on how I was a "very beautiful or pretty girl." Beautiful and pretty were two words eventually I would grow to hate.

My parents told me that at birth I had my days and nights confused. I would sleep well during the day, but I was wide-awake during the night. Daddy would put me in a bassinet by his bedside and with one leg dangling out of the bed, would rock me to sleep with the lamp glowing brightly above my head. This of course was supposed to fool me into thinking I was sleeping in the daylight. As always, Daddy's creativity and inventions would prove to be successful. He was very good at sitting back to evaluate a situation in order to carefully accomplish his goal.

I was the second of four children. My brother Chuck was the oldest of my siblings. He often would play jokes on my sisters and me. He often patterned himself after Bugs Bunny, so you never knew what he was up to next. Linda was the third child. She was very quiet and sneaky and loved cats. We often played together. The youngest was Farrah, who was the most favored, "a spoiled brat." I often kept Farrah by my side. Somehow I managed to play with my friends and to keep up with my baby sister at the same time.

4

My sisters and brother called me, "Kaye-Kaye" (from my middle name, Kaye).

I don't remember much about living in Texas because I was just a small child, but I do remember our family being very happy. My days as a child were spent running outside and playing with my brother and sister. (Farrah had not yet been born.) We lived in a nice neighborhood, in the suburbs, in a 3-bedroom home. Mom would make sure that Dad would provide us with the best that life could afford. A comfortable home with TV, all the appliances, and a new Ford parked outside. Mom had all the conveniences and worked as a window dresser in nearby boutiques, fashionable department stores.

One day Daddy came home and told Mom he had an overseas assignment. Mom was pregnant with my baby sister Farrah and started screaming. We ran into the kitchen and she said, "We're going to Japan!" We were very excited. "Miss White," Mom's third personality, had always wanted to go overseas. Miss White's personality was very aloof. She wished that she had stayed single and never wanted anything to do with a husband or children. Oh boy, did she remind us of this constantly! She was a mystical woman to me. She was always classy, well dressed, and groomed as she headed out the door to lead her free and independent life. She often socialized with the Wives Club at the base and this was what came naturally for her. When my mother was eight or nine years old, she would visit her biological mother. She would often watch from the kitchen while her mother would prepare very extravagant dinners for Dr. Hymen, a wealthy brain surgeon and his wife, who employed her. Although they were millionaires, they would treat my grandmother as though she were a part of their family. They would take my grandmother all over the world as they traveled. There were some places they would visit in England where my grandmother would not be allowed entry because she was a servant, but the doctor and his wife would insist that she be treated as an equal. When visiting England, she sat among servants of the Queen.

Often the doctor and his wife would throw elegant dinner parties. My mother (Miss White) loved to watch from the sidelines as the guests entered their home wearing elegant gowns. She would go onto the porch and imitate them. This is where Miss White acquired grace and poise was that befitting a Queen. Unfortunately at the end of her fantasy she had to return home to her estranged family.

Soon after learning that we would be relocating to Japan, the Air Force packed up our belongings. We began a new adventure. I could see this was going to take some time to get used. This was as foreign to us as it could get. My parents seemed to naturally adjust to driving on the other side of the street, but to me, it was still the wrong side. We soon grew very comfortable in our surroundings and at age four I became fluent in Japanese. We lived there for 4 years. When the time came to relocate again, Anna Mae did not want to leave. She had adjusted so well that she also could speak a little Japanese, and she got along well with the Japanese people. Mae loved to play the slot machines. Miss White loved having the maids wait on her and the Japanese people treated her in a queenly manner. We all liked it there and wished that someday we could return. However, our time was up and we had to return to the States. This time our orders stated: "Relocation to California."

We soon settled into our nice duplex on the base. It took some time to become adjusted to living back in the United States--driving on the right side of the street. Of course, it didn't take much time at all for my brother to become mischievous. My sisters and I really didn't mind his pranks at first because we were having fun. You name it! We pretty much tried it. I recall a time when he convinced us to jump from the roof of the house holding an opened umbrella to imitate Mary Poppins. The house wasn't very high, being a one-story building, but we climbed up to the roof, jumped and found ourselves lying on the ground with collapsed umbrellas and sore butts. This was only the beginning of our brother's daily stunts. Eventually he became more creative and talked us into swinging from the same roof with a rope tied to a tree. Like Tarzan, we were supposed to swing from a tree and land on a chair on the other side. Chuck measured the rope too long and we found ourselves face down on the ground.

On one of Chuck's more ingenious days, my sister and I glanced up from playing with dolls to see him in the nearby field enticing a bull with a red cape. I didn't really think the bull was going to run after him. That was, until I noticed the bull digging his hooves into the ground and bowing his massive head, looking most upset. The next thing I saw was this skinny boy yelling and running in our direction. All I could hear was "Open the door!" My sister and I were so frightened we opened the sliding glass porch door and ran inside, shutting it behind us. My brother had no other choice but to climb a wall that partially surrounded our back porch. When the bull saw the reflection of himself in the glass, he stopped rather than charge through the glass door. Boy, was that a close call!

Being a creative person, my brother developed a way to make a homemade, Slip and Slide®. He accomplished this by using a small ditch that ran beside the house with a small pond of water at the end. I really believed in this exploit, yet Chuck was up to no good as usual. My sisters and I were so excited as we slipped into our bathing suits and ran outside to have fun on my brother's new creation. He instructed us to run together holding hands. He yelled, "On your mark! Get set! <u>Go</u>!" We set off running and slid into the pool of water, only to find ourselves greeted by five or six large, water snakes! Chuck and his conniving friend, Stanley, had so graciously caught and placed the snakes in the water earlier that day. Do you think we were scared? Scared did not describe the look in our eyes, as we stood up yelling, screaming and ran away shaking in fear. My brother and Stanley lay on the grass, crying in laughter.

These stories are never ending and I could go on forever. I've been asked a million times, "Why were you so gullible?" My only explanation was that we were Chuck's baby sisters and he had a way of convincing a snake out of its skin. He could convince a bear that honey wasn't its favorite food. Trust me when I say this, my brother watching Bugs Bunny all the time, taught him all about pulling stunts. My brother was <u>good</u> and we were easy to fool.

# Chapter 3

Soon a family by the name of Mr. And Mrs. Jones moved in next door. They had three small children. They asked my parents if I could baby-sit for them, but my father objected. He felt that 9 years old was a bit too young for me to start working. Mae convinced him otherwise. And besides, I liked the idea of earning some spending money. Our families became very close, and their children loved having me around.

One sunny afternoon, while playing outside in the yard with my sister Linda and the other neighborhood children, Mr. Jones called me over to the white picket fence that he was mending. Mr. Jones was in his 30's, tall, of medium build, maybe 170 pounds. It's tough to explain, but his attitude was different towards me than before. He was friendlier. It was a hot day and he was sweating while working in the 90° California heat. He was drinking what I assumed to be beer and he asked me if I could baby-sit for him. I told him I had to call and ask my mom, who was out with her friends at the time. When I returned to the white fence after talking to Mae, I assured him that it was all right for me to baby-sit. He asked me if I could "arrive early" so that he could give me some instructions about what to feed the children and when to put them to bed. I agreed, and went off to play for an hour with the other kids.

Soon Mr. Jones came calling for me. His kids and I jumped up and joyfully ran into the house. We were so happy that I would be watching them that evening. When we arrived, I expected him to be dressed for work, but he wasn't. He was still wearing an undershirt and raggedy yard shorts. I was so concerned with playing and having fun, that I didn't pay much attention. As soon as we entered the house, Mr. Jones yelled at his three children to leave. He told them to stay outside and play, and not to come back to the door because he had to talk to me. I began to feel ill at ease, thinking I had done something wrong. He asked me to go back to his bedroom. I had no idea why he wanted me to go there or what he wanted to talk to me about. I entered the bedroom and he locked the door. He asked me to sit down on his unmade bed, but I was becoming scared and simply stood next to it. Looking at me with a smile, he said "Don't be nervous, I won't hurt you. "He said he wanted to teach me the facts of life, since he noticed how I was playing with the little boys in the neighborhood. Of course, I pleaded with him. I didn't want to learn about the facts of life from him, my Daddy would explain that stuff to me. I desperately wanted to go back outside, and allow him to dress for work.

He was starting to get upset with me and said, "What I have to teach you is definitely different from what your parents will teach you." Again I exclaimed, "I don't want you to. I just want to go outside and play." He then picked me up and sat me on the floral bedspread next to him. The room was colorful with orange, green and yellow décor. Whining, I pleaded with him to please let me go outside. He acted as though he didn't hear me, stood up, went into the bathroom and shut the door. I tried to climb up onto his bureau and unlatch the door, but unfortunately, I was not tall enough. I climbed up on his bed and started knocking on the window. I was trying to get the attention of my sister and friends playing in the yard. I was shaking in fear and started to cry. When the children saw me, they thought I was playing around and began to laugh and point at me. They were teasing and making fun of the way I was acting. I began to cry even harder. I kept turning around to see if Mr. Jones had heard me and re-entered the room. I started to yell a little louder, but he heard me, and came out of the bathroom with only a white towel around his waist.

He climbed onto the bed and grabbed me away from the window. He pulled me close to him and as he tried to kiss me I began hitting him. I could smell the stench of beer stagnating his foul breath. Again, I pleaded with him to please let me go back outside. I tried to push his chest away but my tiny hands and arms were no match against his powerful grip. I tried so hard to keep him off of me but it was to no avail. He kept pulling me closer and closer to him as he tried to kiss me. His face seemed so big and heavy as I tried to push it away. Nothing seemed to work. He then reached down and removed my shorts and underwear. His body smelled of sweat. I felt so ashamed, although I knew I hadn't done anything wrong. I remember it was so hard for me to breathe as he laid his large, body on top of mine. As I started to scream, he covered my mouth with his large hand. I felt pressure and then an explosion of pain.

I passed out and the next thing I knew, I was in a white room. The room was white all over and well lit but had no windows or doors. I was sitting alone, naked, and clutching my favorite stuffed monkey. I cried out, "Mama and Daddy!" The room was warm and comfortable with no way in or out. I knew that no one could harm me here, not even Mr. Jones. I felt so safe in this beautiful white room that I didn't want to leave for fear that there was someone lurking outside it. There was such serenity, peace, and quiet. It was a room of purity and tranquility. I played with my stuffed monkey for some time, and then I heard the sounds of my friends playing outside the window. "Kaye-Kaye!" They were calling for me to come out to play. I set my stuffed monkey down by my side. Suddenly I was outside my white room, lying in Mr. Jones's bed.

When I looked around, there was no one in the room. I could hear Mr. Jones in the shower; water and more water. The door to the bedroom was now open, unlocked. I slowly rose using both hands only to see that I was lying in a small pool of blood. The lower part of my body felt as though I had been sawed in half. "Am I dying?" I said to myself. I started to cry very softly so that Mr. Jones wouldn't hear me and once again chase after me. I wasn't sure if I could move or not, but slowly I slid down from the bed. I sneaked out the back door to avoid the children playing outside. I didn't want them to see me that way. They would probably ask me too many questions that I was unable to answer. When I reached the house, I slowly walked straightaway to the bathroom and sat on the toilet. Blood colored the water in the bowl. Linda walked into the bathroom without knocking. "What happened? Mr. Jones is looking for you." I told her to tell Mr. Jones that I was going to tell my parents that he had raped me. Being so young, I wasn't even sure if what he did was rape, but I remember remnants of a vague description my mother had told me.

From the way I was bleeding, I knew I was going to have to tell someone. I pulled off my clothes and handed them to Linda to wash for me. I was afraid that Anna Mae might see the bloodstained clothing. Anna Mae had already informed my sister and I that if anyone ever raped any of her children she would kill herself. My mother was so serious, and I was pretty sure that what Mr. Jones did, had to be rape. I didn't want to take the chance of losing my mother. I knew I should keep it from her.

Suddenly, a loud pounding noise came from the front door. I told my sister that if Mr. Jones was the one knocking, to answer the door and tell him I was gone. I quickly slipped on my clothes and hobbled out the back door. I tried running but I was in too much pain. I went door to door in the neighborhood, pounding on doors. Finally I arrived at a house where a woman stood wearing some sort of strange head covering; it was black and looked like a hood a nun would wear. I pled for this oddly dressed woman to open the door and let me in. She was young and beautiful and showed me to her study. She quietly and gently offered me something to drink, but I politely said, "No, thank you."

I felt embarrassed but I asked her if she could give me some advice for my friend. I went on to tell her that "my friend" had been raped and was bleeding badly. I asked her if she thought my friend might die. I explained in detail what "my friend" had gone through. She kindly told me that my "friend" should tell her mother and seek medical care. Explaining to her why my friend's mother should never be told, and that my friend didn't want to lose her mother, I could see that the lady looked puzzled. She warned, "Your friend must tell someone! "At that moment, there came another loud knock at the door. It was Mr. Jones! He was looking for me! When asked if I was there, the lady replied, "Yes." She came back to the study and I told the lady to let him know that I would be right there to baby-sit for him. He agreed and left. I thanked the woman and summoned up the courage to walk back down the hill to Mr. Jones's house. As I walked down a few houses, I saw him drive away. I really didn't want to go back to his house, but I could not leave his children alone. Feeling that I was not myself, I fed the children and put them to bed early. I decided to practice the speech that I would give Mrs. Jones when she returned. She had to know what happened.

I felt very nervous by the time Mrs. Jones arrived, but I asked if I could speak with her. She looked at me as if she were apprehensive, but said, "Yes, sure." I first pleaded with her not to tell my mother; but she said that would depend on what I wanted to talk about. No sooner than that, Mr. Jones walked through the door. Normally he would not return home at this hour, so this was totally unexpected. I immediately stood up and left without saying another word. I left in such a rush that the money she had paid me remained on the table. She was so bewildered by my behavior, that she followed me home. She asked my mother if something was troubling me, explaining that she noticed how upset I had been that evening. Anna Mae called me to the front door with Mrs. Jones and questioned my behavior. I had to lie and tell her that the children were just not listening to me when I baby-sat. Mrs. Jones accepted my explanation and told me she would speak with the children the next day.

The days that followed were so depressing. I finally stopped bleeding and I just wanted to forget that this ever happened to me. My evenings were filled with nightmares. I was attacked over and over again. I broke in cold sweats, and cried myself back to sleep. I wished Anna knew, so she could help me through the trying times. I wanted to be a child again but I couldn't. Mr. Jones had taken my innocence away from me that awful day. No longer did I act like a nine-year-old child. I felt only like an empty shell of my past being. I still played with the neighborhood children, but it wasn't the same carefree feeling I used to have. I was a stranger even to myself. "Where did Cynthia go?" I'd ask myself. "Did I leave myself in the White Room?"

I began acting differently. I started doing mean and cruel things to the children in the neighborhood. I would deliberately beat them up. In hindsight I guess that I was taking out all my aggressions on them because of what Mr. Jones did to me.

One day while sitting in my room playing dolls with my sister Linda, I started acting out a skit with my favorite stuffed monkey and one of my dolls. The stuffed monkey

14

was Mr. Jones and my favorite doll was supposed to be me. My sister sat in amazement as I acted out the roles of each character. I pretended that the stuffed monkey had hurt the doll and made her bleed. I then took a knife and stabbed the stuffed monkey over and over and over. Then I pulled out the stuffing in his body as if I was disemboweling it. I was showing so much anger and animosity that I had to sit back and take a deep breath. My sister and I just stared at each other. She said "I'm going to tell Mom." I warned her that if she did, I would tell our mother that she stole candy from the cupboard. She shook her head, "No, Mama will not believe it, since I didn't do it. "I threatened her again and she had no choice but to keep her mouth shut. Grabbing the destroyed monkey, I jumped up, ran outside and threw him into the garbage can and slammed the lid shut. He deserved to die! I stood there for a moment before I reopened the can and took him out. I took one of the grocery sacks from the can filled with garbage, threw him back in and put the grocery sack on top of him. I had to make sure that my mother wouldn't see the monkey that way. Since later she never asked about the stuffed monkey, I assume she failed to see it there.

When Easter came that year Anna bought us some baby chickens. My brother, sisters and I were playing with them. I kept throwing mine in the air until it came down and hit my knee and broke its neck. I couldn't believe that I had done it at first. I started to cry. I remembered when I was a loving, kind, and gentle little girl who could never be cruel. My father came into the room and looked at me like he could not believe what I had done. He asked me why I did it, but I could only shrug my shoulders. I really didn't know why. He picked up the little chicken along with the others and took them to a farm. He knew that the chickens had little chance of survival if I was around.

Although my father was a loving man and I adored him, I shied away from him. I didn't want him to touch me or come near me because I thought he might hurt me too. I needed help but didn't know whom to turn to. Many nights I cried myself to sleep.

I tried never to cross paths with Mr. Jones again. When I baby-sat I would make sure that he was nowhere around. One day while I was sitting in the backyard playing with our dog, Linda stumbled over to me crying. She said that Mr. Jones had broken the zipper on her pants. I started to tremble in fear because I knew what she was about to tell me. My heart started beating a hundred miles a minute. "Oh no", I whispered.

She told me that Mr. Jones had called her into his bedroom to fix the zipper on her skirt. Suddenly, the children came into the room and he instantly stopped what he had been planning to do. I just sat there and looked at her in bewilderment. I just couldn't believe what almost happened. This time I had to tell someone. No matter what the consequences were, this was my little sister and Mr. Jones had to be stopped here and now! I didn't know how I was going to go about it or what I was going to tell my parents, but I had to be brave. No matter what happened, I was going to my father. Thinking even for a minute that my mother might commit suicide is the only reason I held back all this time. I had to take the chance that my mother might not commit suicide. Mr. Jones had to be stopped before he hurt my little sister.

That evening when my father walked in from work, I waited in my room as he changed his clothes. I had practiced my speech all afternoon a hundred times. The first words I would say were, "Please don't tell Mom!" Then I'd explain how frightened I felt, but I needed to tell him what happened to Linda and me. Telling him had taken all my courage and after I did, he sat there motionless. An eerie sort of calm passed over him. He quietly asked me to take my sisters and go to our room. In the room, Linda began to cry. She thought she was going to be spanked for something she had done. Reassuring her that this was not the case, Linda moaned over and over that she shouldn't have told me. Besides seeing the blood on my clothes, Linda really didn't know what Mr. Jones had done.

Outside of our room, all hell broke loose. This calm and gentle man became outraged, began to cry and told my mother the entire sordid story. Daddy grabbed his hunting rifle and headed for Mr. Jones's house. Mom got on the phone. She called the military police to stop my father from making the biggest mistake of his life. My sisters and I stayed in our bedroom scared and shaking from all the commotion. Suddenly everything went silent. You could hear a pin drop.

We heard footsteps in the hall. The person paused for a minute then entered the room. It was "Mrs. Meany," my mother's fifth personality. Grandmother tried taking my mother back from her adopted mother at 12 years of age, but was unsuccessful. My grandmother was abusive both mentally and physically. She was very dominating, conniving and evil and could be a great threat at times. This is how Miss Meany learned to be abusive to her children. This cruel persona and Miss White had one trait in common: neither of them would have had any children. Only because the other three personalities loved children and wanted a family with my father were we even born.

The words that came from Miss Meany's mouth shocked me! This is where I first took notice of my mother's different or distinct personalities. She yelled and cursed at us for telling what had happened to us. I couldn't figure out what we had done wrong. She then started to whip me with a belt. I cried out for her to stop, but she was so outraged she could not even hear me. She approached Linda with the belt, and I tried my best to stop her. I kept telling her that it was not Linda's fault: "I'm the one who told Daddy!" She said that Linda was getting a whipping for even being at the Jones' house. The reason why we were being whipped was a complete mystery to me. I didn't rape Mr. Jones. He raped me. Then he tried to do the same with Linda, and here was Miss Meany blaming me for destroying our family. Miss Meany accused me of trying to kill her and said that I was a troublemaker. Tears ran down my mother's face. She looked down at me now curled up in a ball on the floor and told me, "I wish you had never been born!" When she left, I couldn't do anything but weep bitter tears. "What did I do wrong? How did I destroy everyone's lives? Didn't she understand why I had to tell the truth; why I had to try and stop him?" I had to tell my father; I had no other choice!

In the days that followed, Miss Meany became even more stressed. Little minute things would make her blow up. One night she became very angry with us. My brother, sisters and I were already in bed when we heard her arguing with Dad. I think my father was trying to calm her down but she kept yelling that she was fed up. Before we knew it, she stormed into our room, shouting. She told us, "Take off your clothes!"

Although we were reluctant to do so, we disrobed, crying and wondering what we had done wrong. She instructed my father to drag my brother screaming and crying into their bedroom and they both tied him to their canopy bed. There my brother hung, crying and naked. I could see the fear in my brother's face as she started to beat him with an extension cord. As she struck him with the cord, she told him why he was being beaten. Apparently, she had walked into the kitchen and found that it was cleaned improperly. The trash had not been taken out and several other chores had been avoided. She kept beating him until he could not cry anymore. I was so afraid that she was going to kill my brother. As they both untied him, I knew I was next. I started to run but I didn't get very far. My dad grabbed me and Miss Meany pulled me up to the canopy bed and tied my hands. She beat me as violently as she had Chuck; and I screamed even louder. Dad yelled, "Stop it! Stop it! I can't do this! "He untied me. This made Miss Meany very angry. Dad told us to put our clothes back on and go to bed.

Miss Meany and Dad argued for hours. The next day Anna Mae tried to kill herself by taking an overdose of sleeping pills. This caused her to go into cardiac arrest, and she almost died in the screaming ambulance on the way to the hospital. The paramedics had to shock her heart awake with the paddles from a defibrillator to bring her back. She stayed in a psychiatric hospital for about a month, where they diagnosed her as suffering from schizophrenic paranoia and a form of acute, manic depression. Dad was never the same. If only I could change what had occurred, but what could I have done differently to change anything? Mrs. Meany was right, our family was destroyed. We started to get harassing telephone calls and threatening notes so the base commander thought it best to relocate us somewhere else on the base. The move was supposed to have been "top secret." However, we were still being harassed by telephone calls and people driving by our home yelling horrible comments and poking fun at us. Those who found us called us, "nigger liars," and accused us of deliberately lying about an innocent white man. People were just as prejudiced on the military base as they were out in the world. Daddy was troubled greatly by the harassment, and with Mom being hospitalized, it made matters worse. I remember the time when he came home and spanked me for not doing the dishes. My father had never whipped me like that before. He screamed that my mother almost died because of me. <u>I never wanted to hurt the family I loved</u>. Later that evening, Daddy apologized to me. He didn't know what had gotten into him. I knew he was telling the truth because I trusted him completely. My Daddy never lied.

# Chapter 4

After the dust settled, Daddy decided that my rape and my sister's attempted rape had to be handled in a court of law. The lawyers involved in our case against Mr. Jones sent psychiatrists to my school to work with me. The investigating psychiatrists would ask me the same questions over and over again. One question they always seemed to ask me related to whether a boy ever kissed me or if anything of a sexual nature happened with me when I was around young boys that I played with. Disbelieving that they could even ask me these questions, I eventually stopped answering them. I was just a 10-year-old girl and sex was not a part of my life – at all! They hammered at me to no end.

They had me doing tests, like putting blocks together. Soon I grew tired of playing their silly games and knocked all the blocks off of the table. They also asked me to look at inkblots and tell them what I saw. I simply replied, "I'll tell you when you tell me why you are doing this to me." Since they did not feel that they had to answer that question, I walked out of the room. The school secretary told me to sit in the front lobby and wait. Finally, one of the psychiatrist told her, "It's okay, just send her back to class. There's nothing wrong with that child besides her frustration. She wants us to leave her alone." At last, someone was on my side!

Mom was finally released from the hospital just in time for the trial. I recall being so frightened that day. It seemed as though I was all-alone in the world. There was no one to hold my hand or comfort me in any way. As I walked down the long hallway the passersby all seemed to look angry with me. I felt that everyone was against me and I just wanted to run away. They guided me into a room where I sat with a lady that was to keep watch over me. I felt transparent. After all that had happened to me, I was almost convinced that I was the one who enticed Mr. Jones into raping me. Maybe it never even happened to me. I simply did not want to be there and I started to leave the room, but the lady sitting with me would not let me go. She told me to go and sit down and I did so. Inside I was screaming, "Please let me go home!"

Suddenly the door opened and my lawyer greeted me with a smile on his face, took my hand and escorted me out of the room and into the courtroom. He told me with a sincere look to tell the truth and everything would be all right. I looked up into his eyes. He smiled and said, "Soon it will be all over and you can go home." As I entered the courtroom I first made eye contact with my father who seemed to be strong and self-assured. Then I looked over and glanced at my mother sitting next to him. From the loving smile and nod she gave me, I knew it was Anna. She said, "Everything's all right honey. Mama's here, Baby!"

I was led up to a chair and was told to place my hand on the Bible. I was asked to swear that I would tell the whole truth and nothing but the truth, so help me God. The gentleman swearing me in asked if I understood what it meant, and I replied, "Yes Sir, it means that if I don't tell the truth, God will be mad at me." The room filled with laughter and people snickered. Looking around, I couldn't figure out what was supposed to be so funny! As the judge brought order to the courtroom, the lawyers asked me what happened on June 5, 1963. I replied that I did not know the date. He asked me again but differently put this time, "What happened on the day you were raped? "I looked over to Mr. Jones as he sat there with a smirk on his face. He was being obnoxious and cocky and I thought to myself, "You're finally going to get what you deserve. I hope they put you in jail forever." I told the court everything that had happened that day. The judge asked me, "Why did you tell the neighbor woman with the head wrap or hood that the rape had happened to a friend of yours?" I replied, "I didn't want her to know that I was the one who was raped." I told them that if I told the woman and she mentioned it to my mother, that my mother would commit suicide and, "I didn't want my mother to die. "I looked over to see my Mom holding a tissue up to her eyes as she wept silent tears.

When the next lawyer was unleashed upon me, I had no idea what I was up against and he tore me apart. He kept badgering me to say words that I knew I was not permitted to say. He kept questioning me, "Why did he do it to you? We know he raped you, but what actually happened?" I finally gave up and started to cry and in a very small voice I said, "He had sex with me." No one heard me. The lawyer yelled at me again, "What did he do to you? Speak Louder." Again crying and even more loudly, I repeated, "He had sex with me!" I guess that's what he wanted to hear. It was tough for me to explain because I really didn't know what had happened to me. I was in the white room after I passed out. In the courtroom I was crying uncontrollably. The judge finally told him to leave me alone and I was asked to go back to the room where the lady was to watch me once again. As I walked out of the courtroom I turned to glance back at Anna. She again smiled and nodded as if to say, "Everything will be all right, honey!" Not long after, my mother and father were led into the room and we were free to go home. ❖

Later that week, we received the verdict. I was ruled a liar and Mr. Jones was released. I heard that the jury made this decision based upon my conversation with the neighbor. They felt that I probably did get the information from a friend and lied about Mr. Jones. I really didn't care whether or not I lost or won at this point. As a child all I wanted to do

23

was to pretend that it never happened and leave that part of my life behind me.

When it was all over, Mr. Jones was assigned to another base. We heard a rumor later that he tried to rape another little girl. I don't know if it was true or not, but we also heard that his wife and children soon left him. At the time, my mother said, "What goes around comes around."

I hoped she was right.

# Chapter 5

By the end of the year things had finally calmed down and it seemed that everything was back to normal. My father was back to work, my brother was back to his old tricks and we felt safe to again play away each day in our neighborhood as children should.

Mae was another personality that arose from Mom's father. Her father always told her that she could do anything she wanted to do. Since she was daddy's little girl, she was free to drink, dance and gamble just like he did. She felt that she didn't have to change for anyone and although she seldom saw her father, she adored him and wanted to be like him. Mae was becoming very depressed which led to her excessive gambling and drinking. Her personality would soon show its true form.

Anna Mae's church was becoming more and more important to her. Soon, Anna Mae found a new friend named, Neona. They spent a lot of time together since Neona was the church choir director at Anna Mae's church. Neona's husband had gone overseas and Anna Mae asked Dad if she could move in with us. Dad disagreed, but Anna Mae wanted her to move in anyway. Dad knew that there would be nights that "Mae" would go off gambling and leave Neona alone with him. Dad was an honorable man dedicated to his own wife, so he wasn't worried about anything happening between Neona and him. But he also knew that Anna Mae was an extremely jealous woman, and eventually there would be trouble. Dad was a good judge of character, he also was fully aware of how much Neona loved her husband. But he also was fully aware that two women could not successfully live in one household. As it turned out, Mae was out and about gambling most of the time. He and Neona would spend time playing Scrabble® and talking. My father had always been a good conversationalist and people were always happy to talk with him and listen to his wise and intelligent advice.

After the rape and ensuing trial, Dad never wanted to be far from his children. He was always there to care for us. Of course, I was never allowed to baby sit again. Daddy told me that if I needed anything he would provide it for me as long as it was within his means. Having his steady eye on us admittedly made me feel safe and secure. In this cruel, mixed-up world the only protection that children have are the watchful eyes of their parents. Sometimes it seemed to me that he was afraid to leave us alone for fear that something would happen to his girls again.

Dad and I had great times together. He taught me how to cook, sew and even showed me how to make a birdhouse. We had a lot of heart-to-heart talks about childhood. Still I would not allow him to touch me or hug me, even though I longed for those days before the white room.

Miss White joined the base's Wives Club, probably to ease the tension that built up in her during the trial. Eventually Anna Mae's jealous streak went wild. Dad and Neona were spending a lot of time together. As usual, Dad was right all along, and Anna Mae did not accept that he and Neona were merely friends. Dad loved Mom so much and now Neona seemed to be separating them, and sometimes even separated mom from us kids. Dad just couldn't take it anymore. Neona was becoming more important to Mom than the marriage. He decided to volunteer for a year in Vietnam.

His decision was based on two things. First, he needed time away from Mom. Second, Dad knew that by volunteering for duty in Vietnam, his family would once again be stationed in Japan.

Mom decided to follow Neona to Colorado. We were to stay there for a year until Dad's return. I was 12 years old when we left California, in 1966. We had to drive to Colorado in order to transfer vehicles. It was a long drive, so Anna stopped at a convenience store where she allowed us kids to purchase magazines and toys. I decided to read. I went into the magazine section, and that's where I discovered a comic book that would inspire me to change the world; "Richie Rich". It was a comic about a poor little rich boy. I never understood the meaning of "poor little rich boy," but I knew that was what I wanted to be when I grew up. The comic was full of stories about a rich kid that fed the hungry, gave to the poor, and was always trying to make some unfortunate little child happy. He would bring the child home, feed him, and allow him to play and have fun at his glorious estate. This of course, made his rich friends laugh and gawk at him because they felt that he should be using his money only to satisfy his own needs. I admired his courage to stand up for what he believed, challenge other's assumptions, and to do whatever it took to accomplish his goal.

I dreamed that someday I too would become rich and have all the money in the world. I would help the poor and feed the hungry. Yet in my dream, I myself would live a humble life. I started collecting "Richie Rich" comic books from that day forward. I could learn all the different ways I was going to help mankind or at that time, "children kind." Being a child, I was going to buy up all the orphanages in the world and hire women that acted like my mother (Anna), who would treat the children very kind. The children of course, would do nothing but blow bubbles and jump in their beds all day. Every day would be Christmas. In addition, none of them would ever have to succumb to the agony and pain that I had suffered in California. I never wanted to return to California.

In Colorado we lived off base. It was very convenient. The stores were right around the corner and we didn't have to show our ID card to go anywhere like we did on the military base. My brother and I had to go to a public school where the majority of the kids were black. We thought this would be neat since we always attended military schools that were filled with kids of all races. We weren't accepted in this new school because we didn't act, walk, dress or talk black. Several of the girls didn't care for me because of my light complexion, but the guys were all over me. There were girls wanted to fight me, and although I wasn't afraid to fight one of them, there were always five or six of them to contend with. The fight would be unfair as it was, but to make matters worse, they wanted to use guns, knives, and chains! In my other schools there were fistfights, but I was not accustomed to this method of warfare. One day, a very cute boy stopped me in the hallway and since his girlfriend thought I was trying to take him away, she started an argument with me. I don't know what his intentions were, but mine were purely innocent, although she didn't think so. I couldn't understand why she felt threatened since I felt she was much better looking than me. I could see that this situation was not going to end there.

One day in the locker room her friends approached me in the shower. They told me that they wanted to fight me after school. I told them that I would meet one of them, but I wasn't going to fight them all. Before the conversation ended the gym teacher walked in. I had no idea about the full intent of their threats, until I attended a school dance that evening.

28

My brother and I were very excited about going to the dance. This was the first dance we had ever attended, and we were dressed up in our best clothes. Mae complimented Chuck on being so handsome and talked about how beautiful we both looked as we walked out the door. When we arrived at the dance everyone was staring at us as we entered the room. Both of us were asked to dance and we were thrilled to show off our California dance steps. The kids watched with envy and excitement as they asked us to show them how to do the dances.

When our glorious evening was finished, my brother and I left to go home. A fight broke out and one kid in particular was being severely beaten by ten other boys. I don't know what he did to incense them. While he was lying on the ground, another boy just standing by watching was pushed in and soon dragged into a fight he had nothing to do with. All the rest of the boys jumped in to beat them both. My brother was behind me yelling, "Let's go home, Cynthia!", but I was so caught up in the moment he had to grab me and persuade me to leave.

I wanted to help but what could I do? I walked away feeling as though it was my fault that the two young boys lay on the ground suffering. I could not believe that they were both beaten until they were almost dead. My brother and I witnessed the ruffians almost literally half-killing them.

The girls that threatened me in the shower still wanted to fight me, and the fun we had at the dance only made them more jealous and upset than before. This is when I realized how great a threat those girls would be to me. Every day I went to school shaking in fear. Anna Mae worried about my safety, thinking I might get into a fight or possibly be killed. She approached the Principal only to be told that there was nothing he could do. The kids ran the school and every day something violent would occur. Not only were teachers' cars being blown up in the parking lot, but also teachers were being thrown out of their classes and sent home. My mom realized that we were going to have to fight for my safety. Anna Mae wanted to be peaceful, but Mae was ready to do battle.

Mae showed up one day cussing out the kids as they stood outside the school waiting for me to walk by. Every day I was to wait for Anna Mae to pick me up after school, and each day the location of the pick-up would change to throw the girls off track. She said not to worry that she would find me, and reassured me that she wouldn't let anything happen to me. Anna Mae continued to do this until one of the girls passed me in the hall and told me, "One of these days your mom won't be there and that's when we'll find you and kill you."

Her prediction came true when Mom got caught in traffic. When I went to look for her she was not outside sitting in the car. Quickly I ran back into the building and up to the third floor where I could watch out the window. Frantically I awaited her arrival. For a moment I thought I was at the wrong location, but it was Wednesday and this is where she said to meet her. "Maybe she forgot the location", I said to myself. I knew if she did, she would be driving around front any minute. Five minutes seemed like an hour. I turned to go to the other end of the hallway to watch out that window. At that very moment, I heard a door shut farther down the hallway.

When I turned around to look, there were seven girls lined up along the hall. Each of them was carrying a different weapon; chains, knives, bats and razors. I tried to go back down the stairs but the door had been locked from the other side. I literally felt my knees knocking together, just like in the cartoons. I was trembling with fear, thinking I would never see my family again. I knew I was going to die. I sensed that death was knocking at my door. I remember calling on God, my mother and my father. I turned, trying to get the attention of the kids down below only to see them waiting and watching for me to fall to my death. I remember the young boys that almost died right before my eyes. Now it was my turn, and in a way I was almost glad that it would be over with because I was tired of living in fear. There seemed to me no greater fear than living my life in bondage, always carrying some kind of worry. I turned back and looked at the girls. A single tear came to my eye. As they began to approach me I was so scared I couldn't even speak. When they were almost upon me a small-framed girl busted through the door.

She looked at me and yelled, "Cynthia, your mom is downstairs waiting for you."

I looked back only to see all seven girls running away as if they had seen a ghost. By the time I got to the bottom of the stairs and walked out the door, my mom still was not there. This strange girl had lied to rescue me! She introduced herself as Keiki. I was so flabbergasted by the whole ordeal; I couldn't even speak to her. She told me that she liked my brother and thought he was cute. I didn't know this at the time, but Keiki was supposed to have been the toughest girl in the school. Everyone called her Crazy. She would actually fight any boy in school and come out the winner. In a way her family was even crazier than she was. All of them had been in jail so many times, they didn't care who they shot or harmed. No one ever turned her or her family in to the police. Everyone was so worried that her family would retaliate for some reason. No one could even utter Keiki's name without her permission. I guess that's the reason I never heard of her previously.

She explained to me that she had been sick and just recently returned to school. She heard that my brother and I were the new kids. She was also told that we were from another planet because we spoke so properly and dressed real nice. "Gee thanks." I didn't think she was very cute saying that, but at that moment she was the most attractive person I knew-- she saved my life that day.

She was blown away by my brother. She thought he was so polite and extremely cute. I was sure that I could interest Chuck in Keiki if I cleaned his room for a year or gave him my share of the steak dinners. I knew I could at least convince him to be her friend.

When my mom finally arrived, Keiki walked me to the car and introduced herself then ran away to see what other mischief she could scare up. Mom was so happy to see that I was all right and apologized for being late. I said, "Don't worry Mom, it's OK." I looked back towards Keiki. I explained to Mom what had transpired since school let out, but also told her that from now on I would be walking home. I was now under Keiki's protection and was labeled "untouchable". I didn't mind this at all because to me, she was a very nice person. People really didn't understand why she acted the way she did. It was a means of survival. If Keiki had not had a family who backed her up when things went bad, she never would have endured. Her parents accepted me like I was a part of their family.

The very next day, all seven of the girls, one by one, greeted me as though I were their best friend. All I could think was, "Thank God, she likes my brother." Chuck didn't realize it but he had rode to my rescue and he wasn't even there.

# Chapter 6

The year I turned 13 proved to be an interesting one for my brother and me. Not only did we become very close, but we also began to rely on one another. We would go everywhere together. While walking home from school one day, we passed a group of boys roughing each other up. Two of them suddenly decided to go after my brother and give him a hard time. He tried to walk away but they just wouldn't leave him alone. The guy who seemed to be the leader picked him up by the collar and lifted him high in the air. They started to call him names and insult him. My brother started yelling at me to go home and get Mom. I ignored him, dropped my books, ran up to the guy holding my brother and began kicking and hitting him. All the time I screamed at him, "Put my brother down!" Mae always had told us to protect each other or die trying, so I didn't trust leaving him alone to fight this group of guys. I was determined to stand my ground, but the guy I was hitting started to laugh at me. He said, "Hey, look at this little girl trying to whip my butt."

He put my brother down and tried to talk to me but I was too angry to pay him any mind. This guy even had the nerve to ask for my phone number as we walked away. As it turns out, his name was Johnny and he was the leader of the Black Panthers on my side of town. I had to admit that he was kind of cute, but I ignored him when he waited for me after school every day. He wouldn't give up because I think he was fascinated by the way I tried to protect my brother. He followed me home almost every day. And every time, a whole group of ten and sometimes twenty Black Panthers would follow along right behind him. I found this to be very embarrassing.

As we would turn the corner towards my house, I would look at him and ask, "Please don't let my mother see them following me home." He would smile, tell them to stay there, and walk me up to the door. I acted as if I minded, but I did think he was cute. I didn't like Johnny's aggressiveness and could certainly do without his arrogance. I would quickly thank him and said my good-byes as I ran into the house each day before Anna Mae could see him.

Each morning he would wait to walk me to school. He would talk most of the way there and I would just listen. I tried to explain to him that he was going to get me in trouble but he smiled as he walked me to my class.

One day as I was sitting in my "Home Ec" class, sewing, when in walked Johnny. He went right up to the sewing teacher and began to talk to her. The teacher was afraid to speak to him and the entire class thought he was really funny. I didn't find it amusing in the least. I liked that class and my teacher, and he was putting her in an embarrassing situation. Everyone in the school was afraid to talk to the Black Panthers because the other students never knew what the activists would do or say. He pulled out a chair, sat in it backwards, and started to talk to me. I went on sewing, hoping that if I ignored him, perhaps, he would go away. He unplugged my sewing machine and asked me, "What are you doing?" It was quite obvious, so I ignored him. He kept on so I decided to try and get rid of him. I promised that if he left me alone and allowed me to finish the dress I was making, I would talk to him later in the day. He finally left but just like he made a scene when entering the class, he also had to make one exiting. As long as he was gone, I didn't care. The bell rang and my dress still wasn't finished. The other girls in class thought he was cute and loved it that he had made such a big scene for me. I didn't! And I was going to let him know it. When school let out, he

34

strolled up to me, and boy, was I ready to tear off his head! I told him not to ever come into sewing class again! I yelled at him and told him that if he had to interrupt a class, next time make it a class in Government or Science! Although I had been dead serious, I was laughing now and so was he. He promised not to do it again. At this point in our strange relationship, we became friends. I was no longer angry with him for what he did to my brother.

Johnny would often call me. We talked about a lot of things, but one in particular were my feelings about sex. I made sure that he understood that I was not going to have sex, explaining about my rape, although I'm not sure how well he grasped what I was saying. I made it clear to him that if he wanted to be my friend; this was going to be the way it was. He must have really liked me, because he agreed. Johnny had many girlfriends. He needed me more of a friend and confidant.

We started spending a lot of time together. We disagreed on one major thing and that was his leading the Black Panthers. I felt that he was using it to push his weight around; made him feel like he had great power. He was not happy with my opinion and expressed it by not speaking to me for several days. I found myself apologizing only because his friend explained that he did do quite a bit of good for the community. That, I was not aware of, but he just wasn't the type of person to boast. After we made up, I felt that it was about time to bring him home to meet Anna Mae.

Upon their introductions, Anna Mae was very bold and told him the same thing I did about sex. His reply to this was, "Yes Ma'am, but you don't have to worry about Cynthia, since she'd probably beat me up if I tried anything."

We all laughed. He went on to tell my mom about what happened the day he grabbed my brother. Johnny became my best friend, spending a lot of time with me visiting museums, walking in the park, and even going on picnics. Thank goodness his fellow Panthers would stay at bay. It simply did not look right, having ten guys hanging around while Johnny and I went out.

One day we were in the park having lunch on a blanket, talking and laughing. We were having a great time until Johnny came from behind me and planted a big kiss on my lips. I jumped as if he was about to rape me. My lunch fell out of my lap and I started yelling and heading for home. "I hate you, you're just like the rest of them, you stupid yellow Negro! How could you? Do you want to rape me too?" I recall staring back at him as he sat there looking dumbfounded. His mouth was hanging wide open while he tried to figure out just what he had done wrong. He ran after me but I would not stop to listen. I'm sure that day showed him what an impact rape had made in my life and personality. I kept on walking and never looked back.

Mae believed that if a girl were raped, she would always want to have sex ever after. Anna Mae believed that in time I would heal. Miss Meany felt that I would become a whore. None of them were right. Some women never forget the shame and the hurt of rape because they're too busy blaming themselves for what happened. I knew at my age that I was never going to let it happen again. What my mother never understood was that I would never look at sex as a normal part of my life. When I looked at men, I couldn't help but wonder if they raped their wives to make babies, and if sex was always as painful as my experience. "How could a woman allow a man to continually do that to her; giving her four or more children? She must really love that man.", I often thought.

I had a completely different outlook on sex than most people. I wouldn't even allow my father to come near me. I missed the days when I would run and jump into Daddy's lap and he would hold me as I cried and talked about things I didn't understand. After my rape, I remember Daddy calling me to sit on his lap. I would shake my head no. I loved him so much, but he was no longer my daddy, he was also a man. At the time I felt that any man was seriously capable of doing harm to me. I knew in my heart that I would rather die than go through what I went through the day I entered Mr. Jones's house. Mr. Jones had killed me sexually.

I didn't talk to Johnny for about a month after the day in the park. He hiked to our house one day and talked to Anna Mae. She tried to explain to him that I was very vulnerable and she couldn't even explain how deeply the rape had hurt me. No one understood. I was so confused. I couldn't even explain my true feelings. Anna Mae tried sitting down to talk to me. Miss Meany tried yelling and humiliating me. Mae told me, "Give him another chance to be your friend."

Thanks to my mom and Johnny's little tokens-- sending me flowers, candy and a teddy bear, and standing in front of my house acting silly--we soon became friends again. Now I was sure that Johnny knew his boundaries with me.

Dad came home for "R & R" (Rest and Recreation) from Vietnam. I believe that Mom and Dad met in Reno, Nevada. This gave them time to heal their ailing marriage. Johnny talked me into skipping school. A friend and I didn't think it was a bad idea, and Neona was watching us in Mom and Dad's absence. All of my friends met in my girlfriend's basement where we stayed until the coast was clear. The master plan was that the one with the deepest voice would call the school and pretend to be Neona. She would explain that I was sick and would not be attending school that day. In fact, there was a rash of sick calls that day. I wonder why? When the school called to verify my illness with Neona, she went straight to the school, found my brother and asked him where was my friend's house. She went to the girl's house and intercepted the party that we thought we were going to have. I don't know how Johnny talked me into this, but I was in deep trouble. She took me home and decided to whip me and told me that she was going to tell my mom that I had skipped school. My ultimate fate depended on "which mom" she ended up telling. If Miss Meany happened to be mom at the moment, I knew I'd literally suffer the consequences. I would have rather died than answer to Miss Meany, so I took every pill in the medicine cabinet. I went to supper drowsy that night, but luckily I didn't take enough pills to do much damage. When I awoke the next morning, Miss Meany was there. And of course, she beat me again, this time with an extension cord. I thought the whipping would never end. As the wire cut into my skin, I kept yelling for her to please stop. I didn't think she'd stop until she killed me. After the beating, I went into my room where my brother put ointment on my welts. Just when I thought it was over, we both heard her approaching our room yelling, "She is not going to kill me! Not if it's the last thing she does on this earth! I'll kill her first!"

After telling me to dress, she went out to the car, followed by my brother. Miss Meany then put a shovel in the car and went back into the house. Chuck asked, "Mom, what are you doing and where are you going with that shovel?" He had tears in his eyes because he feared the worst as she sent him to his room. She then said to me, "Let's go!" I followed her involuntarily; I knew I had no other choice. Whatever she was going to do to me was not going to happen at home. As we drove down the street she repeated to herself again and again, "You are not going to kill me!" I remember pleading with her, "I don't want to kill you, Mommy!" She told me to shut up and stop crying. As we were driving down the road my thoughts centered on my father. I knew that if he were here now, he would stop her. Soon her fussing became faint; somehow I had turned her off.

Silently I cried to myself. After a beating we were always told to shut up and not show any emotions. I reminded myself to hang in there and hold on to my sanity. I spoke silently, "Cynthia, don't give up and don't let go, you can make it."

I literally was shaking in my shoes when she pulled over to the side of the road. She had stopped the car on a dark, deserted street and instructed me to reach into the back and retrieve her gun.

"Mama, please give me another chance, I'll never do it again." I pleaded. She stopped, then turned around, and yelled, "If you ever skip school again, I will take you out to a graveyard and make you dig your grave and shoot you in the back of the head." I climbed back in the car and she drove back home.

Miss Meany got out of the car and laid the shovel against the garage. I quietly walked back to the house and straight into my room. My brother met me as I entered. He touched my shoulder as if he were happy to see I was alive. He started to ask what happened, when we both looked down and saw Miss Meany's feet beneath the door. We climbed into our bunk beds as I silently cried. Chuck hung his head down from the bunk and asked what happened. I explained in bits and pieces what had occurred that evening. Chuck replied, "I told you Mom was crazy."

I could hear my brother's words ringing in my ears that night as we both went to sleep. I had nightmares all through the night. I kept seeing my mother shooting me in the back of my head and my body falling into the open grave below my feet. Morning came and we were awakened to Anna Mae's screaming; listing our daily duties as she dressed for work. My brother and I followed her to the door sleepy-eyed and saw her glance at the shovel leaning on the garage. She bellowed, "Who took this shovel out of the garage? I told you kids never to mess with this shovel and I want it back in the garage where it belongs! Don't ever touch it again!" We were too fearful of the outcome to make any comments, so we kept our thoughts to ourselves and simply looked at each other. Putting the shovel away, Chuck reiterated, "See, I told you Mom was crazy."

This is when I realized that each of my mom's personalities did not know or remember what the other personalities did. I also became aware that each persona called my brother and sisters different names, depending on her current personality. When I explained this to my brother, he couldn't make sense out of what I was telling him. I think it was easier for him to excuse our mother's behavior as "craziness." Although that was easier for him to accept, I started analyzing her diverse behavior patterns. I noticed that Anna Mae called me, "Kaye," Miss Meany called me, "Cynthia Kay," Mae called me, "Cynthia," while Anna had a cute little way of singing, "Kaye-Kaye." Miss White, who we seldom saw, didn't call us anything. Her term for us was, "You kids this, or you kids that." She probably didn't care what our names were.

My brother and I noticed a significant change daily. One personality would tell us to clean the house while another would come home and whip us for cleaning it, or vice versa. Miss Meany came home one day early from work

40

only to catch us playing in the yard. I was dancing on top of our second car and wetting everyone with the hose. The dog was tied to the cat, and they were both tied to a hose. You can guess that this was Chuck's grand idea! My baby sister was running around naked and my sister, Linda, was tied to a tree as my brother practiced shooting her with his bow and arrows with rubber stoppers at the ends. He was the Indian and she was the cowboy. Since we never knew if we should do the housework or not, we just didn't do it at all. I really thought we were going to be spanked, since we deserved it, but when she got home she walked silently into the house and went to her room. I didn't know who she was at the time, but we were really living life on the edge! We all cleaned up as fast as we could and then sat quietly in the front room fearing for our lives. Anna Mae marched out of her room with her revolver in her hand and decided to play Russian Roulette, yes, Russian Roulette. We stood in front of her wailing, begging and pleading for our lives. She finally stopped and let us go to our rooms. We never did know if the gun was loaded. We all began blaming each other. Miss Meany walked into the room and told us to go to bed. When she went back into her room, I lay in my bed wondering about what she was thinking. What was Miss Meany going to do next? Soon, Miss White came out of her room, dressed to go out, and we were all relieved.

A friend of my father's occasionally would stop in to see if Mom needed anything. His name was Billy. He once worked under my father. One day he stopped by while my mother was at work. He said he would wait until she got home. For some reason or another, I knew that his intentions were wicked. Again, I saw the look that Mr. Jones had given me while watching from his fence. My brother, my sister and I ran outside to play Hide-and-Go-Seek and Billy asked to join us. He kept following me and then he would grab my breast or try to grab at me. I tried to run from his passes. I could see that I had to stay as far away from Billy as I could. He began showing up at our house when he knew my mother was not there. I always made sure my brother was around the house with me or I found somewhere else to go. I didn't want to tell my mother about this since I had been down that road before. I feared for what she might do. All I could do was stay as far away from him as I could. Anna Mae thought he was being nice, doing things around the house that she was unable to do, but I knew his intentions. Thankfully, my father would be home from Vietnam soon.

I was so relieved on the day of my father's return. He surprised my mother with good news. We were all returning to Japan! We were so excited. Unfortunately, they left Billy with us to baby-sit. Daddy didn't like it, but Mae reassured him that she had done this before and everything always turned out fine. I stayed glued to my brother all night and was so happy when Billy said it was time for bed. He asked me to stay up and tell him where to put the clean dishes. I said, "No." My brother looked at me as if I was crazy and it really didn't matter to me. I followed him to bed. Soon Billy sneaked into the room, thinking my brother was asleep, and knelt by my bed. He was just placing his hands under my blankets when I sat up and screamed at the top of my lungs. "Leave!" Chuck woke up and asked what was going on. Billy left the room. I stayed up until I could hear my father step through the doorway. I ran into the front room and greeted my parents, hugging them both. I remember my mom telling Daddy how much I had missed him while he was gone. Little did she know that "to miss" was not the phrase to express my feelings! I had longed for his return. I was so relieved that he was home. That night I slept more soundly than I had in a long time. My daddy was home to stay.

When we were moving out of our home, and Mom and Dad were finalizing all the arrangements for the move, Billy graciously invited us to stay at his house. I really did not want to go there, but Chuck and I stayed outside playing all day. Anna Mae cleaned the house to perfection, and the premises passed the inspection with flying colors, as always. Billy informed us around dusk that it was time to come in. Mom and Dad had more errands to complete and Billy said he would fix us some supper. Chuck and I both agreed at the same time that we wanted hot dogs and Billy told Chuck and me to get into the bathtub before supper. Billy told me to go first, so I gathered my clothes, went into the bathroom and closed the door. Billy tried to open the door. I saw the doorknob turning side to side. Just as I thought he had given up, he started knocking, asking me to open the door so he could help me. I ignored him and kept washing myself. Again, he was knocking, louder and louder. My brother wondered what the commotion was all about and walked to the door. I heard them outside the bathroom door talking. Chuck assured Billy that I was capable of doing this myself. I smiled as I heard Billy walk away. I quickly finished bathing and put on my pajamas. I opened the door very slowly and quietly and went in to the front room to join my brother watching television.

Billy now thought that he had me. He told Chuck to take his bath, but headed for the bathroom right behind my brother. Chuck yelled for me to leave and give him his privacy, but I tried to convince him to pull the shower curtain around the tub and let me stay. He would not agree. Billy heard the entire conversation and told me to leave my brother alone so Chuck could take his shower in peace.

I ran to the front room to watch TV and Billy joined me on the rug. He said, "Don't be afraid, I won't hurt you." This was the same thing that Mr. Jones had said to me. Just

43

then, the doorbell rang and I was thrilled to see Mom, Dad and little sisters standing there laughing and talking as they entered the house. I hugged my Daddy. My face was serious this time. My father smilingly asked me if everything was all right and I told him I was just worried. Anna Mae snapped, "Worried about what?" and walked away. I told her it was nothing. I knew that Billy was quite concerned for his safety by now. Anna Mae told me to go on because Dad was tired and hungry. She looked at him and shook her head. I stayed right by my father's side. I knew that now and in the future, I had to stay close to my brother. That night we became best friends.

The next morning as we left, Johnny and his gang of friends greeted me at the airport with flowers and candy. I hated to leave Johnny, my first boyfriend. After I left, we wrote to each other for a while, but soon grew weary of it. It's funny how distance can end a relationship. We both knew that our paths would never cross again. Later I found out that he had gotten out of the Black Panthers and became a homebody. He eventually had surgery for a hole the doctors found in his heart. He soon got a girl pregnant, was forced to marry her, and supposedly became very unhappy. I only wished Johnny the best, regardless of what he had done.

# Chapter 7

It felt good to be in a new place and different world, as beautiful as Japan. The people were so respectful, and honorable, even though they lived among many Anti-American protesters. They also had more respect for blacks even though there were rumors that black people had tails! Crazy as it sounds, some believed the rumor to be true. I remember wanting to stay in Japan forever, and never return to the States.

Japan was so beautiful, especially after winter when the first plum blossoms bloomed. Cherry blossoms would appear in all their glory. Japanese women wore their summer kimonos fashioned in beautiful vibrant colors, their hair neatly wrapped up in traditional hairstyles. Spring begins the rainy season, and July becomes very muggy with more heavy rain. A typhoon can quickly appear and disappear in the early fall, but fall is a very welcome time of the year with clear blue skies. Even though winter is gray and chilly it sometimes brought severe cold and snow.

What amazed me most were the fields of rice patties stretched as far as the eye could see. The patties were green and beautiful as they swayed in the wind. You could see grass on the plateaus along the mountainsides. My brother and I would walk into the little shops that lined the streets to buy delicious Japanese-made candies, carefully wrapped to make a good presentation. As we entered each shop the owner would bow politely and say in Japanese, "Good morning," and "How are you?" People you didn't even know smiled and greeted you on the street. But nothing prepared you for spring, for me, the most beautiful time of the year in Japan. Flowers were everywhere. We watched the children play their unusual games. You could smell the amazing aromas coming from the restaurants as they prepared fried rice and fish cooked on the hibachis.

Chuck and I were inseparable. We were just like two peas in a pod and no one could ever come between us. I felt so secure in our relationship and knew that if someone tried to hurt me, Chuck would be there to be my knight in shining armor. In turn, if anyone tried to hurt him, I would be there for him. We would ride our bikes together and often sit on a hill by the house and have private talks. When he was with the guys I was right there with them. Chuck made it quite clear that wherever he went, I would follow. Even though, his friends probably didn't want me with them all the time. We'd go to amusement parks and Mom would let us run off and have fun together. We were always a brother and sister team wherever we went. Chuck never really said so, yet I felt that he always loved me.

My brother always gave me a ride home from school on his handlebars, but one day, he decided to take a girl home. I was infuriated. I wanted to grab her by the hair and yank her off of his bike. I cried all the way home. When I got there I ran into my bedroom and fell on my bed screaming, "I hate my brother!" I felt betrayed by him and didn't speak to him for a long time. He didn't even notice that I was hurt because he was so busy chasing after the girl he took home that day. I would go to the places that we used to go together, and sit and cry my eyes out. My heart felt like someone had ripped it out. I was so hurt. I didn't care about anyone or anything. The kids at school started to call me the "school bully." I fought dirty and every new kid coming into the school noticed right off. I would always find a way to catch people off guard to win a fight.

In one particular instance, I was playing in the bathroom with another girl. She was turning the lights off and on when a large, heavy-set girl walked in. As I stood near the light switch, she told us to stop it and slapped me. Everyone in the room looked at her in shock because she must not have known my reputation. Holding my cheek as I left the room, I swore that I'd get her back! I asked my brother without him knowing what I was up to, to help me to time myself dropping something from a tree. My plan really was to wait in a tree with a brick in my hand, jump on the girl that slapped me, and hit her in the head with the brick. Then, I'd run away. The next day after school I climbed up in the tree and lay in wait. When she walked under the tree exactly as I planned, I jumped. She didn't even notice my efforts as I landed three feet behind her on my butt. I watched from the ground as she continued onto her bus completely unaware of my efforts. I headed home to go back to the drawing board. "Ah ha!" I said to myself, "I have a plan!" My timing was off, so my next plan would have to be exact! Again I sat on the branch with a large rock, only in my purse this time. My timing had to be perfect. Much to my surprise, I landed on her shoulders. I didn't have much time before she would have a chance to beat me up again. Funny, even after I hit her on the head and ran away to catch my bus, she didn't try to come after me. Instead she became one of my best friends, even protecting me from others. In retrospect, I guess she knew that by being my friend, she could keep a close eye on me.

I still was not the person I used to be. Bullying became a part of my everyday life. I was so mean that I hit my sister in the arm with a hammer. Finally one day when my brother and I were arguing, he made a statement that really caught my attention. He told me, "Everyone hates you because of the way you act". I stopped and looked at him for a moment, "Liar! "I told him that people respected me and he didn't know what he was talking about! He replied, "No, they hate you!" He made a bet with me that day. He said, "You go a whole month without fighting or mistreating anyone and you'll understand what I'm trying to tell you!" I agreed.

I began to realize what I had become. You know what? I didn't like myself much either. I had to pay my brother the bet we made, he was right. No one liked me. And even though my reputation at that time was bad, I still kept my head up high. I'm not going to say I quit fighting altogether but the bullying came to a stop; and eventually kids started to like me again. I organized a drill team and became very poplar at school.

# Chapter 8

On my fourteenth birthday, I decided that I was going to turn over a new leaf. I found a new friend named Keiko. We became best friends in no time. We would always catch the train to her house. She lived off base about 15 miles away. Keiko was a model. One day she told me that she would teach me modeling and help me find jobs off base. Our modeling jobs took us all over Japan, which really began to change my life. We did television shows together and gained attention throughout Japan. In school I became a drill instructor and because I had learned Japanese so well, I began teaching English to the Japanese. During this time I gained a great deal of notoriety at the school as well as on base.

With a modeling career at the age of 14, I was given opportunities that few teens that age could imagine. As time went on, my sister started Go-Go dancing. Linda and I were treated royally, riding in the Japanese version of limousines, signing autographs, and finding our names in the newspaper. We became very popular and made a lot of money doing so. The Japanese people always treated Americans well, and because of that, the notoriety never went to my head. I began to accept it as a part of my life.

All of my paychecks went to Mae. She loved to drink and gamble, and we found her away from home more often than ever. Sometimes she would gamble Dad's paycheck away, but then feel repentant and take on the character of Anna Mae. When this happened, she would get angry at what she had done and want to kill herself. Most of the time Mae stayed drunk. I was so thankful to God that all the personalities called me by a different name so I knew whom I was dealing with. I had to know when I needed to be careful with what I said and did, depending on who was the "personality of the day." As soon as she walked through the door, I would know who had taken over by the name she called me. Sometimes, I knew it best to run the other way, rather than incense one of them. On those days I would go to the Green Wave Cafeteria and stay till I was sure she had drunk herself to sleep or when I knew that Daddy had returned home. I tried not to be around her, except when Anna would surface. I loved the times with Anna. She was never around very long, but sometimes I could tell by the music she listened to. Anna was always out taking food to the poor or just being there for a friend whose husband had just beat her up or something. She was always giving clothing or furniture to a poor family somewhere. And best of all I would stroll in the door and there she would be cooking a special meal for us and baking cookies or a cake. I heard my name ring out, "Kaye Kaaaaye," in a sort of song. I would smile and sit in the kitchen tasting her delicious cooking. If it was gospel music on any given day, I knew it was Anna Mae. This was a good reason for me to stay clear. We all stayed away as much, and as often as we could. My career as a model was not rewarding to me anymore, because it merely supported Mae's gambling habit; slot machines taking all my earnings.

My brother and I would frequent the cafeteria after school since Mom wasn't home most of the time. We preferred to hang around other students, eat and have a good time instead of going home. One day, Anna Mae marched to the cafeteria drunk, swinging her arms around and talking loudly. My brother was so embarrassed that he walked out. I was embarrassed too, but she was still my mother. Somewhere deep inside was Anna, who deserved dignity. I held my head up high and took her home. When I put her to bed that night, I reasoned that no one understood my mother as well as I did; not even Dad. Sometimes I actually believed that Anna was going to come out and stay out for good. I had to show my brother that no matter what she did she still deserved our respect. The kids would see her strange behavior but they knew that with me there, they'd better not say anything. No matter what any of the personalities did to me, I still loved her. I didn't care what the kids at school thought of her because I knew that if they knew the "Anna" in her, they would also love her warm and giving heart. Her generosity was sometimes overwhelming.

## Chapter 9

Sometimes Keiko would spend the night at my house. We'd go to dances at the Teen Center and have lots of fun together. She was very interested in boys at this age, but I wasn't interested at all. I guess Keiko just figured I was too much of a tomboy and probably thought I was a virgin. Military GI's often would go to the Teen Center to hang out and play pool with the high school boys. Sometimes they would flirt with us but I would put my nose up in the air and pass them by. My Father had warned me to watch out for them and I was always wary, but Keiko teased me about it making our friendship awkward at times.

One night after a teen dance I decided to walk Keiko to the train station. I did this often, and it was not unusual for us to walk the mile from the back gate of the base where I lived. We said our good-byes and I turned to walk home. Most of the little shops were closed and it was getting dark, so I hurried to return to the gate. When I was about halfway home, I noticed a GI leaning against the edge of the building. He had one foot against the wall and the other on the ground while smoking a cigarette. He acted as if he didn't notice me, even though we were the only two people on the street. As I walked past him he dropped the cigarette and grabbed me by the throat with one hand, he revealed a razor with the other. He pushed me back into the alley on the side of the building. With the razor at my throat, he began to interrogate me as if he were my father. He asked me questions concerning what men I had been with, where I had been, and what I was doing; as if he owned me. I was too startled to answer any of his questions—asked by a man I didn't even know. "What does he want from me? Should I fight him; try to run? Should I yell? Where did he come from and why is he doing this to me?", spun through my head. "If I were to yell, would anyone hear me?"

When I didn't answer, he started to shove the razor into my throat. I knew if I wanted to make it home alive, I'd better start answering him. He began hitting me. I tried to tell him what he wanted to hear, but that even made him angrier. As he pushed me further into the alley, I was pleading for him to let me go. He kept hitting me. I asked him, "What did I do wrong? What did I do?" I told him that my father would be along to pick me up at the gate any minute, but he told me I was a liar. He knew that my mom was probably at home drunk, Dad was asleep, and my brother was with friends. How did he know all of these things about my family? Suddenly, he looked me straight in the eye and told me that he was going to make love to me right there in the alley. I begged him to stop. I told him I would go back to the barracks with him but he called me a liar. He screamed at me, "Don't patronize me! You hate GI's and you think you're better than we are. I know you're not allowed to be around us!" I could smell the liquor on his breath.

He hit me harder and I pretended to pass out so he would stop beating me, but everything I did seem to make him angrier. He grabbed my blouse and ripped it off of me. I tried to put my hands over my bra, to cover myself. As he reached down to pull my skirt off, he pushed me up in the air against the wall leaving my feet dangling. As one of my shoes fell off, he ripped off my bra. Again I tried to cover myself but it was to no avail. The next slap almost knocked me out, and I slid down the wall into the urine-filled stench of the alley. I could hardly breathe from the smell. The razor was still cutting at my throat while he kept saying "I love you." There were roaches and rats scurrying around me, and broken beer bottles scattered everywhere. He said that he had been following me and knew my every move. By the light of

53

only a dim lamppost, I lay in the alley with glass digging into my back and still, a razor to my throat. I pictured the headlines in the morning newspaper: "YOUNG GIRL KILLED IN ALLEY." I knew that this deranged man would kill me and leave me in the alley to die. "Why was this happening to me again?" I wondered. I felt a pressure and before I knew it, I had blacked out only to find myself in the White Room.

This time I was 14 years old, but I was safe in the room and didn't want to leave. The room brought back memories of being 9-years-old and how I had suffered. My stuffed monkey was gone and I was sitting on the floor of the room not wanting to feel the pain of this man slicing my throat. I didn't want to see my parents or go to court. I didn't ever want to go through the psychiatric testing or the lawyers repeatedly asking the same questions of me. I wanted to stay safe in my White Room.

When I woke up, I tried to remember where I was and what had happened. I was cold but not dead. Abruptly I remembered the stinky alley with rats and bugs crawling around me. I jumped up only to find my clothing scattered around me in shreds. I held my ripped blouse together, slipped on my skirt, one shoe and started to cry. My purse was gone, but I didn't care. I just wanted to find enough clothing so I wouldn't have to walk home naked. Relieved that he had spared my life, I felt sore all over as I slowly walked out of the alley. When I turned the corner, there he was, in the same position as before, smoking a cigarette. What audacity! When I tried to go around him, he told me to go back into the alley because he wasn't finished with me yet. I said to him, "No I'm not going back into that alley! I'd rather die first!"

He pulled out the razor again. I had made up my mind that I would never go back into the alley and I would fight for my life! God must have been there with me because just as soon as he started to grab my neck, three football players from school came trooping along. "Thank you, Lord," I whispered. The biggest of the three, Tibbs, immediately took off his jacket and backed up. He evidently knew the guy who had hurt me and called him, "Raymond." Raymond told him to mind his own business. Tibbs began to wrap his jacket around his arm. One of the other guys moved behind Raymond to take him down. I fell to my knees because I was so scared, weak and hurting. I didn't want anyone to get hurt for me. Tibbs told Lee, one of the other football players, "Get her out of here."

Lee gently wrapped his jacket around me. I was so thankful because I had no idea how I would get onto the base without the guards questioning me. I kept looking back to see if Tibbs was all right. He had somehow managed to wrestle Raymond down to the ground and take the razor away. While Tibbs had him on the ground, Raymond started screaming my name like a madman. He kept yelling, "Cynthia, Cynthia I love you! Cynthia, God I love you please don't ever leave me! Please don't leave me!" I couldn't believe what I was hearing. Who was this crazy man? Trying not to look back too long, I could see that Tibbs had his knee in Raymond's back. Soon the guards at the gate noticed the commotion and went to help Tibbs. By that time I was back on the base and Lee asked if he could take me home. I explained that I couldn't go home dressed the way I was.

Lee took me to his girlfriend Crystal's house. All of a sudden in a big whirl, everything that had happened to me as a child started rushing at me: my mother's attempted suicide, my father's anguish, my family's embarrassment and people harassing us. My mind spinning, I again saw the lawyers, judges, courtroom and people that had called us, "nigger liars." I knew I could never go through that again. Not ever! As soon as Crystal's mom saw the condition I was in, she sat me down and went to get bandages and medical supplies. While asking me what happened, she cleaned up my wounds and I told her that my parents could never find out about it. I explained about my childhood and that I could not go through another trial or any of the circumstances surrounding it. She promised not to tell anyone. I was too sore to talk and had a terrible headache. She told me that I needed to see a doctor, gave me some clothes and took me to the hospital.

When the doctors examined me, they told me I would be bruised and sore for some time. They tested me for venereal disease, stitched me where I was torn, and tended to the cuts on my back and neck. The cuts weren't deep and neither were the bite marks that Raymond had inflicted. My swollen face and split lip would heal. I kept telling myself, "I made it this far, and I can make it all the way. Be strong, Cynthia, and hang on, you'll make it!"

If it had not been for the White Room I would have lost my mind. I may have felt the "battle wounds" when I left the "room," but while I was there I was saved the humiliation and pain that Raymond had inflicted. After leaving the hospital, I returned to Crystal's house. I changed into a turtleneck to hide the cuts from the razor and the bite marks from my family. I was so thankful for Crystal's mother and the three football players who rescued me.

I went home only to find Mae drinking and playing cards with her friends. I tried to pass by without being seen, but she snuggled up to hug me. Luckily, Raymond only slapped the right side of my face. I was able to hide it from Mae by turning my face the opposite way. It was terribly painful even for her to hug me but I didn't let on. Since she was drinking, she wasn't paying much attention anyway.

I went to my room and sat on the bed. As I lay down on the cool sheets the tears streamed easily. I suffered alone. Again, no one was there to comfort me. I promised myself that this incident would follow me to the grave, and once again I had to put something terrible behind me. I always patterned myself after the "little engine that could," and just kept on going up that hill. I never again would experience the terror that I had gone through when I was nine.

I decided to tell Keiko what had happened. She told me that Raymond had been asking questions about me for some time. It was then that I realized that he had been stalking me. There was no other explanation for his knowing exactly where I would turn up the way he did. Several of my other friends told me the same thing. He had approached them acting interested in me, asking where I lived and where I went each day. He wanted to know everything about me, including my television shows and modeling jobs. I started to have flashbacks of seeing him in front of the base store, theater, and post office. I even recalled his trying to talk to me at the youth center, but I only ignored his advances. That probably angered him even more and I wasn't aware of it. The writing had been on the wall and I was too busy being involved in my everyday life to notice. In hindsight I probably should have acknowledged him, and told him right out in public to stop following me and leave me alone. I wish my friends had told me sooner that he had an interest in me. I may have been able to stop him in his tracks. Life is full of buts, what ifs, and whys, so I guess I'll never have an answer.

That night when I was ready to go to bed I recalled changing into my nightie in front of the window one evening. It was dark outside and I turned out my lights only to see a stranger standing and staring at me through my bedroom window. I ran out of the room screaming. My father ran outside to investigate and found no one. The next morning Daddy found a man's footprints on the lawn. I realized then that it must have been Raymond. I had to get these thoughts out of my head, but I just couldn't.

Since I had become a teenager my father and I no longer had a relationship. We were not allowed to be around each other because of Miss Meany's weird and evil thoughts. Somewhere she had heard that at a certain age, fathers would begin sleeping with their daughters. This was the first time I had ever heard this kind of nonsense. This angered my father tremendously but what could he do? I think at the time he didn't know what to think of my mother. What a ridiculous thing for her to think! I had the most decent father in the world and for all the years they had been married, she should have known that! So he just did as she said to do, to keep her from thinking such evil things. He knew something was wrong with his wife, but what? Almost every day, I wondered where my mom had gotten her weird ideas. Some of the things she said and did were stranger than truth. I guess she had gotten them from her odd childhood.

I decided at this time to turn away from God. How could he allow such terrible things to happen to me! Was he against me for some reason? The only person I could depend on was myself. It seemed that everyone I ever trusted had walked away from me, from my brother with his girlfriend, to my dad and mom. I was disappointed in everyone and everything around me. Everything I had seen in Church seemed illogical and wrong. They taught us about the Bible, which showed us how to have good morals, and the way to live a proper life, but in reality I saw just the opposite. There were preachers sleeping with other women, people gossiping about each other, bingo, long meaningless services and begging the congregation for money. It all seemed pitiful to me. I didn't want to be a part of the travesty any longer.

As I wiped the tears from my eyes, I couldn't help but think about how I was going to keep my mother from seeing my bruises and swollen face. When I awoke each day, I quietly and quickly crept out of the house until I healed. Since Anna Mae always slept late because of her constant depressed state, this was not too difficult of a feat. When Anna was around, she would wake us early in the morning to make sure that we had a healthy and very creative breakfast. Every time I thought about Anna, I missed her terribly. "Has she gone forever? Anna, where are you?" I thought.

A month had gone by and life seemed to return to normal. I started to feel sick. I vomited a lot, couldn't sit through school without falling asleep, and even passed out in gym class. I knew something was wrong, but I had no idea what it could be. I went to Crystal's house, which had been a safe haven for me, and explained to her mom what was happening to me physically. She took me to the hospital under an assumed name, "Miss Mae Doe." When the tests were completed, they told me I was pregnant. Yes, pregnant! I could have killed Raymond at that exact moment!

As I left the hospital, I had no facial expression at all. I was totally spaced out, thinking of the fate that awaited me. I didn't speak. As I felt my mind fading off into the distance, I could hear Crystal's mom saying, "Everything going to be all right, just don't do anything stupid." In fact, she told me twice before I could reply quietly, "No, Ma'am, I won't." I managed to convince her that I wouldn't do anything crazy. And I knew if I committed suicide, I would immediately go to hell. Even though I no longer believed in God, I wasn't taking any chances that might make me suffer more than I already had. Crystal's mom took me back to her house and as I got out of the car, I didn't even turn around to thank her. Crystal ran after me and asked again if I would be OK. I didn't answer her and continued to walk home, wondering how I would find Raymond and kill him.

I visited Tibbs and asked if he could remember if the police take Raymond's full name and address. He hesitated, and asked me why I would ask such a question. I didn't answer him, but he gave me the information and warned me to stay away from Raymond because he could be dangerous. Tibbs tried to remind me of what I had been through and that Raymond was completely capable of doing it again. He pleaded with me to stay away yet his words did not faze me in the least. The voices in my mind were telling me to kill Raymond for ruining my life. I hugged Tibbs and left thinking, that even if I wanted to keep this baby, I couldn't. I was only 14 years old.

Now that I had Raymond's name and address, I went to the barracks to find him the next day: bat in hand and an objective in mind. If he were as dangerous as Tibbs had said, I didn't know what state of mind he would be in. I searched for Raymond for a week until Sunday evening, when the base was not crowded and alot of folks were home with their families. I began to ask questions of the people roaming around. I pretended to be a friend of his trying to find his whereabouts. This different approach was the right one--a passerby pointed out his barracks to me. He wasn't there, but I decided to devise a plan and wait. First I hid my bat in the bushes, when Raymond approached, I hardly recognized him. It had been very dark that night in the alley and the man approaching me looked gentler. I found it hard to believe it was the same man. When he lit up a cigarette and sat on the front step of the barracks, I recognized him for sure. When he looked up, it was as if he knew I'd be hunting him. He almost looked peaceful, as if someone had told him I was looking for him. He was sober and looked very different, but I was going to beat him, regardless. He started begging me not to beat him, but I ignored him almost as if I couldn't hear his pleas. I can't remember how many times I hit him. With every plea, I hit him two more times. Trying to escape the beating, he curled into the fetal position. He kept begging me to stop the blows of the bat; all to no avail. He was going to pay for raping me, getting me pregnant and ruining my life. Two men appeared and pulled me away while I was screaming, "Let me go, I have to kill him!" I felt no remorse, only hatred. Emotionless, I dropped the bat and started to walk home. It was as if I spaced out, but when I arrived home, I fell to my knees and started to cry. "How am I going to tell my parents that I have been raped again and am now pregnant?" I wept in the corner of my dark room. I sat for hours and realized that each time I looked at my child, I would remember being raped. I had to come up with a plan to resolve my situation. I debated with myself for a week.

I soon came up with a plan. I would go to Raymond and tell him that I was pregnant. Then make him go to my parents and tell them that we had an affair and that the baby was an accident. We would tell them that we decided to get an abortion, and if he didn't go along with my plan, then I would threaten to kill him. I knew at the time that what I was thinking sounded somewhat crazy, but I thought it was actually very close to being sane. There was not much time and I needed to do something and do it soon.

I went to Raymond, who didn't agree with my plan at first. He begged me not to kill his child. He said he would care for it. He said he loved me and would make me a good husband. Before he could get anymore words out, I assured him that if he didn't go along with what I told him to do; I would tell my father what really happened. He didn't know I

61

was bluffing because I sounded very serious. I threatened that if he wanted to live one moment longer, he would come to my house and do what I told him.

To clarify how serious I was, I told him "You know where I live because you've been there before. I know that you were the man standing outside my window that night when I saw a shadow outside in the yard." He simply looked at me now, without saying a word. I told him I knew he had been stalking me, and then I looked him straight in the eye and told him not to be late.

That night, Anna Mae was in the kitchen cooking. Dad was in the front room reading the newspaper. I was growing anxious waiting in my room for Raymond's arrival. I remember feeling sorry for him after first putting him through a beating and now this plan that was about to come to fruition. This time I hoped that the ball was in my court. When the doorbell rang, I ran to the door and called my parents over to introduce Raymond. I asked them to sit down; they both looked dismayed. Dad shook his hand and all the while I cringed as Raymond touched his hand. My father smiled at him and said, "Nice to meet you." I couldn't help but think, "If Dad had any inkling what this man did to me…"

I sat on one side of the room and Raymond on the other. It was so hard for me to act as though I had feelings for this man who was supposed to be my lover. But my parents didn't pay much attention to my behavior. Raymond stood up and said, "Mr. and Mrs. Nelson, your daughter is pregnant and I would like to ask for her hand in marriage." I was knocked totally off guard. I was shocked and horrified and I jumped up and said, "No!" at the top of my lungs. I raced to my room. Dad asked him nicely to leave while Miss

Meany followed me with a cord that she had cut from an old iron.

She began to beat me and yelled at me to tell the truth. She blamed me for lying on Raymond, and said that he was probably an innocent man and not the father of the baby. "You don't really know who the father is," she bellowed. I pleaded for her to stop beating me. She kept on swinging the ironing cord, hitting me on the back, face, arms and legs. I knew that if I stopped her and told her I was raped, she would've stopped. But I couldn't. She would just have to kill me because I couldn't say the words. She accused me of whoring around with so many men I didn't know who the father was. She was going to punish me by making me keep my "unborn child," then send me back to the states to live on my own. I begged her to let me get rid of it. I told her I didn't want the child. I couldn't believe Raymond wanted to marry me.

The next few weeks were like hell. Anna Mae repeatedly came to me saying she had to carry this burden because she was my mother. This sin would be on her and that she would suffer in hell for it. She drank constantly. Mae would tell me to keep the baby, and Miss Meany would laugh and torment me about how I was going to be miserable as I tried to raise the child myself. She relished the thought that I would have no food or money.

One day, as if out of the blue, Anna came to my room and hugged me. I held her ever so tightly. I didn't want to ever let her go. It had been such a long time since I had last seen her. She asked me if I was okay. I told her that I didn't want to marry him; I just wanted an abortion. At that, she smiled and told me not to worry. She would make everything all right. She kindly said, "Mama will take care of everything."

I was petrified that if Anna left my room, she may never return. She went back to bed and I wondered if I would ever see her again.

The next morning I was scheduled to go to the clinic. I sat on my bed in anticipation, wondering who would walk into my room. I paced the floor, back and forth while I nervously waited. I heard Mom and Dad talking in the other room, but could not hear what they were discussing. I heard a knock at my door. I sat on my bed all dressed up with my sweater in my hands. I trembled at the thought that it would be Miss Meany who would come thru the door. Soon the door slowly opened and there stood Anna. She looked so beautiful as she smiled at me. "Are you ready honey?" Relief flooded over me and I said, "Yes, Ma'am," and grabbed my sweater. Unfortunately, Anna was under the impression that Raymond and I were lovers, so she stopped at the barracks to pick him up, believing that he would want to be with me. Mom felt that since they would not allow me to marry him, she could at least allow him to be by my side. He politely said his "good morning." Anna thought I was being quiet because I was nervous. She told Raymond that he should excuse my behavior, but little did she know he was the last person on earth I wanted to speak to that day.

The clinic was downtown and when we arrived, Anna took my hand. She knew just how nervous I was and held it tight until a nurse escorted me into a room where I was to undress. As I was about to go, Raymond had the audacity to grab my hand. I couldn't believe he would try such a thing, but he was really taking advantage of Mom not knowing what had happened to me.

Anna stayed by my side as they administered the gas to put me to sleep. When I awoke, who was I to see smiling down at me, but Raymond! I turned over so I didn't have to

64

look at him. Anna sat on my other side. She stroked my face and asked me how I was feeling. She told me that it was all over and that the baby had been a boy. I was filled with anguish and started to cry. I admit that it was the first time that I ever stopped to think about the baby and what I had done. "Poor little baby, please forgive me!"

The look I gave Raymond when we dropped him at the barracks was one I'm sure he'll never forget. Anna stayed with me as I recovered, keeping a close eye on me. I stayed out of school for a couple of days while Anna and I spent the time talking about her childhood. Yes, I was glad it was all over with, but I was afraid to go back to school for fear Anna would no longer be there for me when I came home.

After school I walked up to the steps of the house and could hear church music. There stood Anna Mae with her drink in her hands, bawling and telling me how we were both going to hell for what we had done.

# Chapter 10

I changed into my play clothes and called Keiko. I went over to her house and we sat and talked about everything that had happened. Keiko told me to be very careful because she didn't think my dealings with Raymond were over.

One day Keiko and I were sitting in the Green Wave Cafeteria. Tibbs walked to our table and told me that Raymond was going to prison for cutting another GI's throat. The first thing I wanted to know was condition of the attacked GI. What I heard angered me beyond belief. Tibbs assured me that the man was all right, but the reason for the attack astounded me. While a group of GI's were watching TV in the barracks, the show that I appeared on aired. One of the men made a comment that I was cute and he'd like to meet me. With that, Raymond went crazy, broke a bottle and cut his throat. I was angered, but glad to hear that Raymond would be spending time in prison. I couldn't help but think, "It will be difficult for him to stalk me from jail."

I thought Raymond was in prison, so he was definitely the last person I expected to see. One day at a football game I climbed to the top of the bleachers to gain a better view. From my perch I saw Raymond being handcuffed and escorted by the police across the football field. He kept looking up into the stands as if he were searching for me! He ended up standing directly below me, yelling and proclaiming his love for me. I was so embarrassed that to avoid him, I jumped down almost ten feet to the ground. I twisted my ankle and wobbled home. As I left the field, I still could hear him yelling to me, "I love you Cynthia!" Later I was told that they took him back to a prison in the States, and with that, I never heard from him again. My worry now was how to face my friends the next day. They were very understanding when they heard about Raymond and what he had done. I felt as if my life was back on track. That was absolutely fine with me.

Keiko and I soon went back to modeling and I started performing on television again. Although I didn't think of it being more than just a job, I met some of the most interesting children who later would turn out to be teen idols and legends in their own right. Since I was fluent in Japanese, I became somewhat of a translator for the interviews done on the show. One person that didn't particularly stand out to me at the time was a little boy named, Michael. Years later, I would think back and ask myself, "Why didn't I get that kid's autograph?"

Soon I would be celebrating my Sweet Sixteenth birthday with a slumber party. Anna Mae informed me that this would be my last party, since I was getting too old to have them anymore. All my girlfriends showed up, including Keiko. She came with another girl that I hadn't invited. I was upset that she would be so rude as to bring Karen. I thought that Keiko was the only good friend I had in the whole world and now she had chosen someone else to take my place. It made me very jealous. Karen and Keiko invited some GI's to the party without my knowledge or permission. Mae was furious and blamed it on me, as if I would be stupid enough to pull a stunt of that degree. Knowing that this was probably the last of our friendship, I had to ask Keiko to leave. Tears filled my eyes as she and Karen walked away. I knew that they would now be together all the time and that Karen eventually would be modeling with us.

Keiko and I still would have conversations, but when Karen modeled with us, the talks would end quickly and the two of them would go off together. I had to get rid of this new friend who was so important in Keiko's life. One day I went to Keiko's house to talk to her. I found out quickly why she had been acting so strangely. There were two men there with her. I reasoned that Karen and Keiko must have been sleeping with men to get better modeling jobs. Since Keiko was helping to support her mother, I didn't hold it against her. It wasn't long before we stopped seeing each other. Her mother called me to the house one day to ask why we weren't friends as before. I tried to explain that we didn't have anything in common anymore and our schedules were conflicting. I have to admit I was curious about this interest that all my friends were having in boys. What was this boyfriend/girlfriend thing that kept my brother so busy and separated from me? I totally lost respect for Keiko, but still I was intrigued. Was it just for sex or was there more to it?

Coming home from a modeling job one day, I stopped at the post office to pick up our mail. I bumped into someone, whom I believed to be the cutest man on base. We both reached down to pick up the mail, when he knocked it out of my hands again. I was thunderstruck as he looked up at me with the most wonderful smile. I could only stand there with my mouth open. He smiled, asking me if I was the girl on the TV. And all I could do was shyly stutter out a "Yes." He introduced himself, "I'm Sam Jackson."

One evening while Sam and friends had been watching the talk show I appeared on, a friend of his mentioned that I lived on base. All I could do was smile and gaze at him foolishly. He was being very polite. I just thanked him and left. This man was constantly on my mind. I felt embarrassed at the way I was acting, but I was helpless to stop thinking about him. Now I knew what this boyfriend/girlfriend thing was all about. Trying to see him everyday, I even went back to the post office at the same time daily, hoping to bump into him again. I finally did see him; Sam was talking to Karen. They were flirting with each other and she was doing her best to make him notice her, batting her eyelashes and holding her hands on her hips. I was devastated that this pretty girl, who seemed more mature than me, could capture his attention. Those devilish horns of mine started to grow out of my temples and I wondered if that flirting couple had any idea what I might be thinking. I had to get any evil thoughts out of my head before I did something foolish. I glanced down at my skinny, girlish figure--with physical features not nearly as nice as hers--and yet I realized that my chest was bigger!

Eventually he went over to her house to see her. Karen was in the arms of another man and he heard through an open window how she was only using him; my handsome stranger. Not long after, he approached me and asked me why none of his friends had told him what kind of girl she was. I told him that he was so awestruck with her he wouldn't have listened to anyone about whether or not she was a whore. Sam walked away and I couldn't help feeling sorry for him. He really seemed to be a nice and decent man. I found out that he was not trying to see her because she was easy, but because he liked her; and that made me want to get to know more about him.

I found myself fixing my makeup more often and checking myself in the mirror, not to mention dressing up. Dad would comment that I had changed my appearance, no wearing my torn jeans. I would walk in front of my new friend's barracks, hoping he would see me. I peeked in on occasion to see if I could get a glance at him. I even tried dropping mail at the post office. He would kindly pick it up for me but it was as if I didn't exist. Sam always would say, "Hello," and keep walking. So one day I followed him into a movie theater. I was skulking around behind him buying popcorn and a soda. I was so busy trying to stay invisible that I tripped over a rug and fell behind a row of seats.

Popcorn and soda went flying all over everyone's heads and laps. Popcorn was all over the floor. I stayed hidden until I thought the coast was clear. I slowly rose and with my eyes peeking over the top of the seats, I checked to see if he was paying any attention to the commotion. Everyone was laughing at my escapade. I felt so humiliated, I ran from the theater. If I had not worn those silly high heels to look more mature I wouldn't have tripped. Now it was time to use, Plan B.

Plan B would begin the following day. I rode my bike past his barracks until Sam noticed me. Hopefully he would come out and see me and say something. After I had ridden by several times he finally sauntered out; then acting as if I didn't care, I waved as I passed by. Looking around to see if he noticed how dressed up I was; I steered right into an old "Papa son" walking on the sidewalk. I hit the old man and knocked him onto the ground. I flew over the chrome handlebars, head over high heels. Sam helped us both up as the old man cursed me out in Japanese. Sam and I couldn't help but laugh; the old man called me every name under the rising sun. I hopped back up onto my five-speed and swore I never again would ride a bike in high heels.

With only one plan left, I had to succeed in gaining his attention. I was planning to make it simple since I didn't want to look like a fool. The next day I went to a carnival hoping to see him there. He was riding his bike in front of the BX and I stopped him and told him how desperately I had been trying to get his attention. I couldn't believe what I was saying to him. I told him I thought he was cute and added that I liked the way his clothes fit him. I even asked him why he didn't pay any attention to me. His reply was, "I don't go out with little girls." Offended, I told him that I knew more than he thought I did. He just smiled at me and agreed to meet me later in the day for a trip to the park. We sat on the swings in the park and traded stories about my career and his family. I found myself lying in bed that night thinking how I had made a good friend that day. Suddenly it occurred to me that it would be difficult to avoid having sex, which I knew nothing about really, only that it hurt. How was I going to explain that sex meant "rape" to me? Sex was such a big issue at school that if you didn't have sex, you weren't considered "cool." How was I going to get him to respect me for my beliefs that sex was horrible and still keep him interested in me?

Trying to avoid the subject of sex as long as I could, we grew further and further apart. He was going downtown without me and spent a lot of time off base. It was my belief that I caused this by ignoring the obvious. "Maybe he has replaced me with another girlfriend?" I thought. I followed him one day as he was leaving base carrying a teddy bear. I knew it wasn't for me and naturally assumed it was for another woman. This episode proved to me that I had to go to bed with him or I would lose him. I set a date with him, implying that I was an expert, since I already had sex "hundreds of times." He asked if I was sure I wanted to do it, but of course I wasn't. I was afraid of losing him.

He asked me to meet him at his friend's house and I became extremely nervous. I spent the entire day wondering how I would get out of it, but kept reasoning with myself that I loved him and it would be different this time. Not being able to cancel the meeting, my hands were trembling--I was not ready to be put into this predicament, yet I couldn't lose him. When we met at his friend's house, I immediately undressed and jumped into bed. He was so nervous; he took minutes to fold his clothes neatly. Then he climbed into bed and our eyes met. We just stared at each other. As it turned out, neither of us was ready. Of course, I pretended that I wanted to go through with it, but he explained that he felt

71

like he was robbing the cradle. He feared my dad, the law, and the repercussions that this might cause. Both of us laughed as we left the house and decided to try again some other time. Even though I didn't think he was serious about me yet, I did know that this was the man I wanted to marry. His not pushing me into anything physical gave me a lot of respect for him and with this "promise," I hoped that we could wait until we were married.

We really enjoyed each other's company and continued to see one another. I was beginning to fall deeply in love with him and was happy when I could see him every day. Knowing that inevitably we would make love, we started touching each other and began to kiss a bit more. Sam asked me this time if I was ready. Upon meeting at his friend's house, we removed our clothes and climbed under the sheets. We lay there kissing and I began having flashbacks of my rapes. I tried to erase them but I couldn't; even telling myself that this time I was in love. Mr. Jones's and Raymond's faces flashed in front of my eyes. But when I tried to stop Sam, it was too late. I even thought Sam was raping me and when I asked him to stop, he ignored me. I didn't know how to stop what I was feeling. This was becoming nasty to me. As before, I felt a pressure and passed out, finding myself in the White Room. I was so ashamed to be there, because I had allowed this to happen to me. Seeing my body as an instrument rather than something cherished, I had no respect for either Sam or myself. I had been given a body to take care of and gave it away so I wouldn't lose a man I thought I loved. How stupid could I have been to allow this to happen to me again and expect it to work?

When I awoke, Sam was scared to death and had a cool compress on my head trying to revive me, repeating that he was sorry over and over. I told him that I was okay, but he couldn't recognize that I was all right. I felt too embarrassed and too scared of loosing him to explain what had just happened. I guessed that he thought it was my first time and so he excused what had happened. We left each other, without sharing any of our inner thoughts. About a week later we tried it again, and the same thing happened. Because he was tired of excuses, my attempts to get out of the situation failed. Finally, I broke down and explained why I couldn't enjoy sex. I couldn't tell him that I was afraid he would leave me, nor could I tell him that I hated every minute we spent having sex. I didn't know how to explain how my mind took me away to the White Room every time he tried to have sex with me. When I finished describing my past encounters, he said that he would stand behind me all the way. He said there would be no more sex until I could get the help I needed. My feelings for Sam Jackson grew even more strongly than before, and he became my manager and companion at shows.

Sam thought I was being ridiculous allowing Mae to gamble away my earnings, but this was not his decision. He had no right to interfere. We soon began talking about marriage and he made it clear that I would not be giving money to Mae. Even as I described Mom's personalities to him, he had no understanding whatsoever about Multiple

Personality Disorder. Just as everyone else did, he thought my mom was crazy. There were times I thought that I had the problem and my mom was perfectly normal. Why then, could Mom not remember anything she did?

# Chapter 11

Sam and I enjoyed traveling all over Japan together. Sometimes Sam would even dance in some of my shows. He soon discovered that my agent had been cheating me, so he began to negotiate my deals for me. As time went by, I started to hate being a celebrity. I enjoyed all the perks it brought me like the bodyguards and the limousines and getting almost anything reasonable that I asked for. Sometimes the promoters would put us in a luxurious hotel and block off our entire floor. Although I enjoyed all this, I still felt abused; having to pay for Mae's gambling habit. I knew that if I stopped modeling, Mae would get angry with me and Miss Meany would beat me.

Soon I started falling asleep and felt nauseous in school again, but this time I knew the reason. I had Sam take me to the hospital where we found that I was pregnant. Since the previous doctors told me I could not become pregnant again, I had not been concerned about it. The base in Japan was going to close soon and I felt happy that I was carrying Sam's baby. I imagined that we would fly back to the States and live happily ever after with our little fairy-tale family. This opportunity gave me the chance to quit modeling, dancing and doing television shows. All the news was going to be quite a shock to my parents so we decided to tell them everything all at once. They were angry, but since we were going to get married, it would be acceptable.

Mae was furious that I would no longer be supporting her gambling habit, so she decided to take it out on Sam. One day when Sam and I came home from a movie, she was in a drunken state and started to fuss at him. Normally, he was able to ignore her comments but he was angry because Miss Meany had beaten me the previous evening. I told him to leave but he didn't want to go. Little did he know what he was up against, when he let Mom know how he felt about her beating up the woman that he planned to marry, pregnant with his child! Suddenly Mae walked out the room and in came Miss Meany with a gun in her hand pointed it at Sam. I could tell that he was scared but he looked her right in the eye and said, "If you ever pull a gun on me again, you better make sure you kill me." Miss Meany was so drunk; it didn't faze her a bit. I started to think Sam was a bit crazy for facing her that way in her current state. At this point, I began to fear him.

As we began to organize our move from the base, I noticed that we were arguing a lot. The closer the move came, the worse life became. One day, Sam and I were playing around and I started sticking him with a pin. When he told me to stop, I kept it up because he had poked me too. We were laughing about it. Of course I didn't take him seriously and kept sticking him. The next thing I knew he slapped me so hard I could see stars. He didn't apologize for his actions. I thought he should have gotten up and left before he retaliated against me. This was my first inkling that I didn't want to stay with him. Sam was a bodybuilder and had twice the strength of a normal man. I told him to leave and never come back. Being pregnant and alone didn't matter, as long as all the arguing would stop. Being married was a way to leave my mother and her personalities, though. Sex was still uncomfortable for me and I always felt inadequate, yet Sam was my first means of escape from the life I had learned to endure.

Sam decided that he didn't want to be married either, which made breaking up easier. Korea was his next assignment and I would be going back to the States to begin a new life. Things were looking up for me but Miss Meany began to beat me when she heard the news. Dad interfered this time, telling her to leave me alone. He said he would personally take me back to the States and make sure I was on my own and safe. I was his child too and he was not going to desert me. Miss Meany accepted these words with cold silence.

When Sam saw me pass the barracks one day, he asked if he could come to my house that night because he had something important to tell me. I had nothing to say to him but I agreed. Upon his arrival, and to keep him from fighting with my mom, I took him to my room where he dropped to his knees and begged me to marry him. I was getting dressed to go out at the time and didn't feel like talking to him. He pleaded to let him take care of the baby and me.

I started to think about the personalities of my mom, living alone in a world I didn't know anything about, and how would I cope with a baby? If we were married, my baby would have a name and not be considered illegitimate. I didn't want my child to be teased or unaccepted in society. Still loving Sam, I reasoned that he would also want the best for our baby and we would be able to work things out. Sam smelled so good and looked so handsome that night. I admit, I was a bit swayed when he got down on his knees again and promised he would never hit me again. His loving gaze told me he was sincere and I told him I would marry him.

Dad made good on his promise to ensure that I was safe before he went to his next assignment. He drove us to a little chapel in Reno, Nevada where we were pronounced man and wife. Then Dad drove us to a base in Oklahoma where we were to begin our first assignment as husband and wife. Dad dropped us off after making sure we were settled into the base hotel, which was called "BOQ." I knew that I could always count on Dad to keep his word.

# Chapter 12

My wedding band was a K-Mart special, which cost $20 to be exact. Sam promised that he would buy me a nicer ring later, so I didn't mind. The first night in our hotel we talked for hours and planned our lives together. Mr. and Mrs. Jackson. We couldn't help but smile, knowing that we would be spending our golden years together. We could not afford a honeymoon but being together was good enough for us.

The next morning was my husband's first day on his new job. "Husband!" It sounded so weird! I thought this would take some getting used to. I awoke singing to myself as I dressed. The day was clear and sunny which matched my mood. I saw contentment and happiness in my life. I planned spending my day making a wonderful and romantic dinner for two. The Commissary was ten blocks away and I decided to walk there to buy the ingredients I needed to make dinner. As I walked, I thought about how much I loved him and what it would take to be the best wife possible. To me, marriage is a commitment where both partners look out for the other's well being. I was going to strive to make sex a beautiful thing and not black out anymore, pleasing him in every way I possibly could. Now that I was away from my mom, I could be my own person and not worry which personality would appear to change the course or direction of my life. I missed Anna tremendously and wished she could be with me since the baby was due so soon. I wish her life had not been governed by M.P.D., fragmenting her into those five individual entities. Recalling the struggles I had been through with her personalities, I could only imagine what it must have been like for her. Thankfully, I would not have to deal with that anymore. My new family was my only concern now. I was going to make the very best of it.

Walking in the hot Oklahoma sun, I felt that I might faint from the heat as I approached the Commissary. I bought what I needed but before I could reach the cashier, I passed out. The store manager called a medic and when I awoke, I was being tended to in the office. The medic had already placed an ice pack on my forehead and taken my pulse; the store manager had called my husband. When Sam arrived, he was very concerned about the baby. He took me home and put me to bed as the medic suggested. I slept until it was very late. Sam was in the front room watching television when I awoke and went to the kitchen to make dinner. He was furious with me and we began to argue. I still wasn't feeling well and was in no mood to discuss anything. He kept badgering me and finally slapped my face. This was our first big argument, and me not being an argumentative person, I realized that by being married to one, you soon learn to play the game. I yelled back at him, explaining that he was not my father and he had no right to talk to me that way. "I am no longer a child! "He said that I could not go anywhere without his permission. I glanced at him as if he were crazy and reminded him loudly that he promised never to hit me again. Stomping away, I went into the bathroom and locked the door.

I undressed and turned on the shower. Sam began knocking on the door, asking me to open it. He pleaded with me to let him in. I was so angry with him. I ignored his pleas and cried under the running water, never wanting to argue again. All of a sudden thunder boomed in the small room! The bathroom door flew off its hinges and fell onto the floor. Sam stepped over it, leaned towards the tub, and hit me so hard I landed down in the tub with a hard thud.

I trembled to think of marriage that started out like this. I knew we were headed for trouble, but what was I to do? Was this what an abusive marriage was like? Abuse was always something that I had heard about but never witnessed since my Dad never hit Mom. Dad always remained a gentleman when my Mom chose to hit him. Miss Meany bit off part of Dad's nose once and his face got really red. I knew he wanted to hit her but his self-control won out, and he held back. No matter how angry she made him, Dad was taught early on that a man should never hit a woman and he held onto those values. My thoughts kept trailing back to solutions and how I could get out of this marriage. I couldn't go home to my Mom and Dad.

The baby was kicking hard so I checked myself to be sure the baby was Okay. I stood up and slowly walked out of the bathroom, hoping Sam had gotten his anger in check. I put on a gown and carefully climbed into bed. Sam told me to help him get rid of the broken door, just as I settled in. I didn't want to anger him again, so in silence I followed his instructions. I hurt so badly I didn't want to do anything but go to sleep.

Enough was enough for one evening. We dressed and took the door into the room next door, switched them, and hoped that we would not be have to pay for the damage Sam had done. As the task was completed, I threw a blanket and pillow at him like I had seen in the movies. Unlike the movies, he threw it back at me and made me sleep on the floor. Now in my seventh month of pregnancy I felt extremely uncomfortable sleeping on the floor, but it was better than sleeping with him. I wondered how anyone could be so thoughtless as to knock down a woman seven months pregnant. It proved that he was not the man that I thought I had married. There he was, yelling at me about "being stupid and jeopardizing the baby," and yet he was knocking me down in the bathtub as if I were not pregnant. The following morning, I awoke hurting so badly that I could hardly move. I was black-and-blue all along my waist, back, and arms.

There was no way Sam could comfort me and he knew it, so he just looked at me. When he left for work, he told me not to leave the room; making me feel like his prisoner. I stayed there until it was time to make dinner. When Sam returned from work, he kissed me and told me he was sorry. He went on to explain his mind-set about closed doors. Again I fell for his excuses, forgave him and tried to put the violence behind me, but my distrust for him still lingered.

We moved into our new home the next day. This was such a romantic time for us and the next two weeks were picture perfect. Thoughts about fighting were the farthest things from my mind. This was the first time Sam lived in a house in suburbia and we were utterly happy in our new circumstances. Sam would flick the lights on and off, making me quite curious. He explained to me that in his youth he never had light switches. Instead they would go to the middle of the rooms in his home to pull a string cord to turn the lights on and off. He was even amazed at how electricity worked. I would just laugh, but all the time I took pleasure in his curiosity and happiness in our new home. I had experienced all of this growing up, so to me it was simply our new home where we would start our family in a place we shared together.

Sam brought a co-worker home with him the next day named, Terrance. He had a pregnant wife named, Sheila, and a small son. He invited us to his house for dinner so that we could meet. Sheila was very nice but was mentally abused by Terrance. I found in her someone to identify with. Although I was both mentally and physically abused, I felt extremely sorry for her. Sheila's face was disfigured from radiation treatments performed when she was diagnosed with throat cancer. Doctors removed almost half of her throat. The pictures she showed me proved that she had once been a very beautiful woman, but with her change in features, her husband had sent her to sleep on the sofa and began chasing other women. It was nothing for him to parade women in front of Sheila, all the while reminding her how hideous she had become. She was not only fighting the cancer, but also struggling to keep her marriage alive. She was determined not to leave him. Her children were her only reasons continue living on. We stopped visiting them because we couldn't stand the way he treated her, but I would stop occasionally to see how she was doing. Sam's treatment of me was becoming worse. I wondered why he didn't learn a lesson from the cruel abuse Terrance gave his wife.

One day as I sat on the couch watching television, Sam told me he had misplaced some paperwork. He asked me if I had moved it, and I replied "I haven't even seen the papers." He must have become frustrated not finding them, and needed to relieve some of his tension. He walked across the room and slapped me with no warning. This time he split my lip, not knowing his own strength. I was in horrendous pain as I crawled off the couch. I went to my room to pack.

Sam grabbed my suitcases and threw them onto the lawn right in the view of the neighbors. I felt so mortified. I went out to collect my clothes as he yelled at me through the door. People drove by and the neighbors watched, but nobody came to my aid. In those days it was normal "to mind your own business," but this man was threatening to kill me if I left, and no one wanted to become involved. I surprised him and left anyway.

I didn't know where I was going, but with luggage in hand, I walked down the highway to escape this man and marriage. Sam followed me in the car, begging me to reconsider. My fear of the highway was stronger than my fear of him, and with the traffic becoming busier; I knew it was time to allow him to drive me. I asked him to take me to the hospital. I wanted to explain to a military doctor what had happened and ask if they could get me back home to my parents. Miss Meany's abuse would be easier to take than Sam's. The doctor took Sam aside to speak with him. Sam returned with a smirk on his face. Whatever transpired in that discussion was not going to be in my best interest. The doctor told me he could do nothing for me at that moment, but asked me to return the following day. Sam took me home after the doctor released me. I went to bed unable to sleep. I cried all that night, knowing that the two of them would not allow me to escape my situation.

When morning arrived, I called my mom. Miss Meany answered the phone and made it crystal clear to me that I no longer had a home with them. Since I made my bed, I had to sleep in it. Miss Meany wanted to retaliate against me for coming between my dad and her. Explaining that my baby's life was at stake, I heard her laugh and said "You should have thought about that before you married him."

She knew he was mean the moment she met him and reminded me that she had told me that I shouldn't trust him. Everything Miss Meany said was true and I knew it. If it had been Anna, I would be on my way back home. That conversation opened the floodgates. Everything she had been longing to throw back at me came out. She went on about discontinuing my support of Mae's gambling and drinking habits, then to my dad's choosing me over Anna Mae when he drove us to Reno and settled us in at the BOQ. After hanging up the phone, I felt worse than ever and tried to figure out what I could do. The laundry was piling up and the house needed cleaning. I had to be a good wife to the best of my abilities and hang on until I figured what would be my best plan for escape.

That evening, Sam brought home a puppy. He thought it would cheer me up and it did! Sam knew that I favored German Shepherds so that's what he got; making me fall instantly in love with the adorable animal. As usual, there would be strings attached and I was not allowed to play with it. She would urinate and use the bathroom in the garage where we kept her. Sam was so cruel to the dog, not feeding her, hoping she would starve. I would sneak some food to her; he would find out and took it out on both of us. I knew it was better for me to stay out of it, so that the poor animal wouldn't suffer additionally. He would throw her from one side of the garage to the other; there was nothing I could do but wait for him to leave and pet the puppy to ease her pain. She no longer came when he called her and this became a reason for him to beat her more. Her little eyes were so sad. In his presence she would lower her head and keep her tail between her legs. When she and I were alone together she would wag her tail and lick my hands. I had to find a way to free not only my child and myself, but also to keep my dog from harm. I hoped we all would survive.

We would take our washing to the Laundromat weekly. The dryer would destroy some of our clothes, so I would hang them on the line in our yard. My neighbor stopped me and asked if we could talk. As it turned out, she had heard some of our arguments and knew that I was being battered. Telling me to be careful and take this seriously, she added, "If a man hits you and gets away with it, he's sure to do it again." She told me that I could be injured seriously and begged me to be on my guard. Noticing that I was in my ninth month and having three children of her own, she asked me if I could go somewhere until the baby arrived. I shook my head and started to cry, explaining that I had nowhere to go. She told me that after the baby was born, I had to fight back and make him stop his bullying or he would walk all over me. I took it to heart when she told me to call her if I ever needed anything. I made up my mind that I was not going to let him do this to me anymore.

Her words returned to me. I would have to control my temper. I had to cease making the situation worse by fighting back, when he started becoming abusive. At times I would lash out and call his mother a whore or berate his family, which would anger him more. It gave me a sort of pleasure watching him become enraged. He then would lash out about my mother, and he was right. What would hurt me most was his telling me I was "fat and ugly" and that he wished he had not married me. He would tell me that I was "only worth the $20 K-Mart special." I was nine months pregnant and Sam didn't have to call me a fat, lazy pig to make me feel bad. I was already depressed and it made me not want to do anything around the house. I questioned why I should do anything he commanded. Sam was becoming my dictator, instead of my husband. I kept in sight that I was a good person and would allow him to destroy my inner beauty. As far as I was concerned, even animals should be treated better than me in those days. I knew that I didn't deserve this horrendous abuse. We didn't have sex anymore because I would not allow him to touch me. I never understood how he could beat me and then want to make love right after. The very thought of the next time sickened me. I didn't want to punish him but it all seemed so unnatural to feel anything loving towards him. Making love to my husband should have been a very intimate and special thing for us, but how could I lay there bruised and battered and love him? For some reason I still loved this man. There were times when he went off to work that I wanted to run to him, kiss him, and tell him I loved him. There could be no condoning his behavior. I could not allow him to treat me badly. However, I had to wait for the right time when I could find somewhere else to go, where it would be safe. I treated him as if he were a stranger.

I went into the house, after we finished talking. I was so exhausted, being in my last month of pregnancy, and my mind was spinning. I fell asleep and when I awoke, I heard Sam in the next room. Hurrying to get dinner ready, I noticed that he was reading over the paperwork he had lost the night before. It was in his briefcase, but he didn't apologize to me. We began fighting all over again. Every time we argued, he would call his mother to settle it. This made me feel very awkward towards her since she always sided with him.  I apparently had disobeyed Sam about something and we were going through our usual routine of fussing and yelling. He told me he only married me because of the baby and had been in love with someone else at the time. I felt hurt and angry and tried to fall on my stomach to hurt the baby and myself. He thought I was crazy! All this constant yelling and nagging was beginning to take its toll.

The screaming and sleepless nights, along with the physical abuse, made me so miserable I didn't care what happened to the baby or me. I fell into a deep depression, not wanting to leave the bed. My hygiene was always something that made me proud, but now it didn't matter anymore if I discontinued bathing and brushing my teeth.

The time of the baby's arrival was getting close. When Sam came to the door to yell at me I didn't have the strength to yell back. One evening I had an unusual pain right in the middle of my stomach. Since I didn't know what it was, I rolled over and went back to sleep. Asking Sam to take me to the hospital was the logical thing when the pain started again later that night. In the Emergency Room, Sam was making a fool of himself and I was in pain, only to find out that it was false labor. The doctor told us to go home and get as much rest as possible, but the pain kept on through the night. Sam was forced to take me back again. He promised to sue the hospital if anything happened to me. The doctors sent me home once more. Sam was fed up and tired of losing sleep and I was in unbearable pain. He had told me that the next time I had a pain; I'd have to get myself to the hospital.

I had been enduring all night until the pain grew so bad I cried and begged silently for it to go away. I could not bear it any longer, picked up my suitcase and headed for the car. I dropped to my knees in agony as another labor pain hit. The contraction lessened, I walked to the driver's side of the car, tried to get in and the real pain of labor kicked in. I couldn't even sit up once I climbed in. I feared that if I went back to the house Sam might get really angry with me, but I didn't want to have the baby in the driveway alone or take a chance being killed driving down the highway. I made it to the porch only to have another contraction start. As I fell, I waited for the pain to subside and crawled to Sam's bedside, pulling on his arm to wake him. "I'm sorry for waking you up," he was stunned to see me on the floor. I told him that I had tried to go to the hospital myself but as I did, he jumped up, lifted me off the floor, and took me to the hospital. I would spend the next 38 hours in labor.

Most of the time I was cursing the doctors, nurses, my mom, Sam and even God, for my pain. Sam came to tell me that I was upsetting my mom who was in the lobby's waiting room. He had called her when he arrived at the hospital and she came right away to be with me. I became angrier than a hornet at every word he said and the staff made Sam leave the room permanently. I kicked one of the nurses out of the room because she had the nerve to tell me it was easier going in than coming out. I became more aggravated by such crudeness and kicked out the doctors too. I was in no mood for jokes and gave them the ultimatum: "Deliver the baby, or I will do it myself!"

They strapped my arms to the bed so that I couldn't push on my stomach. The way I was behaving, you might imagine that I looked like Linda Blair in "The Exorcist." I wouldn't let the doctor check me, my hair was sticking straight up

on my head, and I acted like someone possessed by a demon. The only part missing was the head spinning, tongue-thing, but I could imagine it would have come to that eventually. Another doctor came in and asked nicely if he could check me, saying that he would deliver the baby if I were dilated fully. I said, "Yes"; and boy, were they happy to see that I was finally dilated! You could see the sheer exhaustion on their faces, along with the pain on mine. When the doctor told me it was time to push I said, "Stand back, here she comes!" September Leana Jackson popped into the world on her due date, September 17, 1971 at 3:24 P.M. No sooner was she delivered than I passed out. I must have slept the entire day away. They tried to bring September to me but I was in too much pain to take her, so they returned her to the nursery to be fed. At times Sam or my mother would feed her but I would immediately fall back to sleep, not waking until the next day.

When I finally re-entered the world, Sam stood at my bedside with flowers and a plaque. The inscription read:

> To Cynthia, My Wife,
> God's Gift
> God gave this child to you to guide,
> to teach, to walk through life.
> Beside a little child so full of charm,

to fill a pair of loving arms. God picked you out because he knew, how safe his child would be with you.

(Below this inscription was listed my daughter's name and birth date.)

I was so amazed and felt so special. This helped me to realize that deep down inside his soul Sam was a loving and caring person. And even though he had treated me so badly, it touched me deeply. I kissed him and thanked him.

All of the other new mothers were jealous and could speak of nothing but the plaque. One of them complimented Sam and told me that the rest of the women had received only flowers that would die and candy that would be eaten. An award was presented to me that I could hang on the wall and would remind me that my husband felt I had achieved and accomplished a job well done. This made me so proud of my husband, and it continued from there, as people would enter my room just to see this famed plaque.

We were back on speaking terms and I began to love my husband more than ever. It's funny how much his charm temporarily could blind me to his abusive ways.

At first, I wouldn't take the baby because I was in such pain. The nurses would bring her in and lay her at the foot of my bed, hoping that I would pick her up, but my need to sleep came first. Deciding to take me out of a private room and move me into one with two new mothers was their way of pulling me into motherhood. I watched as the other women arose early to shower and welcome their babies. They had combed their hair, put on fresh gowns and set out the things they would need to tend to their newborns. They anticipated the babies' arrivals by making themselves look and smell good. I watched as they held their babies in their arms, touching the infants' fingers and toes and speaking softly to them. Their babies were held close as they began to nurse them. Then I noticed that the nurse wheeled September to the foot of my bed. As if they were words from her tiny little mouth, she gurgled to me.

I slowly got out of bed in a lot of pain. I carefully lifted her out of her small crib. I cuddled her into my arms. She was so beautiful. I started to cry; and I told her that her mommy was sorry. I asked her to forgive me and I swore that I'd never leave her again. It wasn't her fault. I kissed her little cheeks and held her tiny hands. I fed her the bottle they had left with me and she gave me a smile and what I perceived as a wink. Somehow I think I imagined it, but I understood then, that my little daughter grasped how I felt and forgave me.

# Chapter 13

When I arrived home with my new baby, Anna was there to greet us. I was so happy to see her. She had cooked a lovely meal and had a big surprise for me. Anna had brought September all kinds of beautiful clothes and an adorable white bassinet. Everything was laid neatly on my bed when I walked into the room. Above all, I was so very thankful that Anna was there to help me. I kissed and hugged her and thanked her for everything. Having a problem standing too long, I went straight to bed. Anna stayed up with the baby that night. Anna was a blessing to us because we didn't have the first idea how to take care of an infant. Anna told me not to worry about anything; she would take care of the house and new baby.

One day while Sam and I were sleeping, the door of our room flew open and in walked Miss Meany. She didn't knock; she just yelled and accused us of making love when she was in the other room taking care of our baby. She told us we were "using her", yet we had no clue what she was talking about. Anna was the one who promised to take care of the baby, cook, clean and allow me to heal. She knew that I had a large episiotomy and had a terrible time moving around. Sam told Anna to leave when she said that he had been cheating on me while I was in the hospital. You would not believe the words coming out of her mouth; demeaning us for trying to send her away when she wanted only to help us, taking advantage of her, and last but not least, insinuating that Sam had tried to rape her while she was there. She also said that he had put something into her head, like voodoo while she was asleep. I had never seen this from her before. She wouldn't allow us to take her to the airport and called herself a cab. When Miss Meany arrived home she told my father all kinds of lies. Not long after her arrival, Dad called to see if it was true. Explaining the way she acted, I think he believed us since he knew the antics she was likely to pull. I knew when he got off the phone he would pretend to be on her side because that's what he did when Miss Meany appeared.

When my mother told me that Sam was cheating on me, I took it to heart and believed that I might lose him, so I made love to him when I wasn't yet completely healed. I thought I was going to die from the pain. I didn't want him to know how much suffering I was going through, hoping that I could escape to my White Room, but this time I had to stay. When he was finished, I walked to the bathroom to sit on the toilet, only to find that I was bleeding badly. I began to cry when I realized that I had reopened my stitches. None of this was worth it and I never tried sex again until I was fully healed. He asked me many times, but I used every excuse in the book. If I lost him to another woman because of sex, then that was just fine. I loved him a lot but I did not want to have sex if there would be that much pain.

Since my husband was not an understanding person, he refused to help with the baby; at all. Because he had to get up early for work, I was expected to stay up with the baby. He accepted no responsibility but accused me of wanting the baby

for myself. He said that September wasn't his because I had been cheating on him. He was in total denial. Our new baby was very expensive. We were forced to take most of his pay to buy diapers and formula. One day he said that the Laundromat was costing too much and brought home a washboard. I had never seen one before, and certainly didn't know how to use it. He took me into the bathroom, and while filling the tub full of water proceeded to teach me how to use the washboard. I ran out of the room crying. I raced to the phone to call Dad and Mom. Anna Mae answered, and after I explained the circumstances, she promised to call Sears and order me a washer and dryer that day. Sam was livid, but I put my foot down this time. Our daughter needed to be first but he thought that his entertainment and such should come first. No matter how much I argued, he wouldn't listen.

Sam decided that September no longer needed formula at one month of age. Although the doctor ordered otherwise, I was forced to purchase regular milk for my newborn. I wanted her to be healthy and I knew that cow's milk would be very difficult for her to handle. As soon as Sam went to work I took a walk to the pawnshop down the street. My ring wasn't worth much but I asked the storeowner how much he could give me for it. He offered me five dollars, which I humbly took to buy formula. She drank the formula so fast I didn't even have enough time to steal any money from Sam's wallet to buy more. I hoped that he would not notice. When the formula got low, I would water it down, but September knew it and just drank more. I needed to pawn something else, but other than wedding gifts still in their boxes, I had nothing. When I offered the presents to the pawnshop owner, I asked for the ring to be returned before my husband noticed. He agreed. I was able to purchase more formula.

Not long after, I needed formula again so I tried to pawn the ring once more. The elderly owner asked me why I was pawning my wedding ring. I explained that my husband would not give me money for my baby. He felt sorry for me and offered me more money. I could not accept his generous offer. I already had enough trouble trying to pay back the money he had given me before. I knew I could not pay it back in time before Sam saw it was missing, so I asked the man if I could have $2.50 more. He was happy to oblige. Thankfully, the next time I went to his store, he informed me that the price of gold had gone up. The pawnshop owner offered to give me more money, adding that I didn't have to pay it back right away. He gave me until the end of the month and said that if I ever needed a witness in court, he'd be happy to testify for me. I thanked him for his kindness and started for home. Soon, September was drinking even more formula. I had to swallow my pride and accept more money from the kind gentleman, but I always paid him back. I could tell he wanted to do something to help me but he never interfered in my life. We became friends after a while, and eventually he was giving me money without my pawning the ring. He wanted me to keep the wedding band on my finger. Luckily, when September was two months old, the doctor told me to add cereal to her formula, and fruits and vegetables to her diet. I was hoping my newborn would adapt without any problem.

That evening I was in the kitchen, warming food for September. Sam strolled in and asked if he could be the first to feed her now that she was old enough to eat baby food. After I warmed her food and gave her dish to Sam, I showed him how to hold her in his arms. I watched for a minute as he fed her. Then I rushed into the kitchen to start dinner for Sam and I. I was standing at the stove putting water on to boil, when I heard a loud slap on skin. I thought Sam had swatted a mosquito. I hesitated to make sure, waiting to see if the baby was going to cry. I knew deep inside that there was no way that Sam would hit my baby. He couldn't be that crazy. How could anyone hit a two-month old? I stood back and hesitated for a minute, but when I didn't hear anything, I went back to what I was doing.

All of a sudden I heard a horrifying scream come from my baby. I was right; Sam had hit her and continued to do so! I dropped everything and ran to September. She was gasping for breath after being hit so hard. I tried to grab her, still screaming, out of his arms and he began to hit me. He stood up and threw the baby down on the couch, while kicking and hitting me. I curled into the fetal position and waited for him to finish. I again reached for my baby. He no sooner would knock me down, than he would begin beating me again. I kept yelling, "You crazy, black #@$%#^%(&. What did she do, to deserve such treatment?" He told me that she kept spitting out the spinach I had prepared for her. "That meant she didn't like it, stupid!" I yelled. He still wouldn't let me touch her. I continued to reach for her. He picked up the screaming baby by one arm and carried her to her crib as he continued to spank her. Of course she wouldn't stop crying for him, so he beat her more, while I begged him to stop. Throwing her into the crib, he pushed me out of the room and slammed the door behind him. He told me, "If you go into her room, I'll beat her again." I pleaded with him to please let me have my baby. The more I pleaded, the more firmly he refused to let me go into her bedroom. She was still screaming her head off! I slid down the wall onto the floor and held the doorknob and wept for my child. I cried hysterically, feeling completely helpless at her door. "I'm going to kill you!" I screamed. I told her through the closed door, "Mama's right here, honey. I'm sorry, baby. Mama's sorry; please forgive me. I'm so sorry!"

I knew Sam would beat her again and I wanted to kill him for it, but I didn't want to go to prison. I knew just how mean and cruel he could be, but hitting a two-month old baby was beyond reasoning. After about an hour and a half, her cry turned to a whimper. I heard her falling asleep. I longed to hold her in my arms but I knew for her sake it was better to stay away. When Sam finished his dinner that evening he left to get something from his office. As soon as he was out the door, I started for September's room. When I touched her she jumped, so I felt it best to leave her alone and allow her to sleep. I covered her with a small blanket, and turned off her light. I reached to wind up her music box; it began playing, "You are my Sunshine." I left out of the room before Sam could walk home. She was still whimpering in her sleep. I avoided sleeping with him when he returned, by staying up late. I noticed too, that he had a tough time getting to sleep. Maybe he was worried I would make good on my threat to kill him.

September never seemed the same after that night. In fact, she was very nervous and had crying spells for no reason--though I tried to comfort her. When she heard his voice get loud she would jump. It seemed at every little noise her eyes would widen in fear. I knew that she had been traumatized that night by the beating her father had given her. Sometimes when the crying wouldn't stop and I became aggravated, I would place her in the crib until she'd stop crying.

At one point she developed a terrible diaper rash. Since Sam refused to pay for medication, the doctors told me to let her go naked so her skin could dry out and heal, but she would scratch herself until she bled. I tried putting gloves on her tiny hands but she would take them off. Nothing I tried worked. I decided to go to the store and steal the medication. The medication proved not to work, and her repeated crying spells annoyed Sam. I kept her away from him as much as I could. Finally one day, Sam had had enough and flew into a rage, picking her up by one arm and beating her. This episode put me into a rage too, and all I could do was fight him back to protect my child. By the time it was over, I was scratched, battered and beaten, but he stormed out of the house and left us both alone. I held my baby and comforted her as we both cried. Not too long after, I met an old woman who told me to put cornstarch into her bath and let her soak every night. When I tried that, her diaper rash cleared up and I had a happy baby again. I decided that the old remedies would always be the best when it came to raising my children.

# Chapter 14

Sam decided that it was time I got out and found a job. He suspected that I was stealing money from his wallet and told me that there were two kinds of people he hated: one was a thief, and the other a liar. This was his way of accusing me of stealing from him. He had no right to keep money from me. The government sent paychecks to the wives to make sure that food was being purchased for the families of servicemen. This was a method of keeping enlisted personnel from spending their paychecks before they got home, ensuring that the children would always be fed. Sam would not let me have the check meant for me. Since he knew I would spend it on bills and food, he would forge my name and cash it. He would pay the bare minimum to the bill collectors and spend the rest going to movies and doing things he enjoyed.

It seemed that every time I went out with him something bad would happen, so I preferred to stay at home. If we went to a nightclub, I had to keep my eyes where he could see them to make sure I wasn't looking at another man. When we went out to dinner I always knew to order the cheapest thing on the menu. Even at a drive-through, I was not allowed to purchase anything. At a drive-in one evening we were arguing about me not being able to buy the snacks I wanted from the snack stand. I just wanted to go home because he started yelling at me right there at the drive-in. Everyone watched him slap me against the car windows. The baby started screaming because she was scared. Sam grabbed her from the back seat and told her to shut up, but being only 6-months-old, September didn't understand. He grabbed a diaper from the bag and shoved it into her mouth until it split her lip. We were pulling her to and fro, as I tried to grab her away from him. Finally he let her go, and opening the passenger side door he shoved us both onto the concrete. The drive-in customers watched in amazement. Of course, nobody wanted to get involved. I thought there was something definitely missing in the picture. No one cared that a six-month-old baby and her mother were beaten in public. What kind of world were we living in and why wouldn't anyone call the police?

Sam told me to get back into the car and I refused. He jumped out of the car, snatched the baby and started to drive away. I held on to the car as long as I could without falling. Finally, I let go only to tumble to the pavement. I was running down the highway, crying for my baby. He drove away. I kept running and crying, worrying about what he was doing to my baby now. Soon, after walking about a half mile, he came back for me. I jumped into the car right away and looked for my baby. Once September was back in my arms again and safe, I felt better. We proceeded home.

I walked around to every store trying to find a job. I would return home with applications, only for Sam to throw them away because he didn't want me to work at any of the places. Sam eliminated any job where I might be around men--which didn't leave much for me to choose from. Deciding that a home-based career in Avon Cosmetics was the most logical way to start out, Sam would watch September while I worked. Soon he grew tired of watching her and he expected me to take her with me. I complained to him, saying that I would quit if he wouldn't watch her. He warned me that she'd be on the street if I left her with him. I didn't care what he said. I was tired of dragging my baby house to house, changing her diaper in the car, and feeding her in the hot Oklahoma sun.

One day I walked out and tried to leave the baby with him only to have him carry her to the door and sit her on the front step. You should have seen her confused little face as she looked up at him and then over at me as if to say, "What did I do?" Next, her diaper bag came flying out along with her blanket and then he slammed the door behind him, scaring the baby and making her cry. I went to the porch to get her. Imagine what the neighbors were thinking when they saw this. In actuality, I didn't care what anyone thought about me anymore. If they were so concerned, they should have called the police.

I didn't feel like working that day. I decided to take September to a park to play. I knew if he caught me he would be angry, but who cared?

Sam did not want me to going to see friends. He hated when I wanted to do anything on my own. One day I decided to visit a friend of mine. He despised my friends. But I left anyway. I needed some time to myself. I marched around the corner to the back of my friend's house and knocked on the door. She was glad that I finally got out of the house, but watched in silence as I sat near the window where I could watch to make sure Sam didn't chase after me. I was right; he walked out of the house. But he didn't come looking for me. In fact, to my amazement, he came out empty-handed and drove away. Maybe my I was talking to my friend and had my back turned when he put the baby in the car. I know that he did not see me go around to the back of my friend's house. He couldn't possibly have known that I was sitting in the house across the street, watching.

I waited an hour for him to return, but something made me feel uneasy. I decided to go home to make sure that he hadn't left the baby. I didn't turn on any lights in case he was watching or passing by the house. There to my surprise, September lay in her crib, fast asleep. Sam didn't get home until the next morning about 1:00 A.M. If I had not been watching, September would have been alone all night. I cringed to think that what if I too had decided to stay out late? After that evening, nothing that Sam ever could do would amaze me. I took September everywhere with me and I stopped selling Avon. It was simply too much of a hassle to sell beauty products and care for a child at the same time.

# PART TWO

## Chapter 15

When my employment with Avon ended, I knew that I still needed a job. Although I had never been a waitress, I found employment in a Mexican restaurant. My boss there was very kind and understanding; we became very close. She was willing to show me around and teach me everything I needed to know about being a waitress. Often Sam would wait outside for me to finish work, in addition to calling me periodically to verify that I actually was working. My boss indulged me with this and understood that he was an abusive husband. Because I needed money for the day that I would leave Sam, I opened a secret bank account. I started saving every cent.

While I was working, Sam would take care of the baby, but his jealousy became worse. He started accusing me of cheating on him. Not only would he follow me but he would also check the odometer on the car to make sure I wasn't going places where he forbade me. One day when he picked me up at work, he didn't have the baby with him.

When I asked him where she was and he simply replied, "I left her with a friend. I need to speak with you alone."

When we arrived home he told me to sit in a chair and wait. I wasn't sure what he was up to but I patiently waited for his return. Soon he walked of out the bedroom with a revolver.

Putting one bullet into the gun's chamber, he said "I want you to play Russian Roulette."

Sam placed the nozzle of the gun in my face. Asking me questions about my actions and whereabouts, he would pull the trigger every time I denied his charges against me. He thought that everything I did or said was a lie. During this game, I could sometimes see the bullet in the chamber. When the bullet was on the top or bottom, I waited for the shot that would end my life. I was crying and yelling, and Sam was yelling back at me. I was so mad I finally said, "Just kill me. I don't care anymore." I wasn't going to play his games. Again I imagined the newspaper account for the next day: "WIFE KILLED BY JEALOUS HUSBAND." And it was all based on nothing, absolutely nothing. He began laughing at me, and I was so fed up I kicked him in the chest with all my strength and knocked him to the floor. He continued to laugh at me as I screamed, "Where is my baby? Go get my baby now! I'm not playing with you!" Again he laughed as he got up, walked out of the room and left the house. I watched for him through the window, pacing back and forth for almost an hour. I was hoping and praying that he would appear with September. I called different people and places to find out his whereabouts. It grew dark.

Finally, I saw the lights of his car flash across the window. Bringing the baby in, he stormed past me and refused to allow me to take her from him. She was sleeping. Inside the house, he still would not allow me to touch her, until he had taken off her coat. She seemed fine. At long last, I was able to hold my baby daughter, thankful that we both were safe after the ordeal he had put us through. I thought to myself, "I hate you, I hate you, you black #$@%(!" I knew then that I had to work as much as possible to make enough money to leave him. I worked overtime and kept all of my tips, saving for the day that I would free my daughter and myself.

Sam's sister was going to be married and he wanted to attend the wedding in New York City. I mentioned to him that we could first visit his family in New York and then my parents in Florida. I was scheming for a way to stay in Florida once I got there, but as usual, my plans didn't always go the way I wanted. I drove most of the way to New York, since Sam was not a good driver and would sometimes fall asleep at the wheel. He also knew that my driving skills were excellent and my navigational process was far superior to his. Before we reached New York, Sam took over the driving and we drove into a terrible snowstorm. I kept asking him to put on the snow chains. Soon the car skidded off the road and into the ditch. The baby was thrown to the floor and I into the dashboard. I yelled at him for being so stupid as not to put on the snow chains. Sam hitchhiked to a service station to get us towed out. Finally, without any more ado, he called a tow truck to get us out of the ditch. We installed the snow chains and continued to our destination.

We took turns driving into the city. I was simply amazed at all the sites. New York City was definitely different from anything I could have ever imagined. It was as if I had traveled to Mars. There were so many buildings, yet no grass or trees. People went everywhere and moved in a rush. This was the first time Sam had driven to the city so he kept getting turned around in the wrong direction, because of one-way streets. We finally arrived at his mom's house. I was in awe at the number of locks she had on her door. First we buzzed to enter the building, then we had to be buzzed in at a second door, and no sooner did we arrive at her apartment door than we heard the bolts being thrown. There must have been 20 locks on that one door, plus a bar.

His mom grabbed the baby and everyone hugged each other excitedly. From the very beginning of our visit, it became clear to me that something was wrong. His family was trying to put on a good front, but I could tell that they didn't care for me. As we sat down to get to know each other, the conversation immediately turned to the events surrounding the visit of Sam's friends with his parents. Sam's mother asked them how well they knew me, and they answered by saying they knew me very well (meaning that they had heard and were told about the problems I had with Raymond). They were trying to be evasive because they respected Sam and did not know how much of the story he had told his mother. They felt that it was our place to tell her. His mother created the false idea, from their conversations and her own evil thoughts that his friends had slept with me. So before they had even met me, Sam's parents already had formed an opinion of who or what I was. They felt that I had gotten pregnant on purpose to trap Sam into marrying me. Evidently, they didn't think that Sam was very wise or that his mother had raised him to know better. It was then that I understood why his parents felt the way they did about me. His mom had misunderstood them. I knew that this would ruin my relationship with his family. I wanted to explain everything, but Sam felt that I didn't owe them any more explanations. I don't know if he was ashamed to tell them or if he thought that they would misunderstand the situation, being that they were always so far away. I agreed only because I didn't want to relive it again by telling them what happened.

His sister, Catherine, and I seemed to get along; even though deep down inside I felt that she was trying to trick me into saying something wrong. I felt that she still thought I was up to no good and refused to trust me. I tried very hard to avoid saying the wrong things, not only to protect myself, but because Sam already had warned me about telling them our business. He told me to keep my mouth shut. That was hard for me to do, considering I had few friends or hardly anybody to talk to since the year Sam and I were married. Each and every day I sat in my house alone with my baby, with no one to talk to or visit. It was like being in a prison with Sam there to abuse me, both physically and mentally. I wanted so badly to share my thoughts with her, but I was afraid of the consequences. I believed his parents knew what I was going through, for it was noticeably obvious. When Sam raised his hand I would dodge or duck in fear. When he would ask me to do something I would jump. I'm sure they could tell by the look in his eyes, exactly what I was going through.

His sister asked me to go shopping for a few, last-minute things for her wedding. Sam at first said, "No," but after his sister got on him again, he finally agreed. She told me this would be a good time for me to buy a new outfit. I smiled at her, but when I turned to look at Sam, he opposed us. His sister again got on him. Sam was trying very hard not to look or act, like the tyrant that he was. Again she convinced him, and off we went to the mall. Walking out the door, I made sure the baby had all she needed so that Sam wouldn't have to do anything extra--otherwise I would hear about it when I returned. He may have been smiling at his sister and agreeing with her, but I knew that once I returned I would be in trouble. I just kept my fingers crossed and hoped and prayed that this time he would let me get away with it. Going out, walking through that door with his sister was so great. I felt like a caged bird that had been set free.

Catherine filled me with instructions about the proper way to protect myself in a huge city such as New York. It seemed that everything I did was wrong. I talked wrong, walked wrong, and couldn't even carry my purse properly. She cautioned me to always hold my purse close to me and not speak to strangers. She told me this was a sure sign that I was an out-of-towner. That was going to be difficult for me, since I love to speak to people and ask them how their day was. Having grown up in places where such caution was unnecessary, I couldn't understand it. Clothing and food were so expensive. I was in awe. Catherine picked out an outfit for me to try on; it was fashionable. When she told me the price, I was in shock. I told her that there was no way we could afford an outfit of that price. She reminded me that Sam said to find something nice. I smiled as she took out the money Sam had given her to spend on me. I knew I was in trouble but since it was her idea I let it go. You should have seen the look on Sam's face. It was sort of a half-smile and half "no they didn't." I just chuckled as I watched him try to pretend that $100 was no problem. "No problem at all." I could see him sweating. I ran off to try on the outfit so I could gloat. As I was trying it on, I kept laughing at the look on Sam's face. It was so funny, and I got so much pleasure out of it.

My first taste of New York cheesecake was so fantastically delicious; and my visit to Coney Island, riding the largest roller coaster in the world, The Cyclone, was very exciting. I've been on a lot of roller coasters in my life but this one was the fastest. Sam and Catherine didn't want to ride and that should have told me something. Catherine's fiancé, Lewis, decided he would ride with me. He had never been on The Cyclone before and felt the same way that I did, that nothing could scare him. Of course, I jumped into the first seat and Lewis jumped into the seat behind me. As the roller coaster started to climb up the high incline we both laughed and giggled the whole way. Soon we were cresting the top. I couldn't even see the bottom, as the roller coaster clacked onward and we dropped over the first hill. Down we plummeted toward earth. The wind hit my face as we traveled down in tremendous speed. I was so scared my face froze into one big smile spread across my cheeks. My eyes bugged out. I looked back to see only Lewis's feet in the air, as he gripped the floor. I, on the other hand, was gripping the handlebars so hard that they too froze in position. I stayed in the same position till we reached the end of the ride. I couldn't yell because there was no time. The ride had ended before it started. I didn't even have enough time to pray.

I was still frozen in my position when Sam and Catherine came over to see if we liked the ride. Of course, they were laughing to no end. I was still trying to unglue my eyelashes were stuck to the top of my forehead and put my lips back into their correct position. I knew my heart was somewhere on the ground and finding it would be no problem, considering it was at my feet. Lewis on the other hand was completely speechless. It took about an hour for him to talk again. I had never experienced a thrill that could compare to it, and for a moment all my troubles disappeared into space. Of course, they asked Lewis and me if we would like to ride it again. I just gave Sam a look as if he was crazy and Lewis just laughed. He joked about saving his energy for another exciting ride.

The amazement soon left when I realized that I had to go back to the apartment and stay inside for my own safety. I missed the sight of trees and fields immensely, and since no one had shown me Central Park, I couldn't conceive that nature was just a stone's throw away. I couldn't relate to this type of life in any way, shape, or form nor accept that it was such a dangerous city. In reality I never would be safe anywhere. I knew that even though Sam was behaving well in front of his family, it wouldn't last long. I knew New York was probably a really beautiful city. To me the experience of city life was like living in a prison within a prison, and I never wanted to go there again.

Fortunately we still had our wedding gifts, which Sam gave to his sister. They were the only gifts that survived the pawnshop days when I needed money for formula. The night prior to the wedding there was a welcoming party for

Sam and I. His sister served me several sweet drinks that were not only yummy but also full of alcohol. Not being a drinker, I didn't know what I was in for. I passed out before the party even began.

The wedding was the following day. It was absolutely wonderful and the bride looked gorgeous. I was so envious that I had never had such a fine wedding. After all the ceremonies were over with, the rest of my night was spent sitting and staring into my glass. Sam would not permit me to look at anyone or even glance around the room. So the evening was quite boring for me. That night was horrible. Sam would watch to see if I was looking at another man. His jealousy was outrageous. I knew that if I didn't keep my eyes in the right place, he would slap me in front of everyone there. He was not ashamed to start a commotion anywhere. After the wedding I was ready to pack up and leave and fly to my family's home in Florida. But Sam decided that we would be staying another week. I gritted my teeth when he told me and tried to bear it, because I knew that once we got to Florida I was never going back with him.

One day his mother and I had a disagreement because I would not serve Sam his meals. She felt that I should wait on him hand and foot, even though I explained that he was a grown man and could take care of himself. I thought she was joking, as was I. Then I indulged her with an explanation. "What I meant was that I don't care how other people feet about the way I treat my husband and I certainly I don't care if anyone likes it." She called Sam into the room and told him what I said. He commenced to beat me and throw me all over the room, and she became the entertained spectator. I tried to explain to Sam that I certainly was not talking about her. But it was to no avail.

The next morning Sam left to go and consult a fortuneteller. This was brought on because Sam really never believed that September was his because of her light complexion at birth. He had a hard time believing that he could be her father, since he was so dark-skinned. He would often torment me during arguments, saying that he didn't believe September was his child. I told him that I didn't care if he refused to believe that September was his. I knew the truth and that's all that mattered. I knew that I loved him and would never even think of doing such a thing. Of course his family didn't make the situation any better. They backed him on his little adventure to the fortuneteller. I told him that if he didn't believe me, then he could just leave us to live our lives on our own. He never brought it up again. But I knew it was always in the back of his mind.

The fortuneteller knew his name and the reason he was there, before he even stepped behind her curtain or told her the reason for his visit. She said that his daughter would hate him for the remainder of his life and never have a relationship with him. This was easy for me to believe, since I knew of all the abuse she had suffered at his hand. She told him that he was wrong to accuse me of having someone else's baby. "Your wife loves you and would never do that to you." She told him that I had never cheated on him. She assured him that September was truly his daughter. Arriving back at his mom's house, he was crying and totally believed what the fortuneteller told him. I could only look at him. It angered me that he would believe the words of a fortuneteller and total stranger over what I had been telling him all along. He wanted forgiveness from me, but I could only hate him more for the accusations he had made in the past.

Sam's mother made my stay in New York miserable. I was so glad to be leaving New York to visit my parents in Florida.

We surprised my mother with our arrival. They were very happy to see us. Sam's First Sergeant had contacted my mother. He told my mother that Sam had received an assignment to Korea. He also told her that Sam was to report back to his base in Oklahoma for further instructions. I was planning to stay in Florida, but was reluctant to stay with my mother. I would accompany him back to Oklahoma, planning to stay there alone with September. Once Sam heard my plans he told me that I would only be allowed to stay with one of our moms. He was afraid that I would find someone else during his absence. I probably would have found someone, after what Sam had put me through that year. But the only thing I could think of at that time was getting as far away from Sam as I could. Neither option was one I felt happy with, but even before I could make a firm decision, his orders were cancelled. The beatings and the yelling continued. My threats of leaving became an everyday ritual.

One day in Oklahoma while standing in the kitchen, Sam walked up to me and announced that he had received another assignment to Vietnam. I wanted to scream out in joy but I kept silent! I contained myself for fear of what Sam might do. He told me that he was the one that volunteered. He went on to explain that he felt we needed some time away from each other. I silently agreed. He was planning to leave everything in storage, which would leave me in the streets. So I decided to call my mother, hoping it was Anna, and ask to stay. It was Anna, and she said it would be no problem. I couldn't wait for him to leave! I was so happy that he would be gone and possibly never return alive. It wasn't long before Miss Meany called and informed

110

me that I wasn't going to stay there, that I had to find somewhere else to stay. Of course, that left his mother in New York. We called and asked them, and I could tell that a heavy discussion was going on between Sam and his mother. Sam wouldn't share it with me, but I knew that it involved September and I. Anything that I might need to start a new life without him was stored so that I could not leave him. I decided to call Dad and beg him to allow me to come home. I told him it would only be temporarily, until I found my own place. He told me not to worry; he would talk to my mother. Soon they called me back and told me it would be all right. I was so relieved.

Traveling back to New York for Sam to say good-bye to his mom was like going back to prison after I had escaped. During our stay, she witnessed Sam slapping the baby's hand so hard that September would hold her hand up in the air for hours on end. His Mom yelled at him but it did no good. He told her, "to mind her own business." She saw the immense cruelty in him; causing such pain to a one-year-old baby. We argued about everything.

Most of our belongings went into storage and the incidentals for September and I were sent to my mom. We left for Florida, where I would be staying with my parents while he served in Vietnam. I put on such a pretense. By then, it really was a pretense when he boarded the plane. I hugged him, kissed him, and acted as if I would miss him terribly, but inside I hated him immensely and was hoping that he would die. I was crying tears--of happiness, that my freedom was near. When I left the airport I prayed that I would never see Sam again. I never wanted to face the terrible beatings again in my lifetime. I watched television every day to see if the name, "Sam Jackson," appeared on the lists of the missing and killed in action.

## Chapter 16

I found a job in a day care center, which didn't last long. A co-worker asked what I would do if anyone broke in. Jokingly, I told her that I would take off running to get help. She told the supervisor who felt that she couldn't have me around if those were my feelings. I had been kidding, but she didn't want to take the chance. I had to obtain another job, ending up in the cafeteria and the snack bar. Mom and Dad told me that I should go back to finish getting my high school diploma. At the time I was complaining, or having nightmares of myself walking across stage to accept my diploma only to find myself never reaching the podium or failing to get my hands on it. In one dream I found myself chasing the principal all over the school, while he ran away laughing at me with the diploma in his hand. I took this to mean that something was telling me to complete my education.

I discovered that there were several people in my same situation. After school my classmates and I sat around talking about how hard it was to go back, but that we were glad we did. I met another woman in my class that was just as eager to get her diploma. We took turns driving each other to school. We never really got to know one another but it was fun to study with her, and we both pushed each other to finish. Soon we both walked onto a stage and received our diplomas. With tears in my eyes, I felt so proud of myself. Everyone yelled and screamed as we hugged each other and said our good-byes. I went out and celebrated by myself. Now I could get a decent job and leave Sam for good. After getting my diploma I got a job working in a chow hall. We would feed 500-600 GI's per day. It was hard work, and I continued to convince myself that soon I would find a better job. Now that I had the diploma I needed, I still was lacking the skills I needed to become what I wanted to be. But I wasn't going to give up.

Soon I started to receive letters and gifts from Sam mailed to me from overseas. He sent love letters, which started to make me miss him. Being lonely, I soon wanted to be with him. I wanted to hold him and love him. I kept telling myself, "Don't be a fool and fall for his tricks again!" But deep down, I was curious. Had he really changed? Did his being away from me make him understand how cruel he had been to September and me? Could I trust him again? Maybe, just maybe he was telling the truth this time. Soon, I got to the point that I couldn't wait for him to return home. Soon I bought him little gifts and sent cookies to surprise him. I stopped wanting him to die, discontinued watching the news and remained faithful to him. He continually wrote to me and called me, convincing me that he really was going to change this time. He said that all the stress of starting a new family made it difficult for him to adjust. He promised that our life together would be better and that he would become a good husband. Of course, my loneliness didn't make it any easier for me to make a wise decision.

I didn't know his anticipated arrival date but one night Sam knocked on my window. I let him in quietly, trying not to awaken my parents. We were so happy to see each other that we talked all night. Later, we truly made love. I didn't go into my White Room. I was surprised that I didn't. The only explanation I could think of was that he was treating me so lovingly. I gave him his gifts and showed him my diploma while he beamed with pride at what I had done. The next morning, Mom and Dad knocked at the door. They had heard a man's voice, and they were glad to see it was Sam who had been there with me all night. They wanted to make sure that I was not crazy enough to sneak a man into my room.

We spent two weeks together when he told me that he was going to finish up his next six months in Korea. This is when he broke the news that he had gotten gonorrhea from a girl in Vietnam. Saying that he had been cured of the disease before he left Vietnam, he watched me become enraged. I began to beat him in the chest and face as he lay in my bed. He pushed me away. I walked into the bathroom. He followed after me, telling me that if I became irritated or had any discharge that I should go to a doctor immediately for an exam. I had already had some irritating discharge from my vagina. I could not believe that he had done such a thing to me while pretending that I was important to him. I recall him saying that this Vietnamese girl looked like me and that is why he was attracted to her, plus he was drunk, as if that was going to make me feel any better. I asked him, "So why did you tell me, Sam, to ease your conscience or to see me suffer some more?"

He just waved his hand in the air as if he expected me to understand. When I walked back into the room, I said with tears in my eyes, "No tell me, Sam, why did you do this to me? I didn't stay faithful for you to return here and give me a disease!" He looked at me and said, "I knew you wouldn't understand and I didn't expect you to." I turned my back, sobbing tears of hatred. If I had a gun, at that moment, I would have shot him. He then announced that we were supposed to be doing our own thing; going our own separate ways. "Trying to find someone else," he explained.

I turned and looked at him and said, "Only you forgot to tell me the rules. How dare you, you, you, Black @#$%#$%#$#$%."

Although you hear about husbands cheating on their wives, you never fully comprehend the pain it causes the woman. It's like a knife stabbing in your heart. As he keeps talking, it's as though he is turning and twisting the knife deeper and deeper. The pain never leaves and you never forget what that feeling encompassed. The anguish and hurt can never be taken back. I had to leave him because things were never going to change. After being faithful to him for six months, how could he come home and give me a venereal disease? I went to a local bar and got drunk. "What is wrong with me? Why am I stupid enough to allow him to hurt me over and over? When am I going to learn that he is no good and is never going to change?" Tears rolled down my face. It suddenly occurred to me that I had nothing to fear but bad luck when it came to men. That night I turned over a new leaf. From then on out, I was never going to allow a man to hurt me. It was my turn to hurt them.

The war ended. The evacuation of Vietnam included all the U.S. military. Sam went to complete his year's tour of duty in Korea. I drove to the ocean and threw my wedding ring out to sea. My belief is that the band signifies a circle of love binding two people together as one. When he cheated on me, he broke the circle, making the meaning behind the wedding ring irrelevant. A wedding ring is supposed to signify unity, trust, and honor melded together within a circle. Now it only signified a $20 trinket. Throwing it into the ocean was nothing to me. I had been told over and over and over in our arguments that I never received a diamond because I was not worth a diamond. His $20 ring along with the gonorrhea convinced me that I was only an object with which he could play. But not any more. The physical exam I went through the following day confirmed that I did have gonorrhea. After all I had gone through; I had never gotten a sexually transmitted disease. How could my own husband do this to me? I wanted to kill Sam. I practiced the scene I would act out when the Air Force told me that he was deceased. I merely wanted him to die.

The treatment consisted of two shots on both sides of my bottom. As I waited for them, the doctor told me that I needed to tell my husband. I informed him that I received the disease from my husband. Too bad the Air Force had not informed me! The doctor was surprised to hear this. He went on to tell me that standard procedures were in place to keep the GI's that were infected in Vietnam there, until they were cured. Somehow they gave Sam a clean bill of health and he was sent home. I later sent him an article explaining that gonorrhea can reoccur in a person who drinks and that the particular strain of the disease from Vietnam really was tough to cure.

My infection consisted of a constant irritation around my vulva, which in turn swelled to the size of a hot dog bun. That area burned like fire. It was as if I had sat on top of a burner. The discharge was so excessive that I continually had to wipe myself. Even wearing large, sagging underwear was so uncomfortable that it was awkward for me to walk straight. The area around my vagina burnt so much that I cried when I urinated, and silently screaming would grip the countertop. I continued to work but with much difficulty.

One day, I picked up a tray from a GI's table and although he was trying to flirt with me I was disinterested. I snapped at him and realized later that I shouldn't have treated him badly. I apologized to him and learned that his name was, O.T. After a time, we became friends. I was able to talk to him and he always was available to listen. He assured me that all men were not cruel like Sam was to me. When I healed, we began go out to movies and restaurants for meals. It was nice to have someone whom I could talk to and at the same time, he understood that I only wanted to be friends. In the meantime, I began double dating with my sister and going out with my brother. O.T. wanted me to move out and get a place with him, but I would not agree to that because I was still married. I also had to consider my child, and the way our life was going at the time I did not want to take on that type of commitment.

Things at home with Anna Mae were not going well. She didn't like me going out so often and felt it was improper since I was a married woman. Although she knew of the abuse I had suffered at my husband's hand and my attempts with a lawyer to get a divorce, she still would not agree with me about dating. My attorney told me that I should not begin divorce action against my husband while he was overseas because it could be construed as desertion. I was in a situation where I could lose everything, as little as it was, and also lose custody of my daughter. I knew that would never happen because I would kill Sam first. I was instructed to wait for Sam's return from Korea. Miss Meany and I did not see eye-to-eye; we were constantly butting heads. She told me that if I continued to see O.T. I would have to move out. It was as if she were trying to find every excuse in the book to get me to leave.

One day I asked her permission to find September a puppy. I had tried everything to get September to talk and hoped that this might do the trick. Maybe a puppy would make her happy enough to finally speak? September loved her little puppy and even though it did not make her speak well, she did start to make sounds, say some phrases. The only things she would say were curse words. I guess because that's all she ever heard Sam and I say to each other. She would curse out her puppy. Thank goodness her vocabulary was limited only to the two words: "damn and shit." I tried

117

not to get on her about it because she did acquire her language innocently.

One morning while laying in my bed sound asleep, Anna Mae came to the door. She started beating on the door and yelling, "Kaye, get up!" I got out of bed all groggy and stumbled to the door, shaking all over because of the way I had been awakened. It should've seemed that I was used to her waking me up this way, considering she had done this my entire life, especially when she was upset. When I got to the door she started ranting and raving about how the puppy had to go that morning. I told her, "Yes, Mother, I promise I'll get rid of it tomorrow."

The next day I got up, threw on some clothes and dressed September who at the time, was looking at me wondering what was wrong. I went over to wake my sister, Linda, and asked her to help me get rid of the puppy. She was half-asleep at the time, but was willing to help me. I walked over to the box to get the little puppy. He sat and looked up at me with his sad little eyes as if to say, "Do I have to leave? I was just starting to get used to September beating me up every day."

I said, "Come on, little puppy, it looks like you have to go." We all climbed into the car and away we went to beg someone to take the puppy off our hands. Suddenly Linda thought of someone, a friend of hers that had commented on how cute the puppy was. We drove to the friend's house hoping the family would take the little puppy. When we got there, Linda's friend was very happy to see the puppy and so were her kids. She would be happy to take the puppy and give it a good home.

As soon as Linda and I walked out the door, Miss Meany and my father drove up. They yelled at Linda to get into the car. When I walked up to the car to find out what was wrong, my father said, "Get home!" I could tell by the look in his eyes that he was very angry. My first thought was, "What did I do now?" After seeing Miss Meany in the car it could have been anything, knowing her and how she loved to make trouble between my father and I. As I drove up to the driveway I saw Miss Meany grabbing my sister, slapping her and pushing her into the house. I immediately ran up to my dad yelling, "What's going on? Why are you doing this? Daddy, Linda didn't do anything wrong." My father led Linda to her room with a belt in his hands. Linda was crying, "Kaye-Kaye, please help me. Tell Mama and Daddy that I didn't do anything wrong."

As I tried to get past my mother to stop my father from beating my sister, my mother accused Linda and me of going out in the early morning to "screw men." I looked at my mother as though she were crazy. Where did she get the idea that we were screwing? I yelled, "Mom, you told me to get rid of the puppy this morning." I still kept yelling for my father to stop, as he continued to beat my sister. "Daddy, please stop!" I pleaded. "Mom told us to get rid of the puppy, and that's what we were doing! Please stop!" My dad stopped hitting Linda. He walked out into the hallway to listen to my mother and me. Pushing me up against the door, she continued to accuse me of whoring, in front of my child and babysitter. I grabbed her hands and looked into her sick eyes and sarcastically said, "Yes, Mom, I laid there screwing a man while my baby and my sister were there lying in bed with me!"

I pushed her away. How could she be so sick? What did my Grandmother do to my mother to make her mind automatically race to the gutter? My father came to my mother's side. I knew I was stronger than her and I could see that I could overpower her any time I wanted. Nevertheless, I

119

respected Anna inside that body and I could not harm her. Miss Meany had pushed me into wanting to hit her several times before, but not as much as she did that day. I wanted so badly to hit her and I think my father knew it. It suddenly occurred to me that it was Anna Mae that had asked me to get rid of the puppy. It was so difficult at times for me to identify my mother's personalities and put them in the right perspective. What I should have done that morning was to wake my mother and see which personality was in control-- before I left the house. I should have known which personality I was dealing with before I acted. "I'm afraid you're going to have to leave," my father said. I agreed as I ran to my room, only stopping to tell Linda I was sorry. I took my daughter to see if we could find a small apartment somewhere, anywhere, as long as it was far away from Anna Mae and Miss Meany.

# Chapter 17

By the end of the week I had found a small, inexpensive but quaint little apartment on the poor side of town. It was dangerous there, but it was the only place I could afford. Daddy helped me move in and I was thankful that I finally had my own place. It was perfect for September but I hated having to leave Linda. She was my best friend and running partner. She was not yet 18 and Anna Mae refused to hear of her leaving home. Miss Meany, of course said that we would have all kinds of men in our place everyday. Little did my mother know that I had no thoughts of men because of the way Sam and other men had treated me. I wanted peace, and I didn't understand why it was so difficult for her to understand that. I had made several friends and found that there were other single women who waited alone for their husbands' arrival from overseas.

One evening, a small banging started at my door followed by a very young voice begging me, "Open the door." I looked through the peephole to see who it was. There was no one in sight, and again, the banging started all over again with a cry of, "Please help my brother!" Opening the door I found a small boy standing at my door, crying desperately that a man had taken his brother into the woods. I ran to my neighbor's and asked her to call the police because I didn't have a phone. Soon the police arrived and I gave September to my neighbor to watch while I went with the policeman. The little boy and I went to where he had last seen his brother. The policeman asked the little four-year-old boy and me to stay where we were and not to follow him into the woods. Another police officer arrived to back him up, and soon they came out of the woods. One of them was carrying a little boy crying and the other was pushing a handcuffed man. I felt so heartbroken for the little boy as they put him into the ambulance. I was so frightened. I wanted to move from this terrible neighborhood, but I could not afford the expense.

The next day the woman living next door, whom I'll call Sandy, and I were sitting in our front yard. We were talking about the break-ins in the neighborhood and about a woman that they found dead in a field next to our house. She also had heard what had happened to the little boy and my involvement in finding him. We decided to set up a code to protect each other if someone broke into our house. Our plan would consist of pounding on our common wall and the other person would know to call the police for assistance right away. I thought this would be a great idea, except that Sandy worked at a restaurant during the day and I worked at night. We then decided to set up the same warning system with our neighbors on the other sides of us. Everyone agreed that we all would look out for each other, making me feel a lot safer knowing that we would rely on one another.

My boyfriend would often visit me. September grew to love him and began calling him, "Daddy." This was a big accomplishment for September, seeing that she knew no other words besides "Paw-Paw" and "Nana," which is what she called my parents. Of course she called me, "Mommy," but every other word in her vocabulary was, "shit and damn." I was afraid when I took her out in public for fear of what she might say. O.T. could not understand how any man could beat a little girl, especially one as delicate as September who had such a beautiful smile and was so tiny and pretty. He was very understanding and would gently and calmly tell her," no," when she said or did something wrong. Then he would tell her the correct word and how to pronounce it. I would watch and smile as he attempted to teach her to talk. Soon she could say, "football," when he played football with her. Before long she could say, "dog," and before you knew it, she was starting to form sentences. Her other famous words, which I tried desperately to get her to stop saying, continued.

One night I asked O.T. to watch September while I went shopping. When I returned home, I found September asleep in his arms and O.T. crying. He sat there with tears in his eyes. I asked him what was wrong. He tried very hard to conjure up the words to explain that September had learned a new word that day. Tears rolled down his face and I started to cry too, because I have always been a sucker for a man that doesn't mind showing his gentle side. Asking him which word it was, he replied, "I love you, Daddy." Neither of us could speak as we both held each other. At this time, September was about 18 months old.

Every morning before September would wake; I would prepare oatmeal for her breakfast and lay out her clothes for the day. I would then shower and get myself dressed and ready. This would allow me plenty of time to spend bathing, dressing, and feeding September breakfast. I thought we would do something different that day. I wanted to take September to the park after breakfast. Just as I was about to step into the shower, I heard an unusual noise. I thought it was September waking up, so I tried to hurry and finish before she started to cry. I began to sing the Marvin Gaye song, "Let's Get It On." I hated taking showers alone in the house after seeing the movie, "Psycho." I turned on the water and as I started to soap my washcloth, a cool breeze wafted past me as the bathroom door opened. I couldn't see through the shower curtain, so I froze, waiting to hear September speak or pull back the curtain. Suddenly it occurred to me that it could not possibly be September, because she would be unable to climb out of the crib due to the way I had set it up. I could feel a presence of someone standing in the bathroom with me. I also heard heavy

123

breathing. I was fully aware that it couldn't have been my boyfriend. He had no key. I didn't want to die like the woman in the movie, so I decided to change the scene, thinking that somehow this would keep the intruder from stabbing me to death. I reached down and flicked off the water, then quickly turned and opened the shower curtain. I wanted to be the first one of us to open the curtain. When I pulled it back, there stood a man about 5'7", weighing close to 170 lbs. He smiled as I pulled the curtain back over to cover my naked body.

I yelled, "Who the $##@ are you, and what are you doing here?"

He would not answer me and this frightened me even more. I tried to smile and asked him to please step out into the hallway and I would be out in a second. I noticed right away that he did not have a gun or a knife. I wondered if he had weapons waiting for me in the front room or perhaps even in his pockets. As he stood in the hallway watching me, I grabbed my towel and quickly wrapped it around me. I then scurried into the bedroom, threw on my panties and jeans, only to turn around and see him standing in the doorway watching me. I turned to put on my blouse and he told me not to continue getting dressed, although I did anyway. I asked him how he got in and he told me that I had left the door open. I remembered then that my husband would constantly yell at me for not locking the doors. On the military installations, we never had to lock our doors so it was a hard habit to break, but I wished now that I had locked it.

I thought that if I didn't act afraid and offered him coffee, maybe he would forget about what he had come there to do. Very calmly I walked to the kitchen to make some coffee, reckoning that I could throw the hot liquid on him. I opened the kitchen drawer to get a knife but just then, I saw that he had walked up to me, so instead I picked up a spoon. He insistently told me he needed to talk to me in the living room. He grabbed the coffee pot off the stove and told me that he didn't want any. I could tell that he was getting irritated. He led me into the front room and I sat down, knowing that he was serious and I had to do as he ordered. He asked me to sit on the sofa next to him, but I got up and moved to the other side of the room. He began to explain to me that I had gone to school with his wife. Then he began to tell me of how his sexual organs were too large for his wife, making it painful for her to have intercourse with him. I tried to end the conversation, mentioning that his marital situation was none of my business. Suddenly, I remembered seeing him when I went to pick up his wife for school. It turned out that I did know his wife from the school I attended; we had carpooled together for a while. I told him that his wife and I were not close enough and I would feel uncomfortable talking to her about their personal problems. He was one of the men that sat on the stoop outside of the house with several other men playing cards or talking when I would go to pick her up.

The more I ignored him, the more I could see that he was getting antsy. His words started to fade as I began scheming about a way to escape him. I could take a chance and run for it, but September was in the other room and I feared for her safety. He wanted me to help him and I told him there was nothing I could do. I told him, "Go home and talk to your wife." He became very angry and told, "Shut up!" He went on to tell me how he had been following me. He knew where I worked and said he would follow me home each evening. He told me how he watched my every move. He also told me he watched me play in the park with my baby, and studied me at the base when I went grocery shopping at the commissary. He got up and walked over to me, grabbed me, and told me that he knew I would be more understanding with him than his wife. We began to fight and wrestle with each other. He chased me around the room and threw me down to the sofa as I clawed at him. I got up and ran to the door trying to unlock it and get out. He grabbed me again and threw me onto the sofa. I was astounded that he admitted to stalking me.

As I begged and pleaded with him to stop, he ignored me. I told him that my boyfriend would be home any minute and he laughed and said, "No he won't, he's at work and I know that he doesn't live with you." I tried to kick him in the crotch but he caught my leg and flipped me into the air. As I fell to the floor, he jumped on me and I began to scratch and slap him. My efforts were futile as he just laughed at me. My strength was nothing compared to his. The more I hit him, the more he hit me. I yelled at him, "You're not going to rape me!" He laughed again and the baby awakened and started to cry. He got off of me and I thought he was letting me go to her, but he was only repositioning me onto the couch. I begged him to let me get my baby, but he had only one thing on his mind. I had been stalked before; I should have been more watchful and aware of my surroundings! I crossed my legs and held the front zipper of my jeans tightly as I kept telling him that I was not going to allow him to rape me. I had already been raped two times before and I was not going to let go of my pants. I was not going to let myself get raped for the third time, no matter what! He continued to beat me in my face and demanded that I remove my hands but I refused to allow it. My eyesight started to go black and finally I couldn't see anything. I thought that he had hit me so much that he had blinded me.

Finally, releasing my grip on my jeans, I decided to take my chances and beat on the wall above the couch, although I knew that Sandy probably was working her morning shift at McDonald's. He was too busy to notice what I was doing, and the baby was still crying hysterically in the other room. Still fighting with me, he began to unzip my pants, as a knock sounded at the door. Low and behold, it was my neighbor Sandy. She kept screaming and knocking at the door for me to answer. She yelled, "Cynthia I've called the police. Are you all right?"

The stranger jumped up and started to pull up his pants. I opened the door. Sandy saw my face and started to scream as the stranger ran past her to get away. I wiped the blood away from my now, swollen-shut eyes and asked her if she really did call the police. She said she hadn't because she was afraid that she would fail to find me in time to save me. She reminded me that she didn't have a phone and that the landlord was away. She said, "Look at your face! It's horrible!" I gasped, "Oh God, my baby!" as I turned to race to September's room.

Sandy asked me if I wanted to call the police and I refused. She asked why and I told her that it was a long story; I would explain it to her later. Sandy was hysterical, even more so than me. I reached for my baby and she stopped crying. September looked at my battered face and started to wipe the blood from my eyes as she asked me, "Is Mommy all right?" I told her, "Mommy's OK," as she sat in my lap, staring at me to see if I was all right. Again September tried desperately to wipe the blood off of my face, and I grabbed her tiny hand. She started to cry.

Sandy gave me a cold towel for my face. We spent the afternoon together as I explained to her what had happened and why I couldn't go to the hospital or call the police. I hugged her and thanked her for being there for me, especially since I thought she was scheduled to work that day. She said that she was, but forgot her lunch and drove back home to get it. We both smiled as I thanked God that she had returned home. While I was in checking on the baby, Sandy called her boss to explain what had happened. He was very understanding, and told her to stay and help me out.

When I walked to the bathroom to look at my face, I could not believe what I saw. It looked like I had just finished one round in the ring with Mike Tyson. I was happy to see that I was not blind, and only that blood had filled my eyes. It was then that it occurred to me that I still hadn't fed or washed my baby. For some reason September never left my side that day; she followed me all over the house holding on to my clothing, sticking close by me. I walked around crying, talking mostly to myself. I felt sorry for myself. I asked myself, "What is it about me that makes men want to rape me?"

I was supposed to pick up my boyfriend from the hospital and give him a ride home. I knew O.T. was going to be upset when he saw me. When I arrived at the hospital, O.T. walked over to the car. Upon seeing my face and how I had been beaten, he grew so angry that he wanted to find the guy and pound him into pulp. I discouraged him from doing anything he would regret. Since the healing process took a long time, I was afraid to go anywhere, especially out at night. I decided I would stay in my house, hidden away for the rest of my life. O.T. did everything he could to convince me that I must go on, but it was to no avail. Anna would call to see if I was home so she could drive over to visit, but I would tell my landlord to tell her I was not there. I parked my car around the corner just in case Daddy and she would decide to drop in. I would make a point to call them in case they were worrying about me, but mostly I lay in my bed, only getting up to care for September or go to work. I felt

that I was not only beaten physically but mentally this time--
I had lost my desire to live.

O.T. would stop over at times and care for
September. Sandy checked on me too and could not believe
the condition of my house. She would busy herself opening
the windows and telling me about her day at work. She loved
to gossip and she knew I hated it, but she felt that as long as I
was fussing at her, I was going to be all right. One day, O.T.
said, "You lay there and die while September and I go out
and enjoy life." He dressed the baby and away they
went. They came home with a small Christmas tree and some
decorations. I was so centered on my woes and myself. I had
completely forgotten that Christmas was coming. O.T. began
to play Christmas music and they were both singing as I
walked into the front room. They were putting together the
worst Christmas tree I had ever seen. O.T. allowed
September to decorate the tree herself and I smiled as
September tried to sing. I hurried into the kitchen and started
to fix dinner.

We sat down and ate dinner that night, and I grabbed
O.T.'s hand and told, "Thank you. I loved you". He thanked
me. He smiled and said, "For a while there, I thought I had
lost you." I knew I would bounce back. It was only a matter
of time before I woke up and realized that my life would go
on, especially with someone there to love me. "Marry me,
Cynthia." O.T. said. I looked over at September and then at
O.T. "Don't be silly!" I replied, "You know I'm already
married." He told me that Sam would be home soon and I
could get a divorce. O.T. and September both said, "Please,
please, pretty please!" O.T. and I laughed at the way
September said it. I told him that I was not going to make
any promises, but I'd think about it. In the meantime, he'd
have to stop smoking, drinking and gambling. He told me

that I drove a hard bargain, but for me, he thought he could manage it. I reiterated, that if he quit, we'd see.

Before Sam flew home from Korea, he notified me that he was to be reassigned to Oklahoma. He begged and pleaded with me to go along with him. I told him, "No," so he left and went back to Oklahoma on his own. He must have talked to my father and asked him to talk me into going. Sam knew that if he asked Daddy to talk to me, I would listen. I had immense trust that in my father. He would not have asked me to go back to Sam unless he was thoroughly convinced himself that Sam was going to change. I told my father that I would think about it. That night, O.T. stumbled into my house drunk. He promised that he would stop drinking, he had broken his promise. I could hardly make out what he was trying to say, but it was something about him being kicked out of the United States Air Force because they had tested him and found traces of marijuana in his urine. I allowed him to stay and sleep on the floor that night, after I cussed him out. I could not believe that he was stupid enough to allow his career to be tossed out the window all over smoking marijuana. It was quite evident that September and I did not play an important enough role in his life, if he was stupid enough to allow this to happen. I cried because I loved him so much, but I had to look out for September's best interests. If I divorced Sam right now, we would have to live on the street. My mom and dad weren't going to take me in. As soon as Sam arrived in Oklahoma, he threatened that he would stop sending me money. My job would only pay the rent with nothing else to spare.

It was time for me to make a major decision, immediately. I could not live on love and love would fail to feed us, with O.T. now out of a job. Sam had never before made a promise to my dad, but this time he had made a serious one. He said that this time, because he wanted to keep me so badly, he would stop beating the baby and me. When Daddy told me this, I cried all night. And the next morning, I put on my happy face and tried to make a wise decision that would change all of our lives. Once I weighed my options, I decided to go back to Sam. Maybe I could fall back in love with the man I once loved so much. And if it didn't work, Daddy promised that he would be there to pick up the pieces. I knew that I could trust my father. I also knew that if things didn't work between Sam and I, all I had to do was pick up the phone. Once more, I would put myself back together and start a new life.

# Chapter 18

In Oklahoma with Sam, I went back to work in the same Mexican restaurant where I was previously employed. Life was nice for us for about three months, and then it returned to "normal." The beatings didn't start right away, but the jealousy started just as before. Sam started to follow me constantly and sit outside the restaurant. September had stopped talking again, so I knew something was happening. She was too afraid to tell me because her dad had threatened her. He told her that if she told me anything, he would either break her neck or kill her. I found all this out later, when my girlfriend told me about the way Sam threatened her. I begged September to tell me what had been happening between her and her father, reassuring her that I was not going to say anything to him.

Again, in secret, I opened another savings account and saved every penny. It was not ever going to be enough, so I decided to steal what I could. I was desperate. Sam had me to cut off all communications with my family and he began to act very oddly. I knew I couldn't trust him because of the Russian Roulette he forced me to play before. Something told me that all hell was going to break loose; and it did. When I walked out to my car one evening, I could see by the look on Sam's face that I was in trouble. O.T. had called and left a message for me. As soon as I walked into the house, Sam wrestled me down to the floor, pulled back my head and banged it into the floor. He pulled my hands behind my back and told me to tell him what I was up to. He continued to beat me. He kept

yelling "No other man is going to have you!" And I yelled back at him. "I knew this relationship wasn't going to last too long." September kept screaming "Mommy!" and crying hysterically. Sam yelled at her to go to her room and he continued to beat me. I kept calling him and his mother every name under the sun, knowing full well that this was only making things worse. I didn't care. I yelled at September "Go to your room!", before he grabbed her. She finally left unwillingly, as Sam beat me until I could no longer hit back.

He told me that since I was away I had become feistier. "I will break you again, just like I broke you before! "He told me that if I thought I would go back to my family again, he'd kill me first. I could not move I was in so much pain, so I just laid there. I mumbled, "That's what you think. You'll never break me!" Sam heard me, and came over to beat me some more. "You're going to have to kill me this time" I told him. He laughed at me as he mocked me and told me "No one can help you now. I love you and we are always going to be together." I finally got up enough strength to make my way into my bedroom. Later that night, he must have thought he could make up. He showed me how sick and demented when he tried to make love to me; but there was no way. We wrestled and fought until he finally gave up and left me alone. I couldn't go to work the next day because of the way I looked, so I stayed home. I knew that I had to get back to work to save all the money I needed to leave him.

I decided to phone O.T. to find out why took the chance to call me. He told me that he had to hear my voice, to know that September and I were okay. I told him he was crazy to get involved, knowing what Sam could do to him. O.T. said he didn't care.

"Do you still love me?" he asked. "I still love you, but you have to let go." I asked him not to call me again because he would get me into a lot of trouble. I could tell he was high. I hung up and went back to work. The next night I walked to a pay phone around the corner from the restaurant and called my father. I told him I needed to fly home because the marriage was not working. I needed money to get home. He put it in the mail the next day. Sam intercepted the letter and ripped the check up in front of my face. I had to get out of there, so I started to steal even more. Finally, I saved up enough money to leave. It was funny, but Sam had learned to read my silence as a sign that I was up to no good. That was the way I got when enough was enough. Talking things out with Sam was useless, especially in a situation such as this; it was best just to leave.

Nothing was ever going to change, Sam still continued to beat September and me. It was time for me to walk out and take my child with me. I called my girlfriend and asked her to take me to the airport. I could see the gleam in September's eyes as we packed our bags and put them into the car. Upon reaching the Airport, I spied Sam standing there waiting at the entrance. I looked at my girl friend and asked her if she had called him. The only thing that I could imagine was she had informed her husband about taking us to the airport, and maybe he had told Sam. Sam tried to give me a gift and begged me to stay with him. Boisterously, he followed me through the airport making a scene, but I continued on, stopping only to tell him he needed to see a psychologist. He continued to yell as September and I continued on through the gate. I looked back in horror as people stared at him making a complete fool out of himself.

Once we had boarded the plane, I looked over at September only to see her watching out the window, afraid that he would follow us onto the plane. As the plane took off, I think we both sighed a breath of relief. I told her to pull out her coloring book and we began to color. "Not to worry everything is going to be all right." As soon as we arrived, I could tell Anna Mae didn't want me there. I told her I would move in with O.T. if she didn't want us at home, but my mother insisted that I stay with her until I found my own place.

To celebrate my arrival in Florida, my family had a picnic. September had a fever that day and I wanted to stay home with her, but my father insisted that I go out and have a good time with the rest of the family. I called Daddy every chance I got to confirm that September was all right. Dad told me that she was fine and my mom was with him, so I should just have a good time. My brother and I left the park and went to a party. Soon I received a phone call from Anna telling. I needed to come home, September's fever was worse and she thought that we should take her to the hospital. So I asked my brother to take me home. Since he wanted to stay, one of his friends offered to take me home. On the way he decided to stop at a rinky-dink motel with a red light on the outside. All I knew was that I was somewhere in Dade County. I had never seen the likes of a place that sleazy before. He told me that if I didn't sleep with him I would have to walk home, I chose the latter of the two. I got out of the car and started walking as he yelled at me to get back into the car. Although I was scared, I ignored him and kept walking. I was being stubborn and did not like the idea of him giving me ultimatum. He drove up to me, laughing and telling me that I should get back into the car, but I didn't trust him. He finally left me alone and drove away.

I noticed a bar with a bunch of drunks standing around. Knowing it was not a safe place to be, I decided to go in another direction. Finally I came to a phone booth in the middle of nowhere and called my father. He asked me where I was but I had no idea, so he told me to go to the nearest corner and read the street sign. I did what he told me and returned to the phone. "Fifth Street." He said "Fifth and what?" I was so scared and nervous. He then instructed me to go back to the same lamppost and read the sign going the other way too. I ran back and told him. Daddy said he was on his way. I stayed in the booth with the door closed, hoping no one would come along until my father arrived. Not much later he rescued me. I felt relieved. I hopped into the car and my father asked if I was okay. I said, "I am now." He looked at me, "As soon as you get a job, Daddy's going to take you down and get you a new a car. Now that you're on your own you'll need a good dependable car so that you will never get into this situation again." I was a single lady with a child who could not afford to be broken down somewhere trying to get a ride home.

We took the baby to the hospital as soon as I got home. Turns out she had an ear infection. The next day my brother found the friend of his that had left me on the street and made sure that he would never, ever do that to anyone else. I got a job working for a dietician at the hospital. Daddy did as he had promised and took me down to a car dealership to find a car. The manager helped me find the cutest little red Mustang. He wanted to give it to me in return for being his friend, since his wife was overseas. He said he would put September and I up in an apartment and get me a maid. I wouldn't have to do anything except to be seen with him around town. This all sounded too good to be true, and when I told my dad about the proposition, he didn't like it. Dad told me to always remember "You never get anything free in life, there's always a catch." Deciding not to take the man up on his offer, we dated each other a few times. He always picked me up in a limousine. He wasn't my type but the butler he had was awfully cute. Not only was he old but we were also from two different worlds. I turned him down again.

Soon I found a job working in a cafeteria on the base. I was hoping one day to be able to save enough money to get my own apartment again. I was glad I hadn't returned to my old boyfriend, O.T., even though I missed him tremendously. He had begun to use drugs and sell marijuana, that, and a number of other bad things he was doing dissuaded me. Sam started calling, threatening to shoot me in the back of the head if I didn't return to him. One day he called me; I felt safe because I knew he was calling long distance. During our conversation a strange woman picked up on the other line in the bedroom. She proceeded to tell me that she was sleeping with him and was, at that very moment, naked after making love to him. It sounded as though he dropped the receiver, returned to the bedroom and yanked the phone from her. I'm sure he didn't hit her; he only got off on hitting me. I felt sure that this torment would never end, I had to kill him.

Calling my girlfriend in Oklahoma I asked her if she still had her gun for sell. I explained that I wanted to buy it. I then told Mae that I needed to get money from my bank account. I asked her for my bankbook that she had been holding for me. She refused to give it to me, stating that I would only fly down there and get myself in a lot of trouble, maybe even shot. I tried to explain to her that I knew what I was doing and told her of my plans. She still disagreed. I begged and begged, she kept getting dressed to go out. Before I knew it she was dressed and on her way out the door to Bingo. I was so upset that I could not control myself. With so many things going wrong in my life, and Sam constantly tormenting me, I decided to kill myself. I couldn't take it anymore. It was either he or I. I decided to slash my wrists. I went into the bathroom and took a razor from the bathroom shelf. I got into bed, lay back, and started to cut my wrist. Soon I fell asleep until I was suddenly awakened by a scream. My baby sister had happened upon me, saw blood all over my bed and ran screaming to my father. My father entered my bedroom and asked me, "Why?" All I could do was cry. "I had to Daddy! I can't take life anymore."" I just want to die Daddy".

Daddy very calmly put my jacket on me, as he listened to my cry for help. He took me to the hospital. As the staff was attending to me they mentioned that the next time I tried to kill myself I should cut up and down my wrist instead of across, and then I would surely end my life. So, trying to be smart, I agreed. That was what I'd do as soon as they let me go home. Sooner than I could think about what I said, they tied me up in a straightjacket and transported to a psychiatric ward. They put me into a room there with mattresses on the walls, blankets and pillows on the floor, and a woman screaming in the next room. My mother appeared at the door. Looking thru the small window on the door, she whispered, "Kay?" I yelled at her to leave. She shut the small window and went back home. I didn't want to see Anna Mae or listen to her lecture me. But to my surprise O.T. showed up in the hospital. He brought me some flowers and we talked. I thanked him for visiting and I never saw him again. Later, I was released.

# Chapter 19

Soon after I was released from the hospital I went back to work at the cafeteria. I was still very confused and angry about my life, but I had decided that if I kept my mind occupied I would eventually get over Sam's threats. I even started to think maybe Sam would be doing me a favor if he shot me in the back of the head. At least it would be all over with.

At work one day a man walked up to me and asked me my name. I smiled as I showed him my nametag. He then asked if the bread pudding was any good. I told him, "No, don't buy it." I knew the bread in the pudding was more than a day old and also had been left out overnight on top of the refrigerator where the rodents had nibbled on it. He smiled and put the pudding back down. He introduced himself as Eddie and asked me for my phone number. I gave it to him and just in time, because the next thing I knew my boss had walked up behind me. Turning around to see my boss staring at me, I giggled. Eddie smiled and walked away.

While playing puppets with September that evening the phone rang. It was Eddie. I rushed to the phone and answered as if I weren't expecting him to call. We talked a little and he invited me to a house party he was having that weekend. I was not very keen about going to a house party. They were always crowded and made me feel too uncomfortable, especially when I didn't know anyone there. But I went along with it anyway and told him, "Yes." He told me it would be that Saturday at 10:00 in the evening. I thought that was a little too late to have a party, but he explained that every time he had a party that started any earlier no one would show up. I laughed because I knew he was right. He asked if he could pick me up but I told him that I would rather drive myself. I asked for the directions and we said our good-byes and hung up.

That Saturday as I prepared to go out that evening I checked with my father to see if he would keep the baby for me. Mae had gone out to play bingo. I smiled as Daddy lay in the bed with his grandbaby by his side. It felt rather weird to be dating, especially since I still was married. However, I already had started the divorce proceeding and knew that it wouldn't be long till Sam and I would be divorced. I found it very uncomfortable, but I reasoned if he could fool around, there was no harm in me going to a party. I needed to make changes in my life. I was tired of going to work, coming home and taking care of the baby every night. "Plus, you never know, this could be the man I've been waiting on to come along and treat me right."

I bought a special dress for the occasion. Looking in the mirror as I rushed out the door, I stopped to fix my hair one more time. I was proud to be driving my own car too, especially after what Daddy had warned me about. I knew I could come and go as I pleased. I was supposed to go early to help out with the hors d'oeuvres, so I left an hour ahead of time. I wasn't surprised when I didn't see anyone else there. As I walked the little pathway up to the house I could hear music blasting. I knocked on the front door and Eddie answered. I could see his friend in the kitchen doing something. I started for the kitchen, but Eddie stopped me, and asked me to sit and have a drink. He said there was plenty of time. I smiled and took the beer from his hand. They had the television and music both playing at the same time. I tried to pretend as if I was interested in the movie on TV while he asked me questions about my life. Our conversation was going well until his friend called him into the kitchen. I had started to wonder why no one had shown up yet, so I followed him into the kitchen. I smiled and inquired about why no one had arrived yet. He walked up to me and asked me if he could talk to me in the other room. So I followed him, expecting him to tell me something was wrong.

When we got to the room he told me how beautiful I looked that evening. Then he started to kiss me. I pushed him away and told him he was being a little too presumptuous. Smiling, he pulled me over to a set of bunk beds, and began talking about how intrigued he was with me and how turned on he was. Again he tried to kiss me, but I stood up and walked back into the front room where I knew I would feel safe. All of the sudden the music got louder. It was so loud we could not hear each other speak. I was trying to tell him it was time for me to leave when he again grabbed my arm and pulled me back to the bed. He twisted my arm behind me and pushed my face onto the bed. I tried yelling, but his friend ran into the room and put silver duct tape over my mouth. They both began to strip me naked. Before I knew it, I was being sodomized by both of them. I could feel my rectum being torn open, the pain was excruciating. When I cried out Eddie told me, "Don't cry, it won't do you any good." Which was true, no one could hear me. I tried to fight as they tied my wrists behind my back. They each took turns holding me down, while the other took his turn.

I soon blacked out and found myself in my White Room. Sitting there, I felt ashamed. I wanted to stay there. This time it was different. I was going stay, nothing was going to make me leave, or so I thought. Maybe I could figure out how this all worked and just stay in my state of unconsciousness? Then I woke up. I was untied, but the duct tape still covered my mouth. Eddie, who had invited me in the first place, was standing above me. He told me that if I went to the authorities he and his friend would say they had never seen me. It would be my word against theirs. They

141

stripped off the tape from my mouth. I was in so much pain that I could not say a word, but I thought to myself, "I will be back to kill you both!" I pulled up my underwear and painfully walked out the room, through the front door, and got into my car.

When I arrived home I poured myself a warm bath filled with Epsom salt. I hoped this would start a healing process. The next day I drove around looking for a gun shop. The law in the state of Florida required a two-week waiting period. Thank God, because if it weren't for those two weeks, I know of two men that would be dead today. I filled out the paperwork, so that I could return later and purchase a gun.

While driving home I felt the urge to yell. I drove and drove and drove far out into the Everglades Park, until I became lost from all the side streets and turns I had taken. Finally, I came to a street that dead-ended into the swamps. I parked, got out of my car, and stood staring into the swamp. Far as I could see, grass was growing tall in a large lake of water. It must have been a place where people drove their airboats. I yelled and screamed at the top of my lungs, until my throat was too sore for me to scream anymore. I sat in my car and thought to myself, "What do I have, a rape sign on my back?" I didn't realize that growing up in an over-protective home and being part of a military family did not help me to develop street smarts. All it allowed me to do was to live a naïve life. It also sheltered me from harm's way, which prompted me to trust almost anyone. I had too much trust in GI's. I seemed to have thought that since these men were in the military that they were different from civilians. But I could see that they were worse. All they had to do was get assigned to another base if they got into trouble. Not being able to learn about death, see murder and cruelty, or know evil people, only made me think that I lived in some kind of Disney World. My perception of society was definitely lacking.

After sitting in my car for about an hour or two watching the sun go down, I decided to go back home and soak in the tub some more. It was hard trying to find my way out of the park. I kept going down all of the wrong roads. Finally, I found my way out and began the long descent home. When I reached my house the odometer on my car registered 65 miles. I could not believe I had driven that far. But the time to myself was worth it.

I continued to soak each day in Epsom salt, and finally the pain subsided. By the end of my two weeks I decided to go back and purchase my gun. I remembered a question on the paperwork I had to fill out to purchase the gun: "What is the purpose of purchasing the gun?" I hesitated because I knew I was going to use it to shoot someone. I wrote down that I intended to buy it for my own protection. I was not lying when I used the word, "protection." I left the shop with a shiny new 45-calibre pistol.

I went back home and felt very strange walking into the house with a gun. I had to pass Anna Mae cooking in the kitchen. I tried to walk as straight as I could in front of her, I didn't want her to notice my limp. When I spoke a few words to her, I could tell she knew that I was up to no good. I was trembling all over. I hurried to my room. Once I was safe in my room I pulled out my new gun. I started to examine the pistol, and put the bullets in it. Suddenly, there was a knock at my door and my name, "Kaye," called out. I knew it was Anna Mae by the name she called me. She tried the door but found it locked. I was rushing around, trying to find somewhere to hide the pistol so I could answer the door. Anna Mae called through the door, "Are you okay or is something wrong?" I replied, "No, Ma'am," as I stuffed the gun between my mattresses. I hurried to the door and unlocked it. She asked, "Why'd you lock the door?" "I was going to sleep and didn't want to be bothered." She stood in the doorway staring at me for a minute. I know she knew something was up, but she did not want to pry. She walked away and left me feeling even more insecure. She did not normally respond this way. I went back and laid in the bed until I thought the coast was clear, just in case she decided to return and check on me. When I heard her talking to my father, I went back to handling and loading my gun.

When my sister Linda came home I heard her in the next room. I went over to get her to show off my gun. She was just as scared of the gun as I was. I only let her hold it for a minute. I had loaded it and didn't want an accident to happen. After Linda left the room I began scheming on how I was going to kill both of the men who had victimized me. I thought I would wait until night, go to the house, find a way in and shoot them both.

I waited until nightfall, and began getting ready. While I was dressing I was shaking all over. I could feel my heart pounding through my chest as though it would burst at any given moment. I knew if I attempted anything, shaking as much as I was, it would more than likely be a failure. To ease my nerves I took two valiums. I started for the door and noticed Mae standing in the kitchen, pouring herself a drink. When I quickly passed by her and told her I was going out for a little while she asked me, "Where is the baby?" I told her, "Linda is watching her." as I grabbed for the doorknob. Mae noticed what a rush I was in to get out of the house. She asked, "Cynthia, are you in some kind of trouble?" I hesitated, "No." She always seemed to sense when I was in trouble. I smiled at her and kissed her on the cheek. I ran out of the house clutching my bag close to my side. I set the purse on the passenger's seat and drove straight to the nearest liquor store. I bought a fifth of gin and sat in my car drinking it straight, all the while thinking, "I have to do this! They don't deserve to live after what they both did to me!" After I had downed almost half the bottle, I started to feel the liquor. I tried to drive to where I remembered their house being, but I kept getting lost.

After driving down street after street, I began to get frustrated. Tears were streaming down my cheeks. I was feeling out of control. I told myself, "Calm down, Cynthia, and try a different street." As I drove down yet another street, taking gulps from my bottle of gin, I saw the house. I could not believe it. There it was right in front of me. It was as if it appeared out of nowhere.

I parked my car and walked up the driveway. I noticed there were no cars parked in their driveway. I knocked on the door anyway. No one answered. I walked around to the back of the house and peered into the windows. The rooms were empty. I walked around the house some more and looked into the kitchen window. The house was deserted. "It can't be! It just can't be!" I said to myself. "I was just here a couple of weeks ago." Slowly, I walked back around to the front of the house and sat down on the front steps. I began sobbing uncontrollably. Holding my face in my hands, I heard someone speak. Looking up, I saw that the voice had come from the next-door neighbor. She told me that they had moved out, and it was a shame since they were such nice young men. Of course, she was old and to her they probably did seem like nice young men. I did not answer her. Instead, I put my head down and began to cry again. The old woman went on to say that she had heard that one man had been assigned to another base, and the other had moved back into the barracks. I looked up at her and began to feel extremely dizzy. The effects of the gin hit me all at once. I stood up, thanked the old woman, and headed to my car.

Once I was in my car, I decided it would be better for me to stay there and sober up a little. I was too messed-up to continue driving. The next thing I knew I awoke to the old woman knocking on my window, scaring me half way to death. I jumped up, wiped the drool from my face, and raised my hand to her to show her I was okay. I started the car and drove away.

Again I drove to my secret place in the Everglades and sat in my car. It was like a sauna inside the car, so I rolled down the windows to let in some air. Mosquitoes rushed into the car as if they had been eagerly waiting to eat me alive. I started the car back up and drove home. I was feeling sick and could not think of my next plan in my state of mind. Part of me wanted to return to the old woman to find out where the guy, Eddie, was stationed. I would have gone anywhere to kill him. But in the meantime I had to focus my attention on the other man that was still there. I asked myself, "If I were a creep like those two, where would I go to pick up women?" Then I remembered the Airman's club. I thought I might begin to frequent it more often to search for my no-good scum of a friend. I started going there every Friday and Saturday night. I had become very mean and it didn't take much to arouse my temper. My friends started calling me Red. I even tried to smoke so I could look cool, but I kept lighting the filter. In fact, it was quite embarrassing sitting in the club trying to light a cigarette while my friends laughed at me. "Try turning the cigarette around the other way and lighting it. It's easier to smoke it that way." After about the third try I gave up. God evidently was trying to tell me something.

One night, while sitting in the club with my sister and her boyfriend, a man walking by caught my attention. My heart skipped a beat and leaped with joy. I grabbed my chest and looked at my sister. I gave her the eye that meant, "I'll be right back." To my surprise it was Eddie's friend! I walked over to him to see if he would notice me, and if so, what his reaction would be. Of course, I was looking sharp in the black dress I was wearing. Believe you me! It was fitting rather well. I pretended to be interested in talking to someone else, when he walked up to me and tapped me on the back. I turned around. He looked stunned at first. I immediately tried to calm him down and told him, "Hey, don't worry. I'm not mad at you, instead I would like to thank you and Eddie for what you did for me that night. I had a very eventful evening, and I rather enjoyed it. In fact, I see sex in a totally different light now." I was smiling and batting my eyes. I asked him to stroll over and join me and my sister at our table. He said he was at the club with someone else, but he would stop over later.

I spent most of night looking around the room for him so that when he left the room I could follow him, of course, trying not to look obvious. I couldn't take my eyes off him. When he glanced at me I would divert my attention onto something or someone else, so he wouldn't know I was staring at him. My desire to kill him was so strong that I could not concentrate on anything else. The longer he avoided me, the worse my anger grew.

Suddenly he left the room. This time he was headed out the door with another girl. I followed both of them out to the car and called for him. He told his girlfriend to hold on for a minute and ran back to me to see what I wanted. He told me he was taking her home and that he would be right back. I told him "I'm not going anywhere. I'll be right here when you get back," all the while keeping a sexy smile on my face. If he only knew how much stored-up anger was behind that smile, he would've raced to the police. This was not an easy task, pretending I was interested in being with this man--yet all along scheming to kill him.

Soon, the dance was over and I stood at the door watching everybody walk to their cars. My sister approached and asked me what I was waiting for. I told her to go home. I said, "I love you," as she walked away. She looked back at me for a moment and then got into her car and left. I stood there and watched each car pull away until they were all gone. Giving up, I started to walk to my car, when I noticed another car zipping through the parking lot towards me. It was him. "Yes! Yes!" I said, as I quickly got into my car and pulled the gun from under my seat. Putting the gun into my purse, I climbed out of my car and walked over to meet him. He introduced himself to me. "My name is Lauren." I immediately put my arms around his neck and pulled him close to me. As we embraced, we started to kiss. Although I detested every moment of it, I had to convince him that I truly missed and desired him. I told him, "Let's go in my car since it's a brand-new Mustang." Lauren agreed and asked me where we where going. "You'll see," I told him with a smile, "you're going to like this place." He told me that he had moved from his house after his roommate left and was now staying in the barracks. I acted as though I didn't know what he was talking about. He told me we could go back to his place because his roommate was asleep. I immediately responded, "No, I just want to be alone with you. I've been dreaming of making love to you ever since that night. Have you ever made love in a car?" He smiled and said, "Yes." We kissed again, and drove off.

Part of Lauren's conversation I tuned out because I was trying to figure out how I would do this evil deed. As I was fazing him out I suddenly heard him say, "So, you like what happened to you, huh?" I hesitated before answering him, because I had to think about what I was going to say. It had to be very convincing. "No, not at first. It wasn't until I tried it with other men and I found it to be better the second time around." He laughingly told me he thought I would be very upset and angry. He went on to say how it was Eddie's idea, but he went along with the plan. It was a good thing that the car was dark because I'm sure my face was turning red and steaming. I laughed with him as I started to step on the gas. He asked, "Why are you going so fast? Slow down we have all night." I told him I was sorry and took my foot off the pedal. I hadn't even realized that I had started to speed up. I definitely did not want to be stopped by a cop. At least not this night!

He started to explain how there were other women but they did not like him that much. I began to grit my teeth, and turned the radio up in order to drown out his voice. After he watched me turn down all sorts of side roads he said, "Wow, this must be a really private place of yours." Smiling, I told him "It's a place I always go when I want to be alone and think, or to make love to some a man." We turned down the last street, the one that dead-ended into the swamp. I envisioned how the alligators would eat up all the evidence. I also thought of the pleasure I would get from shooting him with every bullet that I had. I asked him, "So, how many women have you done this to?" In a very snooty, arrogant voice he told me, "I don't know, I lost count."

I stopped the car and started to kiss him with what I consider, "the kiss of death," and boy did I mean it this time. "Look out, dude, because you are in trouble," I said, as I told him I needed to go to the bathroom. I got out of the car, and hiked around toward the back of the vehicle. I squatted behind the car so he could not see me pull out the gun. I took off the safety and headed back toward his side of

149

the car. When I reached him, he was already in his underwear. "You arrogant, @$#%@#%$#@%!" I pointed the gun at his head and ordered him out of the car. Lauren sat in the Mustang and stared at me. Again, I said in a very conniving, "Get your @#$%$# out of my car! And then I want you to walk toward the end of the street. "He started calling me, "crazy." It made me giggle. Then he tried to challenge me but I told him, "It would be wise if you follow my directions since I've never shot a gun before." He followed my directions. I could hear him begging and pleading and crying. I told him "Don't cry. It's hard enough to kill you as it is."

I climbed up onto the hood of my car as he walked away slowly. He started to turn, and I advised him not to turn around. "I'm not going to let you just shoot me. "I let off a shot to intimidate him. The gun jerked my hand back so hard that it scared me half to death. It scared him as well. I was almost thrown to the ground. The jerking movement hurt my arm. He turned and kept walking. "Stop where you are and remove your underwear." He turned, pleading with me, "Why do I need to take off my underwear?" Looking at him very seriously, I told him, "You will not need them after you're dead. Plus the alligators can't digest briefs."

I continued to point the gun at him as he slowly took off his underwear. I could see the sweat glistening on his body as the mosquitoes attacked him. I ordered him, "Throw your underwear to me! Turn around! And get on your knees!" He begged and pleaded with me, "Please don't kill me!" I asked him again, "How many women have you hurt and humiliated, raped and sodomized?" "One," so I shot off the gun again. "You liar!" I yelled. "Why do you want to know?" he cried out. "I'm the one asking the questions here, stupid" I repeated, "How many?" "About ten, I don't know." "That was ten too many!" I climbed down off the car and started to walk toward him, while he was on his knees. "I hate to do this but you have got to be stopped. Who do you think you are? What gives you the right to use women in this way?" The only response he gave me was uncontrollable sobbing. I told him, "Remember what you told me, don't cry, it won't do you any good." I hesitated for a moment because I knew I had control. I knew he was all mine. I could hear it in his voice as he continued to beg. I also knew this would be the perfect murder. No one saw us meet in the parking lot because they had all gone home.

He then looked up to Heaven and called on God. His calling on God did not faze me in the least. How dare he, anyway? How could God help someone like him? If he did, I didn't want any part of this God. My hands began to shake, something inside kept telling me, "Don't do this," "Don't do this." I walked back to my car and I threw his underwear as far out into the Everglades as I could, where I had thrown the rest of his clothing. Getting into my car, I sat for a moment and watched him. He looked as though he was still praying to his God. I sat and watched him for a moment. Then I turned on the ignition and backed up. I backed up until I came to the end of the road. Turned onto the next road and drove about another half mile. My conscious mind kept telling me to go back and finish the job, finish what I had started. If he got back to the base he was either going to kill me or tell on me and I would probably go to prison.

I sat in the car biting my fingernails. Putting my face on the steering wheel, I raised my head and looked at my gun. I turned the car around to go back, finish the job, and dispose of the body. I got halfway there and stopped again. I said to myself, "So what, let him tell." I did not think he could even find his way back. He was 30 miles from the base and was wearing no clothes. I thought if that failed to teach him, nothing would. Anyway, the only person who would probably get into a lot of trouble was my no good husband because I was his dependent.

Women need to learn to fight back. Knowing I could never go to the police made me take charge of my own life. I drove away drinking my beer and listening to Otis Redding. On the way home I thought to myself," How could I have stopped this from ever happening"? When I thought about it for a while I could have done something different. All I had to do was take someone with me that night, perhaps a girlfriend, my sister, or someone. I also could have told my parents so they could have been aware and dropped me off and introduced themselves to the guys. On the way home I laughed, thinking about all the different problems he was going to encounter trying to get back to the base butt-ball naked. When I realized a smile had taken over my face, I knew I was going to be okay.

Believe it or not, I neither saw nor heard from Lauren again. I assume he figured it would do no good to report me because now it was my word against his. For someone to do what I did to him, the police would have to realize he must have done something too. I would like to think he has mended his ways and is sitting in some church somewhere. Who Knows? On the other hand I became worse. I was now on the prowl, searching for another man who believed he was God's gift to women and he could treat them however he desired.

# Chapter 20

I did not like going to the Airman's club. My wall was up, and I did not trust men. I only went to the club to find victims; abusive, arrogant, and nasty men. Everywhere I went I took my gun with me, just in case someone tried to take advantage of me again. I could not believe I had become what I was.

One night a man came up to me and asked me if I wanted to go somewhere since it was so dead in the club that night. I said "Sure, but my sister will have to come with us, since we're so close and all." He said, "Hey, no problem!" My sister informed her boyfriend and we all went to the car. While driving along the street headed for a club downtown we were all listening to the radio. The man I was with decided to put an 8-track on the stereo. It was XXX-Rated. It was the first time I had ever heard a man and woman making love on the stereo. The moaning and groaning was ridiculous. It was the first time I had ever encountered such trash. I explained to him, "I consider myself a decent young woman and I am not going to listen to such rubbish." He looked at me. "It's my car and I can play whatever I want." I looked back at my sister. She knew I was mad, and she also knew I was carrying my gun. She smiled and winked as I smiled back. I pulled the 45 out of my purse and put it to his temple. The gun was locked, but it was full of bullets. "Pull the car over! Stop! And get out!" He yelled, "What do you think you're doing?" as he pulled the car over to the side of the road. Not caring to repeat myself, I told him, "Get out of the car!" He got out of the car and called me every cuss word under the sun. I then moved over to the driver's seat. We locked our doors and drove away. I turned on the music and we laughed and danced as we drove back to the base. I could see him out of the rearview mirror, running after the car and yelling, "That's my car!" I took the

153

car back to the base and left it at the gate. I told the cop that the guy who owned the car would be there soon looking for it. The cop asked for our identification cards. We showed our cards to him and we walked back to the club to get my car. I really was starting to enjoy myself. I liked being in control.

One day, while working at a part-time job in a snack bar, a man came in and ordered a hamburger. He asked me out. And of course, feeling very protected carrying my newfound friend, I said, "Sure". I was feeling more secure going out with strange men. I was high on the chance to once again scare the mess out of someone. It actually was very easy to say yes without having to worry about the end result. He said he would pick me up at 7:00. I smiled and told him, "Sure. That will be fine." He seemed to be a pretty nice guy. He was also very handsome, and I was hoping that this date would go according to my expectations. I started to leave my gun at home because this guy did not seem as though he was going to harm me. He was too polite. Something kept telling me, though, to take it with me anyway.

He picked me up right on time. He was dressed very nicely and smelled good. He even opened the car door for me. I was impressed. We drove off the base and were headed toward the club when he told me he had to stop by his work for something. "No problem," I said as he drove me up a dark mountain pass. When I asked him where he was going he explained, "I work at a radio site on the mountain." When we reached the top he stopped in front of a building. He turned to give me a kiss. I pushed him back, telling him that he was moving too fast. I heard him say "Take off your underwear."

I was shocked not only because he was so blunt, but he had been acting like the perfect gentleman. As usual, I had misjudged his character. "I think it's time you drove me back home." He told me, "If you don't pull off your underwear, you'll have to get out of my car." I definitely was not going to get out of the car, and I certainly refused to walk home. So of course, I pulled out my 45 and stuck it to his head. "Get out!" His eyes widened as he looked into the barrel of my gun. He reached behind himself to open the door and slowly backed out of the car. I slid right into the driver's seat, closed the door, locked it, and drove away. All he did was stand there in shock and watch as I drove away. I could not help but laugh at his expression. I took the car back to the base and parked it. I gave the keys to the gate police and walked home.

Luckily I ran into my father. He was leaving a little convenience store on base where Mom had sent him to pick up some bread and milk. He asked me why I was out walking, especially since I now had my own car. I explained that I had decided not to go with a friend so I thought I'd walk home. Daddy always laughed and smiled when he knew I was asking for trouble so he very nicely told me, "You know that's why your daddy helped you to buy a car. So you wouldn't be out here this time of night, walking by yourself alone." Getting into his car, I agreed and promised him that I would be careful and drive my own car. However, I was having a lot of fun taking different cars back to the gate.

Every Friday Linda and I would make sure we were at the club on time. While sitting in the club one night a man strolled up to our table and asked to sit down and join us. We said, "Yes, of course." He ordered himself a drink, not bothering to ask my sister and I if we cared for one. I looked at Linda and gave her the eye because I knew we were about to be entertained for the evening. I couldn't stand self-centered men anyway, but we were both bored and had nothing better to do. He told us that the club was slow and that we should go to another club off the base. He told us that it would be his treat. We laughed and said, "All-l-l r-r-r-right-t-t!"

We smiled as we both agreed and got up to walk out. He was still at the table finishing off our drinks and his own. We laughed as we started out the building and to the car. Following us out the door, he put his arms around us and told us how beautiful we both looked. I gave Linda the eye as she laughed at me. I told him "We will take our car and follow you", still remembering my father's wise words. Following him to the club Linda and I were going over our game plans. When we arrived at the club it was very crowded, but we managed to find a table. The guy started yelling and waving at his friends so that they would notice that he was with us. Soon a very tall waitress hurried over to our table to take our order. We all ordered and of course since he was paying, we asked for the most expensive drinks on the menu. As soon as the waitress took the drink orders, he decided he had to use the restroom. In a few minutes the waitress returned to the table and told us our bill totaled $20.00. I told her that the man we were sitting with would pay for them. She informed us that the man had told her that we would pay. My sister and I only looked at each other. I smiled at the waitress and began to search for my money. I asked my sister if she could cover her drink and she said, "Yes." We drank all the beverages, picked up the car keys that the guy had left on the table, and headed for the door.

I got into his car and my sister drove mine. Just as we were pulling out of the parking lot we noticed him chasing after the car. We laughed as we both drove off. Once we got back to the base we left the car at the gate. As I was about to give the car keys to the guard, I noticed dangling from the guy's keys was a dog tag that read: "If you find these keys, please call this telephone, ----------." I called the number and his wife answered. I explained to his wife what had happened. She was not sure if she should believe me or not, but when I said he would come home without his car, she did. I hung up the phone laughing. This time the security police asked who owned the car. I explained that the owner loaned us the car, and would soon be arriving to look for it. Again Linda and I laughed as we climbed into my car and drove home.

I wasn't having much luck finding men that were abusing women--until one night I visited the Airman's Club, looking and stalking so to speak, for my next victim. I did not have to go far because finding another man was very easy. Walking up the sidewalk to enter the club was a GI fighting with his girlfriend. Everyone stared as they walked by. She was pleading him to give her another chance. She said she was pregnant with his child and wanted him to acknowledge it. He was calling her a whore. "It's not my baby! Get away from me!" I could see the hurt and torment in her face as he pushed her away. She sat crying and he returned into the club. Of course, I had to follow him. It was time I paid a visit to my getaway 30 miles off base. I approached him and offered him a drink. "Isn't that embarrassing? It must be hard having some girl hanging around your neck, accusing you of having a child that is not yours?" He agreed to my offer.

We both went up to the bar and I ordered the drink. My sister glanced across the room at me. She knew what I was up to. I gave her the eye and she returned to doing what she was doing, laughing with some friends. Before long we were into a conversation and he asked me to excuse him, because he wanted to go play pool with the guys. I asked if I could watch. We both walked upstairs and I sat through four or five boring games. No matter how bored I was, I was not going to leave. Every now and then, he would stop playing and wander over and talk to me to show me off in front of the guys. As I sat there, I kept imagining how the night was going to end.

It started getting so late that we actually closed the bar. I asked him if he wanted to go to one of my private places to be alone. He agreed and said, "We should stop and get a bottle." We stopped at a convenience store. He asked me what I wanted to drink. I asked him to get me a specific type of beer, but he bought what he wanted. I thought to myself, "You creep! My turn is coming, and you're not going to like it." I smiled and he got back into the car. He wanted to stop some place else, but I convinced him that we should go to my place. Plus, I had to go to work the next morning. That's how cold I had become.

I was driving while he was popping beers left and right, tossing the cans out the car window.

I told him, "You shouldn't be littering because this world is for our children's future. They are the ones that have to live in this environment." He laughed. "I don't care. I'm not ever going to have children." I could see why, since he was so busy denying that every child he helped to conceive was not his. Boy, he was not winning any points with me. "Where are these jerks coming from?" I asked myself.

When we got out to the water I kissed him and told him to go on and remove his clothes. As usual, I made believe that I had to go to the bathroom so I could go back to the back of the car. The mosquitoes were out in full force that night. Swatting the mosquitoes, I pulled out my gun. I stood up and noticed that he was still sitting in the front seat, guzzling beer, so I tucked the gun back into my purse. Things were not going as smoothly as I had imagined. I told him to hurry up and get undressed because I wanted very much to be with him. "Don't you want to make love?" He told me I was moving too fast, grabbed me, and began to kiss and fondle me. What was I going to do to get him to move faster? Plus the mosquitoes were eating us alive, but he didn't seem to notice. I tried closing the windows but it was hard to breathe. He was so disrespectful towards women that he didn't even bother to take the gum out of his mouth. The next thing I knew, he was reaching down, trying to take off my underwear. I realized what he wanted to do. He wanted to keep his clothes on while we had sex. I convinced him that I wanted to take off my own underwear. I had thrown my purse in the back seat, and I had to get to it. I had to improvise. "There's more room in the backseat." I climbed out of the front seat and headed for the back, as he watched me. I pretended to remove my underwear and at the same time tried to get my gun. The tough part was trying to smile and look sexy all at the same time.

As he strolled around to open the back door on his side, I lifted the gun. He stuck his head inside the car, only to find my 45 pointed at his forehead. Forget making him take off his clothes, this was the time to make my move and make it quickly. Instantly, he backed out of the car and dropped his beer. I told him, "Back far away from the car!" He yelled, " @#$%@#!" "That describes you perfectly." I got out of the car and told him, "Walk slowly to the front of the car!" "Why?" I told him, "For that innocent woman and child back at the club. And for any other woman you decide to take advantage of in your lifetime." Again I asked him to remove his clothes but he refused. His reaction scared me. I told him, "I've never shot a gun before. I'll probably accidentally hit you right between the eyes. All I'll have to do is tell the police that it was an accident." After hearing this, he began

159

to disrobe. He kept talking to me, but I tuned him out. I stared at him as he removed his clothes. He stopped just before he removed his underwear, and almost instantaneously I let off a shot. He grabbed his ear as if he thought I had shot it off. Laughing, I ordered him, "Turn around and get on your knees!" He refused. I told him that if he did not turn around, I would shoot out both of his knees. I think he could tell my inexperience with the pistol by the way I was handling it. This man never cried once during the entire ordeal.

I was so afraid of him that I threw his clothes into my backseat, locked the doors, and started up the car to drive away. He jumped up from his crouched position and started screaming at me. I backed up and I could see him searching for his clothes. Just like before, the mosquitoes were torture. I backed up as quickly as I could, turned the car around, and drove off as fast as possible. I kept looking behind me to see if he were after me, but I figured that he didn't want to take any chances, so he let me drive away. That night I was not able to fall asleep. In fact, all night I kept thinking that he was coming to get me. I spent many restless nights without any sleep.

Nearly one week later, I was with Anna Mae at the base hospital. We were there to pick up her medicine. Suddenly, my mother nudged me and said, "Look at that man staring at my beautiful baby." I smiled at her, "Maaaama." When I looked over to see who she was referring to, it was the man I was having the nightmares about. He was standing at the counter with his girlfriend. As my mother walked up to the counter to get her medicine, he just stared at me. He asked my mother how she was doing. She told him she was fine. I thought for sure he was going to say something, but he only looked back at me and smiled. I quickly grabbed my mother's arm and forced her out the door. On the way out to the door she asked me, "What that was all about?" "I haven't the slightest idea." She started fussing, "You frown too much. You're never going to find a good man the way you treat men!" She told me that Sam had made me a cold human being. I said, "Yes, he has Mommy," as I got into the car. Little did she know how true her statement was. I could sleep after that encounter, but I never forgot how close I came to either losing my life or being left 30 miles away from the base myself.

I thought I was a failure on my last journey to the swamp. In fact, I had begun thinking that maybe I should start driving the men one hundred miles away, tying them up, beating them, and then shooting them in the legs. After my last victim I had begun to feel that what I was doing for women was in fact not helping. I was getting desperate. The word failure was not in my vocabulary. Cynthia Jackson a failure? No way.

To my complete surprise I saw the man again the next week. This time he was at the snack bar on base having lunch with his pregnant girlfriend. When I saw this, my heart leaped for joy. I could not believe it. Maybe that night did leave an impression on him? If he was with her again maybe he had a change of heart. I guess I will never know for sure. Sometimes I wish I could turn into a fly so I could find out what goes on in people's lives.

Dropping off men's cars at the base gate was continuous, but going out to my special place in the swamp never happened again. It is not that I wanted to quit, because I was constantly bumping into guys that were treating women badly. It seemed as if everywhere I went, there was some man threatening his wife. Once, I even saw a man slap a woman in a park. Another time I was about to board a plane when a woman walked up with two black eyes and a busted lip. What was going on? I could see what I must have looked like to other people when Sam beat me. But no one helped me. People just minded their own business. I realized that I was fighting a loosing battle. I was trying to take on the world and help all women including myself, but there were just too many men for me to fight alone.

# Chapter 21

I still continued to go out but not for the reasons I went out before. One evening as I was entering the club, several people approached me. They all laughed in my face about my new boyfriend. Even the men asked me, "Where did you find this guy?" I was confused because I didn't have a boyfriend. "What are you talking about?" One woman began laughing hysterically and said, "That's not what this guy Terry is telling everyone!" I asked who they were talking about. Someone finally pointed to a tall, skinny man with his back turned to me. I walked up to him, only for him to turn and put his arm around me. To make matters worse, he kissed me on the cheek. I pulled away and could not believe how incredibly ugly he was. He looked as though he had been burnt. His skin was the color of charcoal. I had never seen someone as ugly as him in my life. In fact, he should have been in a freak show. After I got myself together, I asked "Why are you telling everyone I'm your girlfriend?" I said it as loud as possible so everyone could hear me. He looked at me and asked in a whisper "Can we go outside?" I said, "Okay."

We walked out the door, people stood laughing and giggling. Once we were outside, I asked him again. He told me that he had seen me at my job and heard that I was very a mysterious person. No one could figure me out. The guys around base were always talking about me. "Sooo?" He told me he went around the base telling everyone we were together. He did this so guys would befriend him and girls would talk to him. I was very upset, and boy did I show it! He tried to calm me down as he led me farther away from the building. I told him, "I wouldn't be caught dead with someone like you!" He went on to explain how lonely he was, and how much he needed to have a friend. When he

163

told people he was dating me, it opened up room for discussion. He said, "Everyone is very curious about you because they never see you with anyone. You just come and go." "And what did you say?" "I told them it was because of me." "Oh, I know you didn't!" I put my hands on my hips. I pointed to the door and told him, "You're going to go back in there and clear this up and you are going to do it right now!" I was so angry I could feel "devil horns" coming out of my head. I could feel myself becoming evil. He told me, "Okay, if I do, will you go out with me?" My eyes widened. I could not believe he had the audacity to ask me something like that after what he did. I told him, "You must be crazy."

I knew it would be best to walk away from this crazy fool. I turned and again told him, "Go do it! Now!" "You don't understand how it feels to be so ugly no one will even have anything to do with you!"

I guess he expected me to feel bad. I walked away shaking my head at him, when he yelled, "What about a movie?" I stopped and stood there for a minute thinking, "Anything to get this man to clear this situation up." I told him, "Okay, I'll go to the movies." I figured no one would see us together, and most importantly no one would see him. As I was walking to my car he called, "How can I get in touch with m?" "I'll find you."

That night in my dreams I was the one that was ugly, and I was the one that was trying to get a date. Regardless of how much I tried to get people to see my heart, and regardless of how nice to a person I was, no one could see through my ugliness. I woke up in a cold sweat, shaking. I was so angry and upset with myself, I went looking for Terry.

164

After searching the base, I found him. I walked up to him and told him I would meet him on Saturday at 1:00 P.M. I told him, "Meet me in front of the movies for a matinee," and then I walked away. I turned to glance back at him, and could see the sheer joy on his face. He yelled, "One more thing! Can I bring a friend?" "Go ahead, and I'll bring my sister Linda." This made him even more thrilled. I walked away and told myself I would do anything just as long as I never had another dream like that one.

That Saturday when we met, I thought I was seeing things. I got out of my car and walked up to the both of them. The guy he had brought with him was at least 50 years old. I could not believe what Terry had on. He was wearing a black-leather, bell-bottom suit that had pinstripes down the sleeves. The pants were high waters and he was wearing white socks. I looked at my sister as if to say, "How am I going to get out of this date?" I told my sister to stick with me and I would find a way to get rid of them. As we walked up to the theater, people stared at Terry. Besides his clothing, I suppose they were wondering why he was wearing leather in Florida. He looked ridiculous.

We didn't want to see any of the movies that were playing on base, so we decided to go off base to find one. They walked us to the car and I was shocked again. The car was a yellow convertible. My sister and I both said, "Oh no!" at the same time, and offered our car. They both insisted that my car would be too small to fit the four of us. Plus, the older man had bad knees. I agreed, and we got into the convertible. I insisted on Terry and his friend sitting up front and my sister and me in back. That way if we passed anyone we knew we could duck down in the back seat and hide. Once inside the car, Terry started up the engine and played the radio very loud. I told my sister, "I can't do this! I cannot do this!" She laughed and reminded me that I had promised him. We both pulled out our scarves and covered our heads. It was my sister's idea to bring the scarves just in case. As we were headed to the movies downtown, we passed a carnival. The guys got very excited and wanted to stop. Linda and I did not want to, but they insisted. Both men agreed it would be fun and turned down the street leading to the carnival. I could not even muster a smile. As soon as the car was parked, Terry and his friend jumped. Both came to the back to let Linda and I out. We left our scarves on. We figured we were bound to see someone we knew. We told the guys to go on ahead, and we would follow behind.

Walking through the crowd was horrible. It was as if we were freaks in a freak show. People stood back and parted the way as we walked through the crowd. Most stared, but some people laughed. I was so humiliated, but I knew I had to keep my promise. If I didn't, I knew I would go through another week of having the same nightmare. It was getting harder and harder to stay.

Soon, we came to a ride that had disco music coming from the speaker as people flew by. Some people had stopped to clap and dance. Suddenly, Terry and his friend began to dance. They were dancing as stiff as Frankenstein's monster. Their arms and legs were stiff as boards as they flailed around. I was so embarrassed I thought I would cry. Crowds began to gather around as they both made complete fools of themselves. These guys really thought they looked good.

The crowd started to grow larger. I grabbed my sister and we both ran for the car. We jumped in and laughed our heads off. Linda said, "All right, Kaye-Kaye, enough is enough." Soon, Terry and his friend returned to the car with sweat pouring down their faces. They asked us if we saw the crowd that had gathered. We laughed and told them we had. They both got into the car and my sister and I got down in the backseat. People had started to point toward the car as we were driving away. I told Terry my sister and I was hungry and asked him if he could please stop at McDonald's. My sister and I ordered everything we could think of. They both smiled and said, "Boy, you two sure can eat." I asked Terry to leave the keys in the car so we could listen to music. My sister and I sat in the car debating on whether we should leave them. As they walked out the door with two huge bags of food, we waved and drove off. Now I had gone too far. I was doing it to innocent people. What was I becoming?

We parked the car at the base. A part of me could not help but feel sorry for them. Especially because Terry wore that leather outfit and it was very hot outside. However, it didn't take long for me to forget about the situation. I still continued with my rampage.

I did not hear from Terry again until Christmas. He came to another part-time job I was working at a burger place. When I saw him park his car I ran to the back of the restaurant to hide. I remembered what I had done to him and found it hard to face him. I told the other employees to tell Terry I was busy. The next thing I knew one of the employees came back to the store with a couple of presents. I set down the gifts and ran after Terry. He was getting into his car, which was also filled with several gifts. I told him I was sorry for what I had done that day. He said, "I'm used to people treating him that way." My heart began to swell. He asked me what I was doing for Christmas and I told him I was going home to be with my baby daughter. He said that he was going to the orphanage to be with the children, and to pass out gifts. He went on to say that usually on the holidays he would spend time with kids. He said that the children in the orphanage were the only people that wanted to be around him during the Holidays. The children accepted him the way he was. My heart again began to swell even more. The tears began to roll down my face. I tried to hold them back, but they were uncontrollable. I told Terry I had to get back to work, and he wished me, "Merry Christmas and a Prosperous New Year." Before he drove away, he thanked me for going out with him that day. "I had a wonderful time," he said. I wondered how it was possible for him to have a wonderful time after what I had done to him. How could he find enough love in his heart to forgive me? Why would he bring a gift to someone as cruel as I was? How dare he show me love! What kind of man was he, to not take advantage of me like so many others? As I went back into the restaurant everyone asked me what was wrong. I could not speak. My mouth was in pain from trying to hold back my tears. I felt too ashamed to tell anyone this story. I just walked to the back of the restaurants where I had left the gifts that he brought me.

Trembling, I opened the gifts. Inside one of them was a little Japanese music box with a Japanese doll that spun around. The music that played was "Sakura," a song I had always loved, as a young child in Japan. The next gift was a shirt printed with the phrase: "Love is what makes the world go 'round."

I dropped everything and ran into the bathroom. Once I was there, I cried my eyes out. My heart grew until it could not grow anymore. I looked in the mirror at a person that had gone full circle. I had wronged a man that had not known love, but still was able to give it. This man was not accepted by society because everyone teased and hurt him in one way or the other. Unlike the other men in my life, this man brought me flowers, opened my door, bought me lunch, and even walked ten miles home in the Florida heat without anger but only joy and compassion in his heart. At Christmas time he even brought me, not to mention a whole orphanage full of children, gifts. He did not know what it felt like to be loved, but he was still able show it.

What a monster I had become. He did not deserve to be treated like those other men. He was a human being that I turned into a victim of circumstance. He came into my life at the wrong time. God was trying to tell me something. God had given me a rope, but I had gone a little too far with it. It was time to pull it back in. Every time I tell this story it brings tears to my eyes. I have tears of sadness and tears of joy. I'm no longer the same person. No matter who we are and what we look like, we are all human beings. We need to touch each other with love and understanding. Thank you, Lord, that we have each other because we would be so lonely. For those people out there that are hiding because of the way they look, come out because I love you and so does the Lord. We love you just the way you are.

I never did wear the shirt that Terry had selected for me because I did not deserve to wear it. I am not sure as to what happened to Terry. My heart believes he was an angel sent by God. According to the Bible there were angels, and at one time they came down to earth. Maybe just maybe, when we're about to get into big trouble, as I was about to get into, the Lord sends an angel to stop us before we go too far. I would like to think he does. That shows tremendous love. I also think when we get big headed or reach the point of no return He sends an angel. For all the "Terrys" in this world, the men that treat women with courtesy and respect instead of as pieces of meat, "Thank you." I was the truly ugly person, not Terry. No matter how unattractive or distastefully dressed he was, his heart was what mattered. His heart was beautiful. And mine was cold and gray. I never saw Terry again. I always wondered in my heart what ever happened to him.

After my experience with Terry, I did not feel the need for my gun. I took the 45 to a pawnshop and sold it. I must admit though, I was terrified. I was scared of living without a gun to defend myself. So, instead of going out on dates unprotected, I decided to stop dating and stay home.

## Chapter 22

My two jobs were beginning to be too much for me to handle. So I decided to quit my job at the burger place and continue to work in the hospital, under the Dietician. We would fix food for the patients that were on strict diets and take meals to their bedside. Many would try to sneak salt or other restricted items onto their food so someone had to watch them as they ate. I remember one patient in particular that I loved to visit every day. Maggie was an old lady, but she was very pleasant and told some great stories. Her husband had died many years ago and her children never visited her. Even though she was sick and alone, she always had a very pleasant attitude. I fell in love with her right away. Sometimes I would visit her at night if I weren't busy caring for September. In the morning I would smile as I prepared Maggie's plate and sometimes sneak a snack or two to her. She would become so happy when I arrived and would tell me war stories of when she had been a nurse. She told me how hard it was to lose a man fighting in the First World War; their injuries and their lives being torn apart at home. She told me how they came home to a world that didn't care that they had sacrificed their very lives overseas in a country unknown to them. Sometimes she would nurse them back to health only to watch them go back to the front line and continue fighting. Her stories gave me a sense and compassion for our veterans who were so heroic.

One day I decided to sneak her a piece of cake. I put it on my cart and pushed it down to her room, which was the last one on the ward. I pulled out Maggie's tray with the piece of cake on it, smiled, and pranced in to surprise her. When I got to the door, I found her covered in a sheet with a tag on her toe. I dropped my tray to the floor. A passing nurse asked me if I was okay. This was the first time I had ever seen a dead person. At the side of her bed stood her son. I wanted so badly to tell him that he was too late. She had needed someone to be there for her when she was alive. Tears rolled down my face as I began to pick up the tray of food. Her son came over to help me, but I didn't want him to. I was still upset with the way he had failed to visit his mother even though I knew the reason why he didn't visit was none of my business. It is amazing to think of some of the moms that watch out for their children with love and devotion. Then when they get older, their children are not there for them. Maggie died all alone that night watching T.V. I never got to say good-bye to her but I hoped I filled her life with just a little bit of love and happiness, such as that which she had given her children. For all the nursing she had done for the veterans, all the loyalty, love, and kindness you bestowed--"Thank you, Maggie."

The Vietnam War had finally ended and the veterans were coming back to America. The hospital was overflowing with patients. We were working overtime, trying to feed all of them. I even spent extra time on my days off to help out the nurses. There was so much work for the nurses to do, and each patient had so many needs.

One day I arrived at work early so I could spend time with them. I was told not to discuss or ask questions about what had happened in Vietnam. I avoided asking any questions, but the veterans always volunteered the information. They talked about how they were spit on when they landed at the airport. I found one man in particular that had lost both legs and an arm. Another man had lost both his legs. One man had a small missile shot through his stomach. Fortunately, the missile did not explode, but the man had to have the skin on his stomach grafted. There was so much pain and crying. Some were crying because they were so happy to be home. Some patients repeated over and over again, "God bless America." Even though they came back without any limbs, they did not care as long as they were back home. The biggest fear for all of them was that they would never again see American soil.

I went from bed to bed, realizing that many of the soldiers only wanted to hold my hand or flirt with me. I thought that this was cute considering they had only half of their bodies intact. Some were singing praises to the Lord, and even though I had not accepted His love nor understood Him, I questioned their love and devotion. How could they praise the Lord, yet they were far worse off than me? I remembered the old saying about t he man that complained about his shoes, until he saw a man with no feet. Some of the men were burnt so badly you knew that they were not going to make it, yet they were so happy to be home. If they did die here, they thought, "at least I am on American soil."

One man jumped from a burning helicopter. When he awoke he was looking up into a tree. At first he couldn't make out what he saw. There over the branches a parachute hung and from one corner of his eye, he saw a leg hanging. He looked down at himself to find that his leg was gone. I heard story after story like that until I could no longer handle it. I ran into the bathroom. I sat down in a stall and cried my eyes out. Suddenly I heard a woman's voice ask, "Are you okay? Can I help?" Slowly, I stood up and peeked out of the stall. There stood a nurse with a big, beautiful smile on her face. Again she asked to help. My nose and my makeup were running. I walked out of the stall. The nurse said, "Here, give me a hug." I hugged her as she told that she too knew how I felt. "You must be tired." She knew I had been there almost 24 hours. She told me, "Go home and get some rest." "I don't think I'll be able to come back." She told me if I did <u>not</u> come back everyone would understand.

I left for home, showered and went to bed. The next morning when I awoke I went into the bathroom to wash up. Standing in front of the mirror I told myself, "Today I will just go to the hospital, do my job, and come home No extra working in the hospital wards for me." When I got to the base gate there were news cameras, reporters, and signs everywhere. The signs read: "Women and baby killers!!! Why did you come back?" "Why didn't you stay where you were? We do not want you here!" I drove past not understanding all the commotion that was surrounding the base.

When I arrived at the hospital I went straight to work. How dare they say the things they were saying? Everyone was talking about the picket people. I remember saying, "Why don't they pack them all up and send them to Vietnam? Let them find out what these men and women had gone through." Seeing all the commotion made it easy for me to gather up the strength to go back in there and care for these brave, honorable men. I decided that even though some of society was against them and had turned their backs on them, I was not going to be one of them. So I returned to work. However, I did visit that stall a couple of more times. But when I finished, I dried my tears and went back to work. I wanted to give them back a little bit of what they had given me. Freedom.

The story I believe that touched me the most was the one that came from a Vet who told me about the war babies. He said that he was in charge of taking men from the base out to an orphanage that cared for the babies. These were babies born out of wedlock to women who had slept with GI's, whores that left their babies so they could go back and make more money to survive. The babies were also born to women that were raped, not only by GI's but also by the Viet Cong. These were babies that were no longer wanted,

174

victims of war. They were all put into hundreds of cribs that were comprised of only a hardboard mattress, with no pillows or blankets. The babies lay in them cold and naked. When the babies would relieve themselves the caretakers would come by with a hose and spray down the infants with water. They would then be left to air-dry. The Vet told me that the strangest thing about the babies was that none of them cried. You would hear a whimper and then a gurgle, but that was all. He said that he would bring men from his unit and they would take radios, televisions, blankets and food for the babies--only to have the nuns take the supplies away and keep the items for themselves. He said that every guy he took there either would leave crying or not saying a word.

As far as the eyes could see there was nothing but cribs. The children that had begun to walk were put out into a big, fenced-in yard. They would wander around and go to the bathroom in tin cans. One day the Veteran decided to pick up one of the little infants, as it looked up at him, forlorn and pretty. Its eyes seemed to beg him, "Please hold me." He watched as the little baby played with its feet and hands. Being very tempted, he went against the nuns' demands and picked up the baby anyway. Right away the nuns ran towards him yelling, "Don't touch the babies! Do not touch the babies!" He took the child into his arms, and the baby held on so tight it almost squeezed the life out of him. Gripping his neck the baby seemingly held on for dear life. It seemed as though the child were saying, "Please take me home." Since it had never been held or shown any type of love at all, it was very difficult for the Veteran to let go. The tiny little eyes stared up at him as if they could see straight into his soul. He could hear the tiny heart beat, beating loudly, as he tried tenderly to pull the baby away and give it back to the nun. It was to no avail. He pulled and tugged at one arm, freeing it, but then the other arm would latch on. It took two nuns to finally get the tiny infant away from him. As he watched them put the infant back into the crib he cried. And to this very day, he still wakes up in the middle of his sleep with nightmares of those cribs full of babies. The face of the little infant he held so desperately wanting to be loved, lingering in his mind.

One by one the Vets started to leave for home. Thank God the base cleared the front gate of picketers. I had the privilege talking to and shaking the hands of those brave men that went to war. I don't think there is anyone on earth I would have rather met and shook hands with than the Vietnam Veterans. What an honor and a privilege it was. When I went to 'The Wall' and stood before the ones that did not make it, I saluted them. To all veterans, "Thank you, and Welcome Home!"

# Chapter 23

Tired from my week of working with the Veterans, I called a co-worker and asked her if she wanted to do something, perhaps go to the mall or see a movie? She told me to come over and we would decide when I arrived. Not finding her home, I decided to wait. I assumed she was either in the Laundromat or somewhere close by since she knew I was on my way over. I waited by the door and then walked over to the balcony.

My friend lived on the third floor of complex. Her apartment was across the street from a baseball field where a game was going on. I watched as young men played baseball in the fields across the street. I had just worked a 60-hour week and I was very tired, but I also wanted to get away. I was spending so much time with the Vietnam Veterans that I wanted some time for myself. Not only that, but most of the Vets had already gone home to their families. Not feeling as if I had it all together, I took a Valium and some pain medicine for my back. My back was sore from bending over so much to help the patients in and out of their beds, and carrying the food trays.

As I stood by the four-foot wall watching the game, an attractive guy strolled out of the apartment I stood next to, singing. I could hear the song blaring loudly out of the speakers inside his apartment. He left, went down to the laundry and came back. He asked, "What are you doing?" "Waiting for a friend." He laughed and made a joke about her standing me up. I could see he was flirting with me. "Do you want a beer?" I told him "Yes," but when he asked me to come inside I said him, "No." I was very leery about going into stranger's apartments after everything I had been through. He kicked up the stereo, opened his door, and asked me if I did not mind him joining me outside. I laughed, "It's a free world."

He gave me the beer and I hoisted myself up onto the cement railing, between the apartments. "Aren't you scared of heights?" I told him "No, I want to become a flight attendant." We continued talking and he brought out beer after beer.

After about an hour I noticed my girlfriend was still not back. I told him I had better be going home because I was starting to feel dizzy. He asked me to have one more beer and turned to go inside before I could say, "No, thanks." That is the last thing I remember.

The next thing I recall is waking up inside an ambulance with sirens going and lights flashing. A medic was asking me over and over again if I jumped. I said, "No," as I drifted in and out of unconsciousness. He then asked, "Were you trying to commit suicide?" I said, "No," and blacked out again.

The next time I woke up I was nude and laying in between two cots. A doctor began asking me questions like, "Do you know what happened? Do you know where you are?" He went on to explain what had happened, but my screams from pain interrupted him. The pain was so intense and so tremendous that it knocked me out again.

I awoke again with my face turned, looking at the door to my room. There I saw one eye peeking from a small corner of the window on the door.

I cried out, "Maaama!" In walked Anna with tears streaming down her face, "My poor baby, my poor, poor baby." She tried to hold me but I was sandwiched in between two beds and it was next to impossible. "Maaama's so glad you're all right." She told me she called Daddy and everyone else to tell them where I was. Then she told me how she found out the news. The hospital had called the house and said I had just fallen from a three-story building. Before they could tell her the rest she dropped the phone. She assumed that they were about to tell her I was dead and she didn't want to hear it. By the time her friend had come to the phone the hospital had hung up. They thought my mother heard the whole conversation--where I was located and what my condition was.

Not knowing what hospital I was in, Mom started to call everyone as she cried hysterically. All the hospitals told her they had no Cynthia Jackson. One hospital told her they had a Cynthia Hockson, but no Jackson. So mother continued to call. Soon she had called every hospital. I wasn't at any of the hospitals, so she began calling the morgues. None of them had me either, so she called the police. They had no information so she gave up. Her and her friend sat and talked. "Are you sure she said, 'Cynthia Hockson?'" My mom was positive. Suddenly, my mom jumped up and went to the phone. "I bet that's my baby, in fact I know that's my baby!" She called the hospital that had said there was a Cynthia Hockson. She asked them why she was there. The hospital would not give out any more information until she came down and showed some identification.

My mother and her friend went to the hospital, and sure enough the woman they had brought in had jumped from a three-story building. Again she kissed my brow and held my hands extended from the bed. She rubbed her hands through my hair. Over and over again she told me how much she loved me. "Mama's going to take care of you."

After about an hour she told me she was going home, and wanted to know if there was anything I wanted her to bring back. "No, just be careful."

As she left, I lay there and cried. Soon, I fell back asleep from the morphine.

The next thing I knew I heard, "Cynthia Kaye." I awoke to find Miss Meany. She was dressed differently. She walked over to my bed and told me that she was going to call my husband. She yelled, "If you think for one minute I am going to care for an invalid, you have got it all wrong! There is no way I am going to take care of you!" Tears rolled down my face. "Mama please don't call Sam." "Let him care for you. It's because of his crazy @#% that you are in this mess." I tried to tell her that I didn't jump. She yelled, "If you had stayed home where you belong and cared for your baby instead of going out in the streets sleeping around like a whore, you wouldn't be in this position!" Again the words, "like a whore," rang out loudly as she walked out of my room and left me there crying, begging her "Please don't call Sam." I hated Miss Meany and I was never going to forgive her. "I'll make it out of here on my own, Mama. Please don't call him." I tried to get up out of bed because I refused to believe my back was broken. I could not move. The next thing I knew I had drifted back off to sleep. I was in immense pain.

I kept drifting in and out. I knew if she called Sam he would be there in seconds, even if he had to walk on water. That's how much he wanted me to return. Knowing how crazy he was, I knew he would torture me. I cried, and because I was so upset, the pain became enormous. I kept screaming out in pain. The nurses kept running into my room with shots to try and give me some kind of comfort. I kept holding their hands firmly as they tried to relieve me of my pain. I could see that they felt so sorry for me as they held my hand and brushed my brow, asking me to calm down. One of the nurses took a cloth and wiped the tears from my eyes. She tried to soothe me by telling me not to worry, everything would be all right. Soon I started to calm down and go back to sleep. Being frantic was only making my situation worse. Usually as soon as the morphine hit me, I was out. I woke up hours later to find Sam at my bedside, rubbing my forehead tenderly. Stroking my arm, he told me of his love and devotion to me. I looked over at him and again tears rolled down the side of my eyes. He kissed me. "I'm here now and I'm going to take care of you." Tears ran down my face. I couldn't speak a word as I told myself, "Oh no! What am I going to do?"

My girlfriend came over to visit. Right away, she began to cry. She blamed herself, and I told her, "Stop being silly." She told how she had left to go to the store and was coming right back. She didn't think I was coming directly over to her house. I told her not to worry, she was blameless. People from my job and all of my friends stopped by the hospital. There were tons of people coming in and out. I was surprised by how many people really cared for me. So many people were coming to see me that the doctors put a stop to it. Flowers, cards, and teddy bears decorated my otherwise solemn room. It's funny how so many people think of you when you are down and yet when you are perfectly healthy no one takes the time to call or stop by. *Interesting*

When Sam returned to the hospital he came with Anna Mae. After Anna Mae left, Sam and I had a serious talk. I told him, "I did not ask my mother to call you and I am going to lay it on the line. I did not want you back. And as soon as I am well, I will leave you again." Sam tried to explain to me that he did not care; he only wanted to help me. I told him, "As long as you understood that we are not going to get back together, then you can help me."

He was being so kind and gentle that I wanted to believe him. I honestly wanted to trust him. But, my guard was up. Sam would have done anything to get me back. Leaving his girlfriend to come be by my side was nothing to him. I meant the world to him. He just did not know what to do to keep me. His love was too sick for him to understand. He needed to treat me like a human being and not an object he owned, if he really loved me.

The next day the doctor's took me to run tests to see if I was paralyzed. They didn't tell me what was going to happen to me and I learned later why. They put me on a metal bed; face down, with my hands tied down. Then they lifted the bed straight up in the air. While I was watching a monitor, another instrument moved slowly towards me. All I could see was a sharp instrument on the camera. I thought that by the time it reached my back it would stop, but it didn't. The large needle started to enter my back and the pain was so excruciating that I lifted my head straight up and yelled at the top of my lungs. I screamed until I could not scream anymore. Finally, the needle was pulled out. Very quietly I kept telling myself, "How dare they do this to me without warning!" The bed slowly went back down into its original position. I lay crying as the technician came into the room. He told me he was sorry, but that was the only way he could do the test. I cried like a baby as they rolled me out of the room on my gurney.

I would not even talk to the doctor when he came in to see me the day after my horrible ordeal. He would ask me questions, but I ignored him. He asked me if I was angry with him. I did not respond. He said he would come back at another time when I wanted to talk. The test had shown that I was not paralyzed.

Sam was with me every hour, morning, noon, and night. Soon we began to speak like two sensible human beings. At least he did. But I was still filled with anger. He told me that because of the emergency situation he was going to join me in Florida. The next day the doctor came in and told us of a surgery that was going to cost over $30,000. The military was going to pay all but 25%, but it was still too for us to afford. The military decided to pick me up in an ambulance and take me to a military hospital in Mississippi. There, a Christian doctor decided to put me in a body cast. He told me that he believed God could heal me. His faith was very strong. I did not believe him as I asked, "What will happen if God doesn't heal me?" "God will because I have faith in God and what God what he is capable of doing. Just trust in God, and He will heal you." I told the doctor, "I don't believe in Him. He may heal my back, but He will never heal my soul. I don't believe in God, nor do I believe in Satan. So many things have happened to me that I could not tell you all of it in a day's time." He smiled and told me, "I'll pray for me anyway, and put your situation in God's hands."

I was sent downstairs the next day and a body cast was molded from the bottom of my neck down to half of my thighs. This made it very hard for me to sit or stand. Two days later, after they perfected the cast, they sent me home. Sam was given base housing where we were to live.

Sam took very good care of me. He helped me in and out of chairs and in and out of bed. He also took me to my checkups, helped me bathe, and fed me. He did practically everything for me. As my mother had said earlier, I was an invalid. I had to completely rely on Sam, and luckily Anna would come by to wait on me too. Mom and Dad's house was right around the corner from our house on the base.

Soon I was able to manage a little on my own. Sam went back to work and Mom would come over to get me and take me grocery shopping and to my doctor appointments. One day Anna Mae came over to take me to the commissary to buy groceries. I had already been instructed by Sam not to buy too many groceries. The task of buying groceries was hard enough without having to watch what I bought. I really didn't care what he said anyway because I was my own woman, even if I was in a body cast. He could ask me to do something but I didn't like him to demand that I do what he asked. Mother and I spent hours in the store shopping. Since I was having so much trouble walking around in my body cast, looking like a robot, it took even longer for us to complete our shopping. Once I got home I went into my bedroom to take a pain pill. Mother wanted to stay and help but she had ice cream and meats out in the car that she had to get home and put away. Sam drove up just as she was leaving. I was so glad to see him because the task ahead was going to be next to impossible for me to complete on my own. As soon as he came in he started to help me put the groceries away. I prepared his lunch. While he was putting the food away he stopped and asked, "How much for the groceries? "I hesitated for fear of what was about to happen. I knew he would be angry, but how angry I didn't know. I figured since I was in a body cast, and he knew I would leave him, he would never touched me again. So feeling a little hesitant, I turned and told him, $120.

He immediately dropped what he was doing and started to yell at me to take the groceries back to the store. He said, "We can't afford it!" I started yelling. "We could if we didn't go out to dinner and the movies!" We had always argued over this. I always felt that food and bills came before us going out, buying marijuana, or anything else. Not only that, but he didn't realize the pain and how difficult it was for me to spend almost three hours shopping for food. Again he yelled, "Return the @#$% groceries! "No! I won't! If you want these groceries to go back then you take them back!" I poured the groceries onto the floor. He walked over to me, grabbed me and knocked me down to the floor. I lay there immobile as he began to kick me and slap my face. I started to kick him back and yell and called him all kinds of names. After he had finished he walked back to the bedroom. Then he left the house.

As I lie on the floor, the pain from my body cast hitting the floor was tremendous. I listened as the car door slammed and he slowly drove away. "Please come back," I begged, "Please don't leave me like this! Okay, I will take the groceries back. I will do anything but please don't go back to work and leave me on the cold, hard, floor." "He can't be this cold!" "I know he'll be right back." "He's only playing, I know he is." I held my tears just in case he came back through the door. I didn't want him to see me cry. "I'll just lay here. He'll be back because he knows there is no way for me to get up. He knows it takes his strong arms to lift me out of bed each day. He knows I cannot sit because the body cast goes half way down my thighs." I kept telling myself that he would return. There was no way that he could be that cruel. He loved me too much. "He knows I'll leave him for sure if he leaves me like this."

No one was home and I was unable to reach the phone to call for help. The neighbors couldn't hear me yell because they are all at work. "He is not that crazy. Maybe ignorant, but not that crazy." "How could he do this to me over some stupid groceries? No way!" "I will just lie here for a little longer and then he will be back, kissing me and wanting to make up. He just left to go eat lunch. He'll be back."

Five minutes felt like thirty minutes. Thirty minutes felt like hours. I started to get sleepy and eventually passed out. I slept for about an hour, only to wake in horror. As I jumped, I realized I was still on the floor, lying on my back in the same position he had left me in. It was time for my medication. I glanced at the clock to see that I had been lying on the floor for over an hour. "You stupid S.O.B.," I said. I managed to turn over and I started to pull myself down the long hallway. It hurt so much. I had to reach my room in order to take my pain medication.  Pulling with my hands, using the tips of my toes to push myself along, I dragged myself and my body cast down a long hallway. Finally, I started to cry. It was apparent that he was not returning. I reached the end of the hallway only to realize it was connected to another long hallway. I had to turn my body cast around and inch down another long hallway. Finally I entered my bedroom fitted with thick, plush carpeting. I could hear the carpet ripping away from the floor as I pulled myself forward towards my night stand. My back was in tremendous pain. But I could see the table ahead of me. I no longer moved inches, now I was moving only a quarter of an inch and gritting my teeth all the way. Crying and pulling, pulling and crying.

My entire body was in pain. I pulled myself over to the nightstand. I tried drastically to pull myself up on the bed, but it was to no avail. I lay there for a minute trying to figure out how I was going to get my medicine. I decided the only way I could get my medicine was to pull the end table over on top of me. I pulled and pulled and soon the table turned over nearby, spilling the pills onto the floor. Unfortunately, my water glass from the night before also fell, splashing my face and arms.

I grabbed the pill bottle and took out two pills. Now where was I going to get the water? I put the pills into my mouth, and as they started to melt, they left a horrible, rancid, very bitter taste in my mouth. I used my saliva to try and swallow them, but it did no good. They were bitter and all I wanted to do was spit them out. I knew I couldn't. I lay on the floor for several minutes. Then, again I started to maneuver myself back down the long treacherous hallway. I had to find a way to pull myself up, so that I could stand.

Turning around in the small space was very hard, but I managed somehow. I pulled myself back across the carpet and onto the hard floor dragging my heavy body behind me. I only stopped to listen for the sound of a car pulling up, maybe Sam getting out to come into the house to help me. Inching myself along, each minute felt like an eternity. Crying and cursing the day I fell and broke my back! Cursing the day Miss Meany called and told this cruel man to return into my life. I wanted so badly to bend my knees and stand up. But I couldn't, because of how low the body cast was formed. "I have got to get up off this floor! Not for myself, but to show him that he may knock me down but he can't keep me down. I will get up, and when I do you will never knock me down again!" I felt that if I did not manage to get up, he would use it against me forever.

Tired and worn out, I made it over to the table, and again tried to pull myself up. This time the table fell over onto me. Pushing the coffee table out of the way, I pulled myself over to the couch. I grabbed the end of the couch and I pulled myself up a little ways. Then my hands slipped off of the soft, velveteen couch. I tried again and again, each time hitting the floor. Crying and gritting my teeth, I tried over and over again.

In pain I lay on the floor desperately searching for something to help me up. In my heart I knew it was useless. Suddenly, I noticed the doorknob. I dragged myself toward the door, hoping I could open it and someone would help me. Finally, I made it to the door, but the knob was too high for me to reach. I burst into tears. All I wanted was someone to help me. Again, I cursed Sam. "You just wait! I will show you I can get up!" I looked around the room in utter dismay, knowing it was of no use, but refusing to give up. I lay there because I could feel the pain coming back. I pulled myself partway into the kitchen, to look at the clock. Four hours had passed and soon September would be home. "What will she think? What will she do when she sees me like this? How far back will this push her mentally as she sees her mother lying on the kitchen floor with tearful eyes? How much more can this little girl take? What physical effects will this leave her with?"

"First, I must stop crying. I have got to pretend that I fell, that her daddy did not do this. I will tell her that I slipped and fell. She'll believe this. After all, her daddy is nowhere around. She will believe me and then everything will be fine. I cannot let her see my pain and suffering. She will be all right." I made myself comfortable and awaited her entry. I had done all I could do. As I lay on the floor I kept looking around the room to see if there was anything that I could use to pull myself up.

Suddenly the door burst open and there September stood with her little book satchel in her hands. She immediately fell to the floor by my side. Grabbing my neck she started to pull and tug to help me up. I asked her to run back outside and find my friend that had just dropped her off at home. But she said my friend had already left. I told September to stop. "Don't get behind me or the body cast will fall on you and you will get hurt." She started to cry,

"Mommy, who did this to you? Daddy did, didn't he? Daddy did this to you, huh Mommy?" "No sweetheart, I accidentally fell." I knew she did not believe me. She certainly was not used to me lying, but I could tell that this is one time she knew I was lying to her. Finally I asked her to stop and she did, with tears in her eyes. I started to cry as I began to feel sorry for myself. "We've got to find a way to get Mommy up. September, stop crying now and be brave. I'll pull myself over to that chair, and I want you to sit in it and we'll try to pull Mommy up."

I pointed to the chair. She ran over and climbed up into the chair and waited as I rolled over and pulled myself, again, across the carpet to the chair. I wasn't moving quite fast enough so she again jumped down and grabbed my hands to pull me along. I begged her, "Please, let Mommy do it by herself," as the poor little thing kept crying. I moved closer and she again jumped up in the chair. We tried, and it was to no avail. The chair only started to tip over onto me. September jumped down and ran to a chair that sat catty-corner to the dining room. She called, "Come on, Mommy, try this one." I pulled myself over, still in so much pain, but trying very hard not to show it. "This may work," I told her. Because the chair sat catty-corner to the wall and could not turn over without hitting the wall, I thought this just might work. I grabbed the chair and pulled as hard as I could. It was very painful but I pulled with all my might, and sure enough, I pulled myself up enough that my head was next to the wall. I pulled again and finally I sat up. I cried and laughed at the same time. I was so happy! September jumped down and grabbed me around my neck and gave me a big hug. We both sat there and cried. I pulled her close and told her that I still needed to stand up. "So get up into the chair again." I curled my legs underneath me, and again pulling with all my might, I finally stood up.

I admit I was in a lot of pain, but nothing compared to the sheer joy of being able to stand up after five painful hours of being on the floor. I didn't want Sam to know that I was down there that long, so I told September to help her mommy put away the groceries. I could start fixing supper. As I was standing there preparing supper, September came up to me at the sink. With a Cookie Monster hand puppet over her hand she said in her best Cookie-Monster voice, "Daddy did that to you, didn't he?" I repeated, "No, Mr. Cookie Monster, no. He did not knock me down."

September began to frown as she always did. She walked away only to turn to me once more and give me a stare that I translated into meaning: "Why are you lying to me, Mommy?" She turned and walked away. At this age she would talk to Sam and me through her Cookie Monster. It was her mixed-up way of telling us what was on her mind. She seemed to think that if the Cookie Monster asked, she could get away with asking her father things that she knew any other time she would be beaten for. Trusting in me to tell Cookie Monster the truth, she had tried it on me. I always wondered if it would have been better to tell her the truth, because as wise as she was, lying did no good anyway.

When Sam walked in that evening he saw me preparing supper. I could tell that he was surprised but he didn't let on. And of course, there was no way that I was going to tell him what he had put me through. I relished the thought of not saying a word. Why give him the satisfaction? That secret was September's and mine to share forever. That evening after dinner September went to her room to play. Sam and I sat in the front room and watched television. September entered the room with her cookie monster on her hand. She walked up to her father and said in a cookie monster voice;" I hate you." I was shocked and started to get out of my recliner. I was afraid that Sam was going to hit her. Again September using the cookie monster voice said "I hate you".

Her father said," September, go to your room!"

Sam sat there for a minute. Then I could see the anger in his face. He jumped up and went to September's room. There she sat in her bed talking to her cookie monster.

Sam said, "Girl don't you ever talk to me that way again!"

September replied, "Cookie Monster said it."

This angered Sam more. So he took Cookie Monster away. Then I entered the room and told Sam that he cannot be angry at September.

## Chapter 24

When it was time to remove the body cast, boy was I ever to glad to have it taken off. In fact, I had started to remove it myself. The Air Force sent me back to the same hospital that put the body cast on me six months earlier. By the time I was taken downstairs to the tech to have it removed, I wore a smile on my face a mile long. The tech started to cut it away with his saw. When he removed it from my body it was as if I could finally breathe for the first time in my life. He asked me if I wanted to keep it as a souvenir. I told him, "No thanks." Besides, it reeked with a foul smell. The same doctor that decided to put it on walked into my room with some other doctors. Everyone in the hospital was talking about the miracle that had taken place. I couldn't see the excitement of course, but I was very thankful for him and his God. I left the hospital and looked back and said a little, insignificant prayer anyway. "Thank you, God, wherever you are."

Sam and September were awaiting me as I got off the plane. Finally I was walking normally! Of course, it took some time for me to sit properly and stand upright on my own. The adjustment didn't take me long. I don't know if Sam was expecting me to leave or not, but he was treating me great. It had been months since our last argument. He started giving me an allowance. In fact, I ran the house and was surprised that everything went my way. He was taking me to dinner and buying me nice things. I couldn't believe that he was the man I married.

I didn't know it at the time, but it turned out, Sam was smoking marijuana again. One day he brought the stuff home. I was so afraid that someone was lurking outside our door, ready to take us to jail. I argued but he didn't listen. He told me that I should try it. I told him how I was satisfied

192

with beer and felt no need to try it. "No." He kept pushing and pushing me to try it. He told me it would give me the high I wanted without me gaining a pound. I had gained quite a bit of weight since being in the body cast. All I did was sit around the house immobile. I couldn't exercise and he knew how I felt about my weight. I felt very uncomfortable and was extremely upset.

It was about 5:00 P.M. and I had begun preparing dinner and was about to bathe September. She had just come in from school. I filled the tub and put September in along with her floating toys. Sam again asked me to try the marijuana. He approached me in the kitchen while I was preparing supper, "Take a puff." I took a puff, sucked in the smoke and coughed and gagged while Sam laughed at me. Feeling nothing, I went back to fixing supper. Normally, nothing controls me, but the marijuana made me totally high. Soon I joined Sam in the front room and we began to laugh and party our behinds off. With the music blasting I soon forgot about what I was doing. We talked about what effects he was feeling and how I was feeling. We laughed at everything and ate everything in the kitchen! Suddenly, the marijuana started to wear off. It was now 5:00 A.M. and the sun was just coming up. I looked at Sam and said, "I know it's not morning yet?" He laughed and lay back on the couch about to go to sleep. He answered, "Oh wooe, yes it is." I exclaimed, "Where is my baby?"

Then it suddenly occurred to me that I had put September in the bathtub to bath her before dinner. I ran desperately to the bathroom. I didn't hear a sound. As water flowed under the bathroom door, I stood by the door taking a moment to say a prayer. I promised God that if my child were still alive, I would never again touch marijuana as long as I lived. When I walked into the bathroom, September was lying in the empty tub alive, all shriveled up, with every toy

193

in the house in the tub with her. The water had drained out and she didn't know how to refill it so she played in the tub with her animals. As I reached down to grab her she gave me one of her beautiful smiles. I held her in my arms and hugged her. Sam and I just stared at one another. I could not believe that I had allowed something to make me so high that I had forgotten my motherly duties. I surely learned a lesson that day, and I never allowed Sam to talk me into anything so foolish again.

After I fed September I put her in bed to sleep. Sam and I went to bed also. It felt weird to be going to bed at an odd time. Our whole day was messed up. We were all sleeping long into the day, from our episode from the night before, when Mrs. Meany stormed into the house unannounced. She saw the baby in the bed and started screaming and burst into our room saying, "Why is the baby in bed and not dressed? Why are you still in bed?" Sam told me to get her out of the house that minute or he would do something that we both would regret. Guiding her to the door, I explained that we were all up late and just needed to sleep as I sent her on her merry way.

Life with Sam went smoothly for over a year. Watching September playing alone and talking to herself, I decided that it was time to have another child. Our marriage was finally going well. September and I had not been beaten during this period. Sam didn't want to have a child now, especially since I had wanted to wait, not wanting to have one child after another. He wanted four in a row when he wanted them. The pain I experienced during September's birth was so bad that I hesitated to have another right away, and with the way Sam had treated us, it just wasn't the right time. My marriage wasn't stable enough. I also wanted to get to know each of my children individually. I wanted to spend time getting to know September and allow her to get to know me before I brought another child into the world. It would allow her to tie her shoes and go off to school. I didn't want two babies in the house at the same time driving me crazy while Sam worked everyday. It was I that had to raise them at home and felt that it was I who should make the decision on how far apart they should be. I knew just how much noise and crying I could take. With one gone off to school, I would be allowed to get to know my second child. I also observed how an infant and a five-year-old played together; they got along much better than two infants that had no idea what the other was crying about.

I told him I wanted to get pregnant and I was going to remove my IUD. Nothing was holding us back from having another child except Sam's childish ideas about me having them exactly when he wanted them. I couldn't comprehend why he refused to understand my reasoning. We went without sex for a while because it was the only way he could avoid my becoming pregnant. Not being able to abstain any longer, he finally gave in. We made love and I knew that I had become pregnant that same night. In my dreams that night, I was told that I would have a baby boy. I even went out and bought a shirt that said, "BABY BOY," with an arrow pointing to my stomach. Early pregnancy tests were not readily available at that time, but I knew I was pregnant. I told my husband that it would be a boy. Of course he thought I was crazy, but he smiled to think that he was going to have a son.

Things were still going well between Sam and me. In fact, I was rather impressed that it had been over a year since our last fight. I knew that part of the reason things were going so well was because of the marijuana. Even though I detested Sam smoking it, I loved the way he acted. He was so caring and spent a lot of time with September. Sam wanted to take me to a movie and dinner one evening and I really didn't want to go. At his insistence, he took me to the club. My husband ordered chateaubriand, and although I didn't particularly favor raw beef flame-broiled in front of me, that's what we had. It was the first time I saw sherry used to start a fire. How interesting! I jumped when the young man set it on fire. Our evening turned out to be an interesting one.

The next day I walked in on Sam beating September for something. The beatings began again and September was bearing the brunt of it. Sam again became nasty and there would be no stopping him. He would abuse my daughter, I would get between them and I'd be beaten. Soon he stopped giving me an allowance and fussed about grocery money. He accused me of cheating on him. Again, he started checking the car to see how far I had driven, same as before. When we fought terribly Sam could turn on a dime, and then act as if nothing had ever happened.

He began to accuse me of cheating on him with his friends. One of his friends had dropped by when Sam was not at home. I thought it was weird that he came to see Sam when he knew Sam was at work. After that day, Sam started mistrusting me again. He would call all around to find me. His jealousy was becoming outrageous. I couldn't understand why, because I was in my seventh month of pregnancy. I soon discovered that he had received an assignment to the Philippines and he feared I would not go with him. He was also told that the base would be doing a random urine check on all GI's, to see if they were smoking marijuana. It started to make sense now why he was returning to his old ways.

One day I happened upon him beating September for writing on her bedroom wall. I walked in on him yelling at her, "Don't ever write on this wall again!" As he picked her up by one arm and commenced to hit her, I rushed to her aid. There I stayed, by her side for the rest of the night. The next day I heard him grab her to beat her again. Of course, as always I interfered, grabbing September away from him as he yelled at her, "Girl, I'm going to kill you!" He pulled her out of my hands and told her to go to bed without any supper. I went into September's room to ask her why wrote on the wall again. She got down from her bed, grabbed me by the hand, and showed me the wall that she had written on the day before, "Daddy told me not to write on this wall, Mommy." I looked at the wall that she had cleaned the day before and then glanced over to the wall for which she had just been beaten. It was then that I realized that she understood her father to mean only one particular wall, so she wrote on the other wall. If you stopped and thought about it, she was right. He should have told her, "Do not write on any wall in the house." I sent September back to her room and went to Sam, yelling at him about what he had done. He declared that September had understood him, "She was just being sneaky."

I refused to believe that at 4-year-old would purposely ask for another one of Sam's beatings. She was only thinking as a young child. It's very important that parents are perfectly clear about what they ask their children to do. Again that day I learned something else from my little daughter about parenting. We're not born to be parents. We are ever learning to be good parents, as our children in fact, are learning to be children. We as parents should be careful about the decisions that we make. I learned not to jump to conclusions. To ask questions first, why they did what they did. It's a lot easier to make a decision on what their punishment should be, when you fully understand the facts.

After Sam and I finished arguing I went to the kitchen to fix September some supper. Sam came into the kitchen and found me going against his wishes. He grabbed the pan from the stove and poured her meal down the garbage disposal. I grabbed another can of spaghetti and started to open it when he jerked it out of my hand and threw it against the wall. He then grabbed me and started to hit me. Soon, I was knocked to the floor. As he started to kick, I kicked him. He was hitting me, slapping me, and kicking me as I lay on the floor. I began kicking him and I even tried to bite his leg. He pushed my face into the floor and kicked me. After he accidentally, or so I thought, kicked my stomach, I curled up into a fetal position to keep him from kicking my unborn child any more, or kicking me in the face. After he finished, I kept yelling, "I'm going to kill you!"

Whenever Sam would beat me during my pregnancies, he never thought about the child. He only thought about beating me up. After he left the room, I got up and went and sat on the couch. I sat there in the dark as he went to our room and watched television. When I heard the television go off, I knew he was going to bed. He had to be to work very early the next morning. I went into the garage and found suitcases for September and me. I went into her room and packed her clothes. Then I left and went to the liquor store, the first part of my plan. I remember the man's face as he looked at me buying six bottles of sherry. He had a look on his face that seemingly said, "I hope that's not for you." It was obvious I was pregnant. I looked at him and replied, "No, this is not for me, it is for my husband."

I left the store. The entire way home I kept imagining what it was going to be like for my husband when he woke up to find himself burning up in his own bed. I had to make it look like an accident.

I went back home and woke up September. She had fallen asleep with her Cookie Monster on her hand. I dressed her and put her into the car. I gathered up a few other things that I wanted to keep, and put them into the car. Now to do something that I had always wanted to do, kill Sam. I stood at the bedroom door for a minute and stared at him. Then I opened all six bottles of sherry. I started quietly pouring them all around the bed. I tried to soak the rug as much as I could. Then I went to the front room and looked into his secret hiding spot where he hid his marijuana and tried to roll a joint to look exactly like he might have rolled it. It was so hard because I had never rolled a joint before. I must have tried to roll it at least ten times, and still, I could not get it right. It had to look convincing to the police.

I was sitting in the house with all the lights off so if Sam happened to wake, he would not know what was about to take place. I sat there trembling still trying to get the joint rolled right. The house was so quiet, it was creepy. My heart was beating a mile a minute. Suddenly I heard in a very deep voice, "Mommy, I have to go to the bathroom."

I must have jumped a mile high. The tiny leaves of marijuana flew everywhere. I looked down to see September with the Cookie Monster on her hand, talking to me in a Cookie Monster voice. I was so intent in my desperation to kill my husband that I hadn't noticed that September had crawled out of the car and into the house to go to the bathroom. She scared me half to death. I grabbed my heart and told her, "Oh my God, September, you scared me." I took her to the bathroom. Afterward I kept telling her, "Shhhh!" with my finger to my lips. I did not want her to wake up her father. I told her I was taking her somewhere to eat, and if she woke him up, she knew her daddy would not let her eat.

I put her back into the car and laid her on her pillow and blanket. I went back into the house. Again I went to my room to make sure that all the commotion did not wake Sam. Standing by his bed I was thinking how he will never beat my child or me, again. Just as I started to light the joint and set it down on the nightstand, Sam turned over and began to wake up. I immediately started for the door. As I was walking away he woke up and stepped out onto the rug. He called out my name, "Kaye?" I turned and looked at him, putting the lighter into my sweater pocket.

"Why is this rug so wet?" he inquired. I told him it was because I was shampooing the rug. Sleepily, he went to the bathroom and then got back into bed. He asked me if I was coming to bed soon. I told him, "No! I'm watching television." He asked me what was on and I told him a late night show. Turning over, he immediately fell back to sleep. As I went out to the car to bring September back in, all I could think of was how I had failed in my attempt. I put our luggage back in the garage. Sadly, I fed September a sandwich and put her to bed.

I made a bed on the couch that night because I didn't want to be next Sam. Most of the night I sat up talking to myself. I needed to talk to someone else or I thought I would go insane. Kristie!!! I knew that if I went to her I would be able to talk to someone that I thought would be very understanding and not judgmental about the situation I was in. The next day after Sam left to go to work, I went over to my Christian friend's house. After telling her what had happened the night before, she hugged me and told me, "It is a good thing that it didn't happen the way you planned it, because just what if Sam had lived through it? "I would have been sent straight to prison, and he would have finished raising September and my unborn child. He would have been beating them the rest of their lives with no one there to protect them. When I thought about what she said, it made a lot of sense.

So it was back to the drawing board. If I was to get rid of him I had to find a way to leave and take my children with me. After giving her a look of despair I told her that this would never end; he was going to torture us forever, that she was right. I told her that I was scared that one day he was going to succeed, and actually kill me.

She said, "No. God is not going to allow that to happen." I ignored her because I felt she did not understand my situation. There was nothing I could do but go home and try to work out another plan.

# Chapter 25

Sam came home from work with a bottle of champagne. He had just found out that we were now assigned to the Philippines. It was 1976. At first I got very upset, till I thought about it for a second. I realized that it just might be the best thing that had ever happened to me. It just might be the break I'd been waiting for.

I wasted no time calling my brother in California to ask if I could stay with him and his wife. I knew that we would have to fly to California first on the way to the Philippines and this would prove to be the way I would leave Sam. Eventually, I would find my own apartment, but I would not tell Sam any of this until he was already stationed far away. Sam and I packed up the house and away we went. I could smell freedom in the air as we reached California. As soon as we arrived, Sam and I were already at each other's throats. We were arguing, and even though I was in my eighth month of pregnancy, Sam was still hitting me even within my brother's house. Staying in my brother's spare room now, Chuck could hear much of what was going on; including Sam's knocking me around the room.

Chuck asked to speak to us, "You are both going to die. And when you do, you're going to go to hell." It took little to convince me, by this time, because I believed that if there was a God and he gave us His Son, Jesus Christ, who died on the cross for my sins, and I did not accept Him, I would go to hell to pay for my sins. I had been through enough hell in my life here on earth to never go through it again.

We both fell upon our knees and accepted Christ.

Soon the day arrived for Sam to leave. When we got back to my brother's house I decided to go for a walk and

Stacy, my brother's wife, decided to go with me. We took the kids and started walking down a little path. Once I got there I sat on a swing. I was finally free and couldn't wait to find my own place. Stacy looked at me and asked if I was okay. "I'm fine and even more, now!" "Are you still planning on leaving Sam?" "Of course, I am." Stacy told me that soon I would see a significant change in my husband, a change that I had never seen the likes of before. Stacy said, "Once both of you start going to Church, Sam's going to become a man of God, and when he does, he will never touch you, fuss with you or hurt you again. You may have some fights or arguments, until he becomes strong enough in Christ, but you will have the happiest marriage you could ever believe you'd have in your life. Give God a chance to show you what he can do in your lives." I told her that Sam would never change. She told me that if God can move a mountain and bring the Jews out of Egypt, He surely could change Sam. "Just trust in God and stand out on faith." Hugging her, I decided then that I would go on to the Philippines with Sam.

Once I arrived, Sam told me he couldn't make love to me because he had gotten another venereal disease. He had gone over to a friend's house and fell asleep. When he awoke, a woman sat on him and made love to him, giving him the disease. I just looked at him like he actually thought I was stupid enough to believe that crap. Not wasting a moment, I went to the base and told them I wanted to go home. They refused because the orders would have to go through first, so I stayed. Sam started becoming involved with the Church and was going there a lot. Sam never touched me until after the baby arrived. In the hospital Sam was a totally different person than he had been with our first baby was born. When he knew it was time to go to the hospital, he got dressed and drove me to the base hospital where I went into an easy labor. I roomed with four other women, who were also in labor. When the pains started in earnest, I had one great pain; I sat up in bed and announced that every woman in that room would have a baby boy and that for the next seven days there would only be boys born in the hospital. Sam looked at me and the other women a little oddly, as if to say, "Well, you know how it is, she's in labor and not thinking very clearly." Our new baby boy arrived shortly. Everyone that came into the hospital that week gave birth to boys and the doctors and nurses were so awestruck, they kept count and informed me daily, for the remainder of the week. We became friends with the three women. They were always telling people that I was the one who predicted that they would have boys and that there would be a whole "week of boy babies!" I have no idea where my comment came from to this day.

The baby and I were in the hospital that whole week because Sam and I kept fighting over the name we were to give our child. I wanted to name him, "Samuel," the name of a king mentioned in the Bible. Sam wanted him to be named, "Samson," after himself and Samson and Delilah. I would never want my child to be teased or made fun of and I felt that to name him after his father would only open him up to taunting when he went to school. The staff at the hospital grew tired of our fighting for the five days I was there and finally told us, in no uncertain terms, that the child's name would be chosen by the father, since he was the serviceman and it was a military hospital. "Enough said!" I was crushed, but I knew that he would not go through life with that name forever.

I did not want my child to grow up living the life that Sam had gone through. I did not want that for my son. Sam claimed that it was because of his name that he fought his way through life and became a bodybuilder and he was as strong as he was. I asked him, "If you're so proud of your name, than why do you call yourself, "Sam," instead of Samson?" He never answered me, but I knew he was ashamed of his name no matter what he told me. He was always the butt of a joke, and had people constantly laughing at his name. In fact, I purposely used to introduce him to people by his full name so I could prove a point. I used to watch him get mad at people as they made a joke out of his name.

I knew that one day I would change my son's name, and in the meantime I would try to fight his battles for him.

Sam decided that we should have a house girl. Her name was Nene. In the Philippines, a house girl is a maid. I'm very thankful to the Lord for his decision. Her presence in the house, at first, prevented Sam from beating September and I. But of course the day finally came when he did beat September. Nene was traumatized at first and wanted to quit working for us. So Sam would wait till she had gone home on the weekends to beat us. Some old Filipino lady that lived around corner from our house decided to give my son the name, "Pogie." It meant, "Handsome." I was glad because I didn't have to call him Samson. Nene, in the meantime, would do anything and everything to protect both of my children. Sam never took Pogie out of his room to allow his friends to see him, because he was a light-skinned, baby. Yelling at Sam one day, I asked him "Are you ashamed of our son? Should I re-dip him or put him back in my body till he turns dark?" We argued about that for a long time. Sam explained that he didn't want a light-skinned son, because they always thought they were better looking. But it wasn't until people started telling Sam that his son was a cute baby that he changed his mind. Then Sam started sticking his chest out in pride.

I started out breast-feeding my son. He seemed to enjoy the breast milk at first. It was a very beautiful experience to be able to give my child fresh, healthy milk from my body. It was a time I could spend holding my little son in my arms and watching him enjoy the milk that I produced myself. One day while breast-feeding my son, Sam came in and stood over me watching as I fed Pogie. I could not believe the next thing that came from Sam's mouth. He asked, "Is Pogie turning you on by suckling your breast?" At first I thought I didn't hear him correctly, until I asked him to repeat himself. Again he asked me the same question. I had to discontinue feeding my baby because I was so mad I just wanted to slap his face. All I could do was look at him and walk away. How dare he ask me a question like that! Who was this person I had married? Who was he and what planet did he come from? How could he be so demented and sick? Sometimes I didn't know who I had married.

Pogie sat up at three-months and at five-months-old he was crawling around a lot and I thought that it wouldn't be long before he was walking. So I decided to buy a rug and a walker so we would be prepared when he started walking. The rug was 12'x12' and as I was on my knees straightening out the creases, Pogie crawled over to the couch, pulled himself up and started to smile at me. "Hi, Mommy's baby is standing up!" He looked at me, turned, and walked straight across the room and patted me on my forehead. I was so shocked, I could only cry; he was so cute. He pushed the walker around, never used it to walk in. From that day on he was on the run.

Nene became very close to Pogie and was like a second mother to him. Together we kept the baby away from Sam so that he would be safe from abuse. We eventually moved to base housing and Nene came with us.

When Pogie was six-months-old, he was quite an active baby and would crawl out of his crib and keep Nene up most of the night, so we decided to move him into our room. Pogie was in the crib next to our bed and one night he sat playing quietly with his teddy bear and sucking his finger. Sam jumped up and laid him down. "Go to sleep!"Pogie sat up and then stood in the crib as if he were daring Sam to lay him back down. Sam hit him on the diaper and laid him back down, but Pogie stood up again and refused to lie down. Sam's anger showed itself and he started hitting Pogie's leg and spanking him hard. I jumped out of bed, grabbed my baby and took him into the front room where we stayed up together most of the night. Pogie could not sleep during the night, and it became an ongoing problem. I decided to move him to Nene's room so that she could care for him during the night and protect him from Sam's beatings. Nene agreed because she loved him very much and did not want to see him harmed. They became very close even though he would stay awake at night and keep her up also. It was very difficult for her to do her work the next day but she did her best. She looked forward to leaving on the weekends for her free time.

When Nene did take off, she always asked if the children and I would be all right in her absence. I always assured her that we would be fine, but she didn't like to leave us and she and Pogie had become extremely close. Once she told me that she feared that one day she would come back and find us dead because of what she knew went on at our house when the beatings began. Every time she left, she would become very sad and cry as I pried Pogie's little hands from around her neck. He hated it when she left and would cry for hours after. He would climb into his bed and watch out the window calling her name for hours on end, as Nene walked away--but she had to go home to her family to get some rest. At times, she would come back and find me in bed with my face beaten. As it turned out, Pogie was an insomniac and kept Sam and I up. Sam was not going to tolerate this and began beating my precious baby. I did all I could do to keep Pogie away from his father. I stayed up all night to keep them apart.

My daughter, September, began showing signs of a mental illness that I didn't recognize at the time. The entire trauma she had gone through was starting to show in her personality. Carrying her brother to the ladder on the bunk bed one day, she waited for us to find him so that he would get into trouble. Not speaking much, she would sit around and frown a lot. The signs were there, but I just didn't know how to read them.

Sam had certain rules that the children had to follow on Christmas morning. Before they could unwrap their presents, they had to make their beds, brush their teeth and get dressed. But that was not all. They also were instructed to open one gift, put the bow in a bag and the wrapping paper into another. Then they had to wait till Sam took a picture or two. The frowns on their faces showed how unhappy they were. One Christmas September didn't like what she got and made a comment. The toy was taken away and she was sent to her room where she sat crying. I got up and started dinner since there was no sense in the rest of us enjoying Christmas. Soon Sam sent everyone to his or her rooms as we argued. And like always, if he didn't get his way he started to beat me. I was just as stubborn as he was and if my kids were not treated right, then I was not going to give in. It was a horrible thing to do to them. I remember when I was a child, finding my presents Christmas morning and tearing into them haphazardly, wearing my new pajamas and having a wonderful time every year. Dad and Mom would try to take pictures as fast and as best as they could. Every time Sam would take pictures, he would take forever to make sure that everything was perfect and everyone was dressed flawlessly to his expectations. No one ever wanted to have their picture taken because of the way he turned things that should be fun into something far from it.

Sam continued to go to Church. We had been attending a church started by a man that Sam really looked up to. Sam was still beating me and I reminded him that we were not living in a Christian house. I was disappointed that things weren't working out the way my brother and his wife told me they would. Sometimes it seemed to be worse since he became a Christian. He thought I should be submitting to him as he felt was proper for a Christian wife. Yet he started withholding money from me again, mistreating me in public, and the beatings went on. I think he only used Christianity to try to control me. September would wait at the door for us when we went out because she wanted to see what I looked like when I got home, whether my face was bruised or battered.

Upon going to Sam's First Sergeant for help, everything I told him would be turned around; making me look bad and having Sam come out smelling like a rose. Sam even hit me in front of the First Sergeant and they would tell me that my mental abuse of him was as bad as his physical abuse of me. Nothing did any good. Turning to the Church, I found there was also no solace for me. One day I showed up at this church Sam found, only to be told that I could not attend because of the braids in my hair. The church decided to excommunicate me. Citing Scripture, they decided that the braids in my hair were against the teachings of Peter and Timothy. (1 Timothy 2 – 8, <u>I wish, then, that the men pray</u> <u>everywhere, lifting up pure hands, without wrath and</u> <u>contention. 9, In like manner I wish women to be decently</u> <u>dressed, adorning themselves with modesty and dignity, not</u>

with braided hair or gold or pearls or expensive clothing.)
They excommunicated me although I tried to explain that the
Bible was talking about whores that braided gold and pearls
into their hair to adorn themselves. God wanted their beauty
to come from their hearts and not their outward appearance. I
didn't mind being excommunicated from that church. They
could not even show me biblically where their teachings
were coming from, but expected me to follow them anyway.

I started taking the children to a different church
on base. I liked the preacher there and could relate to his
teachings. Although we enjoyed this particular church, Sam
would become angry with us when we arrived home. Sam
decided to stop going to church altogether. He did not want
us going to church and would find something to argue about
completely unrelated to Sunday worship, just to start a
fight. I would ask the church to pray for Sam and for
myself. I would ask for the constant pain and sickness to go
away that I suffered with each day. It was then that the
preacher told me, "Cynthia, I think the pain you suffer with
is the hate that you carry each and every day for your mother
and your husband." I told him that I didn't think so. But he
begged to differ. He went on to say that when we keep hate
bottled up and we don't forgive one another it causes us to
suffer stomachaches and all kinds of abdominal pain. It's
easy for humans to be consumed with hatred. God's love is
unconditional. He loved us so much that he gave His son to
die on a cross for the sins of this world. Forgiveness is
something I knew I could never feel. I hugged him. "I guess
that I will always suffer this pain in my stomach then,
because I could never stop hating them both. So from now
on I will ask the congregation to pray that I release this
hatred and learn to love them again." For my mother this
would not be hard, because it was "Miss Meany" and "Anna
Mae" that I hated, and not Anna. Learning once again to like

her, would not be difficult. Letting go of this hatred for Anna would be very simple. For both, it would be a difficult task, but I was willing to take it on.

First I started by writing Anna a letter and at the end of the letter I wrote: "I love you, Mom." It was very difficult to do, but I forced myself. And with every letter after that I did the same. Soon I found myself being more understanding of her needs. I started to understand the suffering she must have been going through living as 5 different people, pulling her in 5 different directions. No one believed in her and trusted her. She needed someone that comprehended her suffering and loved her just the same. Even though she had Daddy, she needed her children to stick beside her as well. More than anything, she needed our support. So from that day forward I made a pact to try a little harder to look over Miss Meany, Anna Mae, Mae, and Mrs. White--and only see Anna.

One day the kids and I were throwing water balloons at each other. Sam decided to join in. Sam and the kids and I were laughing and yelling and a neighbor called the police. I knew which neighbor it had to be because only one would be brave enough to call. I walked over to her house to thank her for looking out for me. She told me to get away from him but I told her it was not as easy as she thought it was. I had nowhere else to go, my mother said that I had made my own bed and even she refused a place for me. The shelters only gave women three days to find another place and I always winded up coming back home. I told her that I would be fine and not to worry about me. "Someday," I promised her, "I will find a way out." I could see that she felt sorry for me as I walked away, but before I left, she hugged me. "I wish I could do more." "Keep calling the police and someday someone would listen." I knew that she wanted so badly to help but didn't know how. Walking back

211

to my house, I started to feel sorry for myself and started to walk slumped over. Just as I was about to go back to our house, I straightened my back, stuck my head into the air and marched back into the battle zone. Sam never talked to her again. That neighbor was the first person in my life to ever become involved.

# Chapter 26

Soon another problem started to surface. I kept getting sores in and around my vaginal area that would not heal, regardless of how much I applied ointments, soaked, or used topical medicine. I went to my gynecologist only to find out that I had a bad form of Dysplasia. It was a form of cancer cells in and around my vulva. The doctor had to cut away skin and examine it to find the problem. They told me it would require an operation. They were going to burn away all of the cancerous skin and then remove skin from my inner thigh and graft the skin to make another vagina. Of course, this would be painful but they were pretty certain it would rid me of the cancer and I could carry on a normal life.

I had to fly down from the Philippines to Hawaii for the surgery. Before I left I had a dream that the cancer was cured but that I was to go there to be used as a tool to talk to a fallen child of God. I knew what my mission was, but didn't know what I was to do. I just left everything up to God, and unlike Moses, didn't argue.

I did not want to leave my young son and daughter with their father for fear of what might happen to them during my absence. I knew that God would take care of them. I had prayed for a long time that God would use me in his work. And finally, He gave me an opportunity and the honor to fully serve him. Plus, I was excited. I felt like the people on "Mission Impossible." I packed my bags and off I went.

Being a new babe in Christ I was very gung-ho and ready to spread God's words. With Bible in hand, away I flew to Hawaii. I checked into the hospital and right away started praying and asking God which person he sent me there. Of course I got no answer, but as soon as I unpacked my bags and finished talking to the doctor about the procedure of my surgery, I went to work.

Going from room to room I began to take water to patients, bring them food, and sit at the ends of their beds reading my Bible and praying for them while they slept. Only if they were curious did I tell them what I was doing. I did not try to impose on them but waited for their curiosity, which would open the door for my ministry and allow God to prepare the table for me to speak to them. I knew that I was not there to save them, for I was only a human being and could not save anyone, only God could. I was just there as a messenger. I did not know it at first but I was in a ward of about fifty women and they were all diagnosed with cancer. Most of them were very ill and unable to be cured. Some had just found out or were waiting to be diagnosed. Some were on their deathbeds, and some were being treated with radiation. They were scared and alone and crying. They were begging me to go to their beds and talk to them about Jesus Christ and His love. Some were in comas and were never to come out of them.

I worked by day and night. I cried as I assisted some of them with bandaging themselves. Maybe I was there for all of them. Some of them would not accept the Lord, but just wanted to hear me anyway. They were scared to leave their gods and their beliefs to take a chance with mine. I knew that there were many that would die in their sins and that there was nothing I could do for them.

Sometimes their stomachs were infected and they would have to open them up and let them lie exposed to the elements in order to heal. Often, they never knew that the cancer had spread so far that there was nothing that could be done. One lady I remember loved spaghetti-and-meatballs in a can. Her husband knew that this was her favorite meal so he brought her cases of it. I opened the shelves by her bedside one day and they were filled with an abundance of what I would call, "love from her husband." It was her last request while she lay in the hospital to die. Even though he knew she would never finish them, he put several cases there to make her think she would. I cried as I opened one of the cans and she ate it cold, only to throw it up. I dared not show her the tears.

When the night was done and all the lights were turned off and all the families had gone home, I returned to my bed, crying and tired. I wasn't happy about my mission anymore. I wanted to go home.

I climbed into the shower stall and stood under the hot water and cried so hard that I could not breathe. The Lord had sent me into only one other battle zone that I could remember ever being in--that was when I worked in the Florida hospital with the Vietnam Vets. I kept reassuring myself that God is good. He gave His only begotten son for every one of these humans. His love was deeper than mine and His tears had to be more painful for He created each and every one of these women. If it hurt me, how much more, I imagined, it must have hurt Christ? That is why when He hung on that cross. He covered each one of us with His blood and asked His father to forgive us for we knew not what we were doing. I told myself as I have always done before, to be strong. God is with me all the way; just hold onto His unchanging hands because He will help me make it through.

The next morning when I woke up it was time for the doctors to discover that God had already healed my cancer. The anesthesiologist came in to tell me about the shot he was going to administer in an hour. I explained that it would require an elephant dosage to put me out because I had fallen and broken my back in 1974 and they had fed me morphine.

Of course he did not adhere to my words. Who was I, to tell a specialist his job? Soon they came up and gave a shot to the lady in the bed next to me. She was asleep within a matter of minutes. I laughed as they carried her away. They had asked her to count down from 100, and she fell asleep before she had hit 90.

Next, they came for me. They gave me the shot and I started to count down. I was still counting as I got into the elevator, still believing that he had given me enough. I had completely counted down and was sitting on my gurney outside the operating room. I kept telling all the technicians about, The Greatest Story Ever Told. I ministered about the Lord. Soon my doctor came by, "You're supposed to be out of it right about now." I laughed as I went on to tell him that I was cured of my cancer and that I was just there to talk to a fallen child of God. So he asked, "You were sent this far to find that person and tell him of God's love?" "Yes, for I've been cured of my cancer." Well, that's not what my charts are showing, young lady. So this is what I'm going to do, I'll send you back upstairs and tomorrow we'll try this all over again. Only this time we will administer an elephant dose like you told the anesthesiologist to do the first time. Then we'll see if that knocks you out."

The next day the anesthesiologist came to my room to administer the anesthesia. "Okay, young lady, this should put you out. If it doesn't, I've brought along a mallet in my little red box." He grinned. I laughed, "I tried to tell you that the first time." After he administered the elephant dose I again started my count down. I don't even remember getting to 98 and I was out. I only remember waking up with drool streaming down my mouth. A nurse walked in and I asked her if they had to graft skin for another vagina. She told me I would have to talk to the doctor, "He is on his way into your room." In walked the doctor with a big smile on his face. He greeted me with a pleasant "Hello." Then he said, "Well, you were right. You don't have cancer and we don't have to operate. So I guess I'll be sending you back home. We did, however, remove all the Dysplasia and you should be fine. But I'm afraid you won't be able to leave till next week." "That's was fine with me" He walked to the door, turned, and asked, "Did you ever find the Christian that God sent you all this way to find?" "No Sir! But I haven't given up yet." "Good luck!"

He walked out the room and the lady next to me asked, "What were you talking about?" "I had told how I was here on a mission for God. To minister to a Christian who has turned away from God. "Then she told me, "I was a Christian, but I turned my back on God because of the cancer." She went on to tell me of how strong her faith used to be. But after the cancer, she didn't want anything to do with Him anymore. She had two young children and a wonderful husband. Leaving them was too much for her to handle. She wanted to see her two little children grow into adults. She told me of how she smoked a lot before she accepted the Lord. The cancer was now in her lungs. Just yesterday she had found out that it went into remission and she still might have a chance. She felt bad that she had blamed her cancer on God. God has given us freedom to do what we will with our bodies. He has told us how to take care of those bodies in the word of God but we choose to not take His advice.

"I hope now he has given me a second chance," she continued. "He could not have proven his love to me as much as he has by sending you here to leave a message with just little old me. I didn't realize how important I was to Him

217

and how important each of us all are to Him." I told her, "That's why He hung upon that cross for you and me." We both started to cry, and as we fell upon our knees, we prayed and thanked Him. I thanked Him for making me a messenger and for giving me a rare privilege to be able to do His work. She thanked Him for not only giving her another chance but now if she were to die she knew how tremendous His love was and that He would take care of her children and her husband. We both laughed and smiled. We hugged deeply and told each other "I love you". The rest of the night we spent reading the Bible and singing praises. The next morning before leaving she invited me to her home for dinner. She was going to fix me some enchiladas. I said, "Great!" She presented me with a small, handmade doll that was a little Hula girl with a green skirt, red top flowers in her hair, and red lei around her neck.

I went back to work assisting the ladies in the hospital. I remember one lady in particular that had to have a radical mastectomy. The removal of both breasts made her so sad that she lay in her bed alone. Her husband was great. He stood by her side every minute. She blamed herself for neglecting to examine her breasts breast and failing to obtain a Pap smear. Her husband saw me tending to the other patients and asked me to please come over and talk to his wife. I told him that I was ill prepared and I didn't know what to say. "I trust you, and I know that you will say the right thing." I was so nervous that before I approached her I said, "Lord, talk through me and let me say the right things. Give her Your message and what you want her to hear." The next thing I knew, words were pouring out of my mouth. In fact, I was wondering where they were all coming from. I told her that unlike about five or six of the women that were lying in there dying. "God caught your cancer in time to allow you to finish living out your life." She looked at me, "I do not feel whole." "You know," I told her, "I can relate. My husband had beaten me so much in the last ten years that I'm surprised that I am whole too. But we have to keep on pushing and keep our heads up high because God hasn't finished with us yet. He has a perfect plan for each and every one of us and until that day He comes back to get us, we have to keep trusting and believing that He knows what He is doing. Like I always tell my kids, each day trust and obey, for there's no other way. Give Him a chance to prove Himself to you. You will see that you have been truly blessed." As she lay there and cry, I wasn't sure if I had helped her in the way that she needed. But I had no problems checking out my breast as often as I could.

The next day my newfound friend came to the hospital to pick me up. We had a wonderful day in the Lord. They first took me down to the beach where I had to ask them if we could leave because some of the Hawaiian men were gorgeous and I was only human. They laughed as we left and went to their home. We ate and had a great time. That evening when they brought me back to the hospital I quickly ran into the room and put my stuff away, deciding to check on my friend with the spaghetti. When I entered her room, her bed was empty and the sheets had been removed. On the side of the bed in a squat-down position, kneeled her husband. He was carefully placing each one of the cans of spaghetti into a box. One of the cans fell to the floor and rolled over to me. I reached down to pick it up and handed it back to him. He turned and tears welled in his eyes. He took the can from my hand, but he did not say thank you. In fact, I could see he was too choked up to utter a sound. I dared not ask questions, I knew that my little friend was gone. For the first time in my life I had no comforting words to say. I walked back to my room with tears in my eyes. I started to pack so I could fly home the next day. "Lord, I'm not going to ask You why, because You are all-mighty and powerful and I trust in You all the days of my life."

Before I left the next day, an old lady, with whom I had the privilege to pray with at her bed, called me into her room. She told me that she had seen me sitting at the bottom of her bed praying. She asked me, "You mean you were here for surgery too?" I said, "Yes, Ma'am, I was." "I thought you were an angel sent here by God?" I smiled. "No, Ma'am, I'm no angel, just someone who cares. And I would not be who I am today if it were not for Jesus changing my life, for I am not even worthy to tie His shoes. But thank you very much. That is the greatest compliment anyone ever could have given me." It was hard to leave that hospital of dying women. But my job was done. I knew that God had sent me and I could trust that, He would send another messenger.

Returning to the Philippines, I noticed that Nene still tried to do all she could for me and protected the children while I was gone. Sam really changed after my cancer scare. He was afraid that he would loose me and decided to go back to church. At this time there was a Christian retreat for married couples that he wanted us to attend, which hopefully would help our marriage. We went through a ceremony to renew our vows in the Church. While we were there, we argued and he became angry when I said that I wouldn't make love to him. He was yelling, "You won't make love to me! That's what our problem is, and why we can't be happy!" I knew he was right, I did deny him sex. We made a pact, that he would stop beating the children and me if I would do my best to love him. Even though both our tasks were going to be difficult, I would have to say mine would be the hardest. I had lost my love for him and I found it very tough to get it back. It was going to take more than stopping the abuse, Sam also needed therapy. Sam thought that once I got back into his arms again, things would be fine. I tried to explain this to him without actually telling him that I didn't love him anymore. I tried my best to make love to him that night, at the retreat. But I lay there with no emotions. I knew he could tell. It was too late. It was all over with. I could tell I had no feelings. He had beaten all my feelings out my body and my soul. That love I once had for him was now gone forever. Afterwards, I lay there silently, in his arms.

I became pregnant with my daughter that night. I had removed my IUD because of the surgery. I hadn't put it back in because the doctor had wanted to try another contraceptive. This time I had a baby girl that I named, Camille. She was such a beautiful baby. Sam simply adored her. Why he felt the way he did about her I could not explain. But I know she was very special to him. Everything she did he thought was cute. This made September very angry. Of course, Pogie was too young to care. Even Nene noticed his ardor for Camille and asked me about it. I told her, "I don't know. But at least he isn't beating her." That's all I cared about.

# Chapter 27

We moved to another house on the other side of the base. The house was much nicer than the last. I tried with all my might to make our relationship work, but I just could not do it.

As always the abuse went on day after day. I guess Sam felt that I did not keep up my end of the deal so, being angry with me, he decided to start mistreating us. My son was subjected to more physical abuse than ever. Pogie started experiencing a lot of sleepless nights and would stay up all night and sometimes the entire next day, only getting two hours of sleep. I decided to take him to the base hospital where the doctors ran tests. They could not determine why Pogie went sleepless through the night. They told me to withhold from him anything with red dyes, caffeine, and definitely no candy. This regimen did not work. Pogie still wandered around the house late at night getting into things and going into Nene's room, as she tried to get her sleep. We bought a child's gate and locked him behind it at night.

One night while we were all in bed resting, Pogie was fooling around with the gate. Sam and I could hear him. Sam jumped up, grabbed his belt and the next thing I heard was a "Thump!" I heard Sam yelling for Pogie to stay in bed, but heard nothing else. Sam came back to bed. Somehow, I felt uneasy. If Sam had hit him with a belt, why wasn't Pogie crying? I pretended to go to the kitchen for some water. On the way back, I stopped at Pogie's room to check on him. I found Pogie laying in bed with blood running down his face. There was blood on the pillow and he was sucking on his bloody fingers, not even crying. I went into a rage, turned on our bedroom light and started yelling. I yanked the covers off Sam. "How you dared to hurt my baby!" Sam followed me into the room and saw the blood. He had tried to surprise my son by hitting him with the belt, but had cut his head open with the buckle. Sam said, "He deserved it, he was trying to sneak out of his room." I reminded him, "He has a sleeping problem!" Still yelling and fussing, I cleaned up Pogie's cut. I saw that it was very deep, so I got dressed and planned to take him to the hospital's Emergency Room.

Sam refused to hear of this and told me that I was not leaving the house. I put a cold compress on Pogie's head and climbed into bed with him. I held him all night as I cried silently for my son's pain, making sure that he did not hear me. The next morning Sam and I took him to the hospital. Sam of course did not leave my side for fear I would tell the doctors what really happened. I knew it wouldn't do me any good. Telling some one about our abuse always left me back where I was before and that was in the hands of Sam. We told the doctor that he had fallen accidentally during the night. We explained Pogie's difficulty in sleeping, and they decided to try giving him one week's dosage of sleeping pills. When the week's supply was gone, Pogie began sleeping through the night.

Sam stopped asking me to go out to a movie with him. He would just order me to do things, and rather than arguing with him, I'd do as he asked and try not to make any comments that would upset him. Nene was ready to quit again. I tried to argue as little as possible to keep the peace. September had a hard time accepting our house girl as an adult that was there to help raise her and her baby brother. She didn't like for Nene to tell her what to do. One day Sam had to whip her to make her listen to what Nene had to say. He told her, "You better listen and do whatever Nene tells you to do!" When we got back home that night September came running to me, screaming and yelling and crying. "Mommy!" I didn't know what could be wrong, thinking maybe something had happened to my newborn baby. I ran

223

past her into the house where I saw Nene calmly feeding the baby. September said, "No, Mommy, it's me."

As it turned out, Nene had told September to heat a bottle for the baby. Normally we would put scalding hot water into a cup, place the bottle in it for a while and the bottle would be warmed. In our absence, September had dropped the bottle into the cup of scalding hot water. The water had splashed onto her chest and burned her badly. I grabbed September to comfort her. When her dad came in, he started laughing at her and yelling, "That's what you get! That's what you get for being stupid enough to listen to Nene." I screamed, "You told her to listen to Nene or you would beat her. Now you're calling her stupid for listening to her? You don't make any sense to me, Sam." As I walked away September said, "Mommy, but he told me to do what she said." I could only agree with September. "I know, sweetheart." We both tried to hurry and get into the car and drive away before Sam joined us, but it was too late. "Move over. I'm coming with you. September, get in the back!" But I insisted that she stay in my lap until we were at the hospital. As we drove to the hospital Sam kept yelling at September. Couldn't he see that she was in enough pain already?

When we arrived at the emergency room I immediately carried her in. Her burns were third-degree, so she had to be hospitalized. The doctors right away asked her if her parents had burned her. But September explained what had happened and the doctors ruled out child abuse. They tried very hard to examine September but she kept crying and laying her head upon my chest. Sam very nicely said, "Come on, honey, let the doctors check your chest." A few minutes ago this man was calling her stupid. After she was given a room, I helped her to get into her hospital gown. Looking up into my eyes sadly, she pleaded with me to keep her daddy out of the room and away from her. She screamed, "Mommy I hate him! Please don't let him in here!"

Of course, I couldn't keep him out, especially since she was admitted for third-degree burns which kept her there for a week. We had to wear masks and gowns to prevent her from getting infections. Sam would try to talk to her and feed her in the hospital, but she would not respond to him. I would sit and watch them and see the sheer hatred in her eyes. I actually had to force her to speak to him rather than to anger him and give him a chance to yell and get at her in the hospital. After I had been there for a little while, I would rush home to check on the baby. Then I'd returned to be by her side. When September was released, I knew that her physical scars would heal, but the emotional scars given to her by her father, would stay with her forever.

Sam seemed to torment September. She could never do anything right. Even when she ate supper it was a battle over the dinner table. Sam would force her to eat everything on her plate and if she asked for seconds, he would pile her plate even higher than her first helping. I think he was trying to teach her a lesson about asking for more to eat, forcing her to finish every morsel. If she didn't eat it all he would leave it on the stove all night, for her to eat the next day. Of course, this was after he whipped her for not finishing the meal.

Then there was the time he wanted September to became a concert pianist. Against September's wishes Sam signed her up for piano lessons. His reasoning was that kids did not know what they wanted out of life and it was up to their parents to push them beyond their potential. Sam believed that September had what it took to be a pianist, so he signed her up. I on the other hand felt that we should ask her if she wanted to play and if she enjoyed it. Then we should stand behind her and make sure that her dream came true. I never believed in forcing kids to do anything except go to church, which was never a problem for my kids because they enjoyed it. At first September was enjoying herself. She did very well in her piano recital. Sam and I were excited and very proud of her. She came home one day and asked us for a piano so that she could practice at home. I was glad that she wanted to continue with her lessons. Sam told us that it was too expensive so we dropped the subject. One day while I was in the kitchen cooking, September came in looking very serious. "Mama," she said, "didn't you say that if you had the faith of a mustard seed and if you asked God for something, that you would receive it?" Hesitating I said, "Yes, but you must also realize that sometimes God does not give us the desires of our heart because He knows that sometimes it will not always be in our best interest or help us to grow." "What does that mean, Mommy?" Trying to explain to September I said, "He already knows if the piano is going to make you truly happy or if it will cause trouble. So you're supposed to ask and wait and see if God will give it to you." "Well, I'm going to pray and ask God and I hope he will give me a piano." I smiled and kept on cooking. September ran off to play.

Sam overheard the conversation and the next day, a piano was delivered. He saw an advertisement in the newspaper where someone had a piano for sale and he bought it. September was so excited. You should have seen the look in her eyes when they delivered it to the door. As soon as it was set into place she jumped up onto the piano and started to play. "Thanks, Dad!" she yelled. "Thank your mama, too." She yelled, "Thank you, Mommy!" I smiled and walked over to Sam, gave him a hug and kissed him on the cheek. "Thanks, she loves it." Then I went back into the kitchen to finish cooking. Something still was not right. I felt very uncomfortable about the piano but I didn't let on to September. September played for about thirty minutes, until she started to just bang on it. Sam yelled, "OK, that's enough playing for now. This is not a play toy. It's for practicing only." September snapped back, "But I want to play some more." Sam's voice started to get deeper, "No, I'm getting tired of it. It's time to get off now." I ran out of the kitchen because I felt that September was about to get into trouble. "September, you heard your father. It's time to stop." September sighed as she jumped down and ran off to her room.

Early the next morning September was playing at her piano. Sam jumped out of bed and ran to the front room and yelled at September to never touch the piano without his permission. "The piano is only here for you to practice!" I jumped into the conversation. "Sam, how is she going to learn the piano if she is not allowed to play around on it and discover the keys and how they work?"

"She is too young to play around on it." I answered, "Then you should not have bought it for her if you felt she was too young to play on it." We only had the piano a day and we were already fighting. Soon the piano teacher reported that September was acting lazy and was not practicing the way she was supposed to. So when September got home she had to practice without dinner till she got it right. Next she was being yelled at because she left fingerprints on the piano and was told to clean it. One day I awoke to her getting a spanking because Sam found fingerprints on the piano. He knew that she was on it without his permission. September was pretending to play with the piano closed, since she knew she was not allowed to play on the keys. I told Sam, "It's time we got rid of that piano. I don't want anything in my house that will cause my children to get more beatings."

The next thing I knew September followed me to the bathroom and closed the door behind her. "Mommy, can I talk to you?" "Yes, honey, what is it?" Looking up with a sad look she said, "Now I see why God didn't want me to have the piano." "Yes, and I see why now, too." "I don't want it anymore, Mommy. Next time, if I don't receive something that I ask for, I'll understand." I agreed. "In the meantime, September, until I convince Daddy to sell it, please don't touch it so you won't get anymore spankings, OK?" I gave her a hug and away she ran. September always liked a big hug. Soon Sam began to yell at September that he bought her a piano and she never used it. How it was a waste of money. He yelled, "I'm going to sell it!" September and I just smiled. Soon the piano was sold and taken away. I winked at September and she winked back.

All of the family photos he took during those five miserable years showed how unhappy everyone was. The smiles on the children's faces were so artificial. When September began to gain weight, he teased her mercilessly and talked about it to everyone. I took September to the hospital because I could not understand her weight gain. The doctor said that she had built up fat cells and it would be hard to make her lose weight. I tried to help her lose it, but it did no good. Sam encouraged her to eat more than she wanted, possibly to make her feel self-confident. She would decide to eat less on her own. It just didn't work.

Sam and I were arguing one night over who was going to get the kids if I left. I yelled, "There isn't a court anywhere in the United States that will take my kids away from me." Sam yelled, "Yes, they will if they know that you don't have a good job and are unable to support the kids. The courts will take them away." Even though I knew he was lying I still stood my ground. After arguing for hours I started to get a big headache. I got so fed-up and tired of arguing that I would have said or done anything to get Sam to shut up. "Fine," I told Sam, "take the kids! I don't care! Just shut up and leave me alone!" Of course, I didn't mean it because I would kill Sam if he even thought about taking my children away from me. Sam finally shut up and left me alone.

One day I received a call from September's teacher. She sounded very mysterious on the phone. She told me that she wanted to have a meeting with just me, alone. I told her I would be right over. As soon as I walked into the classroom I was asked to have a seat. I questioned the teacher about what was wrong. She began by asking me, "Have you noticed a significant change in September's attitude and behavior lately?" "No, is something wrong?" She told me of how September would ignore her when the she talked to her or called on her, that she seemed to be in her own world. The teacher asked, "Would you please be truthful and answer a question?" "Of course, I will." She asked, "Did you tell September's father that you were going to give September to him, if you got a divorce?" "Of course not! I would never do that." Again she questioned, "Were you and your husband arguing and he said, 'I'll keep the kids,' and you said, 'Go ahead,' just to shut him up?" My argument with Sam had been over a month ago, so I didn't remember and again I answered, "Never"! "I would never say that-t-t-t!" "Y-Y-Yes," I paused biting my finger, "I did! Oh God-d-d-d, yes I did! But I was only trying to get my husband to shut up." "That is what I figured happened. I've seen this go on with other children. September must have overheard your conversation and now feels that you have deserted her. Is her father abusive?" "Yes he is!" "She feels that you are all she has to protect her from him and now you told him he can have her." "But I never meant it, she knows that." "No she doesn't. To

229

her you have never said it before until now, so she believed you. And you probably don't lie to her, so she's scared." "So what do I do now?" I said." Now you have got to convince her that you didn't mean it. Start by telling her that you love her and that you made a mistake. Hopefully she will understand."

That day after classes I decided to walk to the school to pick up September. When September saw me she ran up and hugged me. Trying to hold back the tears, I got down on my knees and hugged her back. I told her I came to the school to walk home with her. A big smile came over her little face. As we walked along I told September that her mommy really messed up, and I needed her to help me fix my mistake. Looking up at me she said, "I'll help you, Mommy." I went on to tell her that I had opened my big mouth and told her daddy that I didn't care if he took the kids. September bent down to pick up a stick and started to drag it along the sidewalk. Concentrating on her stick she had just picked up, she tried desperately not to show her emotions. I continued, "I was so tired of Daddy fussing that I just said anything to shut him up before he started beating me. And you know what? It worked. I had to lie to him to shut him up. But you know, September, between you and me there is no way I would ever let him take my children away from me." Stopping September in her tracks, I got down on my knees in front of her again. "This is where I need your help. We must never tell him this. Because when I get ready to leave him I will be taking my children with me. That's our secret, OK? One of these days you and I and your brother and sister are going to leave your daddy for good, OK? "With a big smile she shook her little head. I cried silently and we again hugged. "No one will ever take you away from me September, I promise. I love you, sweetheart." "I love you too, Mommy." I reached down and grabbed her little hand and we walked home. September I said "Thanks for helping me to correct my mistake." "You're welcome, Mommy" September didn't have any more problems in school. In fact her grades were even better than before. I'm pretty sure she got the message.

I kept having problems with my back and Sam had begun teasing me about my weight gain after having the baby, making me feel self-conscious and uneasy about my appearance. One day while looking in the mirror, I agreed that I had begun to let myself go. I was so depressed and had such low self-esteem. I had no confidence in myself and really didn't care what I looked like anymore. I was not only out of shape but my breasts had begun to sag. I had not worn a good support bra, as I should have. A friend of mine recently had breast-reduction surgery and after speaking with her, I decided to have it done too. Sam disagreed, but I had to do this for myself. I wanted to feel good about myself again, and I knew that I wouldn't have so much back pain. Sam told me I was doing it to get attention. I didn't really care about other men looking at me because I was so unhappy with Sam. I had no intentions of marrying again if we should ever divorce. I wanted to improve my body because I needed to re-build my self-esteem and look like the woman I once was. I no longer wanted to look like someone who had been beaten down so badly that even I lacked the ability to see who I was.

I made an appointment with the doctor. He told me that I was definitely a candidate for breast-reduction surgery, since I had a petite frame and was experiencing back pain from the large size of my breasts. Sam and I argued about this decision over and over, but my breasts were in very bad shape. I could feel Sam's insecurity and knew I was going to have a very difficult time with him.

When it was time to go to the hospital, he refused to take me and refused to let me go through the surgery. I decided that this altercation was not going to dissuade me so I used reverse psychology on him. I kept trying to explain that I no longer felt beautiful when I undressed in front of him (which was a lie), hoping to convince him into taking me to the hospital. Inside, I knew that I was soon going to leave him and I wanted to start my life all over again, not only with a new heart, but a new look.

Finally, he agreed to take me to the hospital, but all the way there we argued. He accused me of having another man in my life, and was supposedly having the surgery for his benefit. I kept praying that I would get to the hospital without him stopping along the way and beating me. I stayed very humble because I wanted the surgery really bad. I also knew that the back pain would go away forever.

The surgery went very well and it wasn't painful to me at all. When Sam came to pick me up, I still felt the tension between us, even though he smiled and agreed that he might just like the new me. I went home and immediately took my pain medication, going to bed as the doctor had instructed. I didn't lift the baby nor did I do anything strenuous, so that I would heal properly.

On the second day after surgery there was a commotion going on with September and her dad. I called Sam into our room and asked him what was going on. He told me that September had walked home from school and had a leftover peanut butter and jelly sandwich that she did not eat for lunch that day. Thinking that Nene would be upset that she didn't eat it, she threw it into the trash by her bed. By the time Sam came home, he followed the trail of ants that was crawling over the trash can and up the wall of the house through the window. I could see the anger in his eyes as he stormed back into her room. "I'm going to kill her." My surgery was not healed and the stitches were fresh, but I gingerly climbed out of bed and walked to my daughter as quickly as I could.

I heard her screams and saw him pick her up by the chest and throw her across the room. My breasts were so tender and painful, yet when I saw September fly across that room into the mirror, sliding down the bureau and landing on the desk, with him standing over her ready to throw her across the room again, I went crazy. I had to save September! I no longer felt the pain in my breasts as I began beating him, hoping he would beat me instead. He pushed me up against the wall, slapped me and knocked me to the floor. My house girl begged me, "Please Cynthia, you just had surgery!" She held September back and clutched my son, who was now crying hysterically. He tore every single stitch I had and scarred me terribly, but I had saved my daughter the pain he would have continued to inflict upon her. Sam stormed out of the room as I sat on the floor bent over in pain. September fell to the floor and hugged my neck, asking me if I was all right. I asked if she was okay because she was my only concern. There we were, both sitting on the floor crying, as our house girl joined us. They struggled to help me into bed. My house girl said, "Why, why didn't you stay out of it. All you did was make it worse. You know how angry he gets when you interfere with his disciplining the kids." "You just don't understand because you don't have your own children."

Blood was draining through my bra. We tried to remove the bandages and put medicine on them, but it was too late. After I was bandaged back together, I took some pills for the pain and laid down. I refused to allow September to see my wounds. She needed no more anguish, but my son saw some of the blood. I sent him out of the room crying. I

233

asked Nene to put the children to bed. September came to my bed to show me the welts on her skin where she had been thrown and hit with Sam's belt. I sat up in excruciating pain and asked her to get me some alcohol to put on her welts. "Why, September, after passing fifty or more trashcans on the way home from school, why would you throw the sandwich away at home where your dad would see it?" She shrugged her shoulders and walked away.

I went to the doctor the next day and he could not believe what he saw. He tried to put me back together with surgical tape to the best of his abilities. Telling me that I would be scarred for life, he said that I should have laser surgery again to repair the damage. The scars meant nothing to me because I believed I had saved my daughter's life. No one would see them anyway and I considered them battle scars. I was just concerned that I would get an infection if they were not properly treated.

I decided to try to do what Nene suggested. From now on I would try to stay out of the way and maybe Sam would not be as abusive. Sam told me after the incident with the sandwich that when he was beating September he saw red. He also confessed to me that he saw red when I would pray or read my Bible during our arguments. I would try not to fight back anymore. Instead I would read my Bible or rebuke his spirit, only making him angrier. I had heard of people actually seeing red before, so maybe it's not just a saying. I still tried to stay as calm as possible and be a good Christian wife. Not interfering with him when he disciplined the children was one of the hardest things I ever had to do. I would walk out to the back fence when he would whip the children for something bad they had done, that was all the strength I could muster. I told the base chaplain about my problems once a week when I would visit him. I would never let Sam know where I was. I attended a wives' group that met to study the Bible every week, but no matter how much we prayed, my situation at home was only getting worse and worse. I refused to believe that God would allow a woman to experience the torture I was going through.

Once Sam found out what I was doing and where I was going, he started torturing me more just to see how faithful I was to God and my Bible. As days and weeks went by he continued to find every reason he could to beat the children or me. I found myself on the floor several times, beaten down and crying. And of course, to get back at him, my only defense was to not have anything to do with him. I knew this was the only weapon of defense I had. Of course, Sam constantly would cite quotations from the Bible: (1 Corinthians 7: 1-5) "The wife's body does not belong to her alone but also to her husband. In the same way, the husband's body does not belong to him alone but to his wife." I think that was the only scripture he learned.

The next day I brought this to the chaplain's attention. He told me that one day my husband would see my obedience, realize how bad he felt for what he's done and fall to his knees, apologizing to the children and me. He also told me to call him the next time Sam went into a rage.

And Sam did go into a rage, not long after my talk with the chaplain. I ran to the phone to call him. He came right over to our house. He was my husband's superior and outranked him quite a bit. With one snap of his finger he could have sent Sam to jail. The chaplain walked up the sidewalk, and could hear the fighting in the house. He rang the doorbell and I went to let him in. Sounding very disrespectful, Sam loudly asked him, "What are you doing in our home? "I could see that the chaplain was very frightened by Sam. Sam advised him to turn around and go back where he came from or Sam was going to take him down. The

235

chaplain looked at me. "Sorry but I have to leave. Do you want to come with me?" I looked at Sam. "If you do, I'll come after you and the chaplain." I looked back at the chaplain and told him, "Thanks, but no thanks." As he left our home, Sam continued to beat me.

The chaplain called me the next day and apologized for not being more helpful. "Sam scared him so bad, I could feel his knees knocking." "I understood because the first time he beat me, I felt the same way. But I've become used to it." "What made Sam angry?" "It was something very minute, but his anger is getting much worse since I started to submit to Biblical scripture." The chaplain told me that there was no way that God wanted one of His children to suffer so badly and told me that I must leave him until Sam got his act together. I agreed. He told me to visit with him soon so that we could make arrangements to leave him. I disagreed. I needed to get a divorce. "A divorce will not be possible, even though Sam has committed adultery several times."1 Corinthians 7:10-16, NAB: To the married, however, I give this instruction (not I, but the Lord): a wife should not separate from her husband--and if she does separate she must either remain single or become reconciled to her husband--and a husband should not divorce a wife. To the rest I say (not the Lord): if any brother has a wife who is an unbeliever, and she is willing to go on living with him, he should not divorce her; and if any woman has a husband who is an unbeliever, and he is willing to go on living with here, she should not divorce her husband. For the unbelieving husband is made holy through his wife, and the unbelieving wife is made holy through the brother. Otherwise your children would be unclean, whereas in fact they are holy. If the unbeliever separates, however, let him separate. The brother or sister is not bound in such cases; God has called you to peace. For how do you know, wife, whether you will save your husband; or how do you know, husband, whether you will save your wife?

The chaplain replied that if Sam did not want a divorce I would be unable put him away. I began looking for a scripture that would set me free.

# Chapter 28

I continued to jump in between my children and my husband, and refused to have sex with him. I felt that if I had to be there he was not going to take away all of my dignity. No matter what he demanded of me, if it was wrong, I rebelled and regardless of how he begged me to love him, I fought him off. I stood strong and I stood proud. I told him that he could do whatever he wanted to my physical body but he was not going to take down my spirit. I was going to fight till I could not fight anymore.

You can ride a wild stallion and ride it until you break it, but as soon as you got down off its back it will very proudly stick its heads back up and prance away. You can not break its spirit. I continued to read the Bible daily for I knew that somewhere in the Word of God there was a verse or verses that would set me and my children free.

I knew that when we left the Philippines, it would be very hard on my second-born son, Pogie. He loved our house girl Nene as if she were his mother. Nene had given him a lot of attention and love that I was not able to offer due to the deep depression I had fallen into because of the physical and mental abuse. She was very fearful of Sam and wanted to leave but she had become a part of our family and wondered if it would make things worse. When Sam and I would leave the house, you could see the fear in her eyes for me as the children stood at the door, sadly watching me go. They never knew what condition I would be in when I arrived home. Nene always pleaded with me not to say or do anything wrong that might insight Sam to want to kill me. I would tell her each time not to worry because I would be fine. She and September never believed it and were still frightened for me to go. I couldn't get her to understand that I had to be strong. I could not let him see that I was weakening each day. If Sam and I went to the commissary, I would come home with a busted lip because I wanted to buy snacks for my kids. I felt that I had a right to buy snacks for my children while he was buying them for himself. He would take the snacks to the house and point them out to the kids, telling the children not to touch them. To make matters worse, he would sometimes eat them in front of the kids but never let them have any. When he ate his snacks, I would call them into my room to play, or Nene would bring them snacks and I would hide the treats. This worked until Sam got wise and asked Nene to leave everything she bought off base with his money out where he could see it.

If we went to the hospital, he would beat me when I told him he was being cruel to the kids or me. One day while we visited the doctor, I let it slip out that he had hit my son. I tried to cover it up by telling the doctor that Sam did not hit him hard, but the doctor kept questioning how hard it was. I knew I was in trouble. We walked out of the hospital and Sam started yelling, and though people were walking into the hospital staring at us, he only grew louder and louder. I even tried walking faster to get to the car before he could hit me. Usually, before I got there, I ended up knocked to the ground. As he yelled to the kids to get into the car, he continued to beat me while my children watched, crying for their mom. No one ever helped me. People only pointed and stared. I looked around hoping that just one person would stand up and come to my defense, but they kept on walking and minding their own business.

One time Sam asked me to go to a movie. I didn't want to go and I was afraid to leave. I knew he was mad at me and I heard the door slam. He walked into the bathroom and started yelling at me. "Why do the kids get all of your attention?" "They don't! I just hate being with you!"He pushed me away from the mirror, so I started for the bedroom door. Nene was very good at protecting the children and I saw that she had put the children into her room and told them to stay there. Just as she came to the door to help me, Sam pushed her away from me, and told her to go back into her room, but she refused. Little did she know that this did not help me. Actually, it made it harder for me to handle Sam. When I saw him getting angry with her, I agreed to go to the movie with him so Nene would be left alone. I could see the frustration in her eyes because she too, had reached her limits. Previously she would run and hide from him, but she had begun to stand up to him. She was tired of his abuse and tired of him beating the children and me. I was afraid for her, trying to be so brave, just as I was scared for anyone who tried to come to my rescue. I knew how crazy Sam was and didn't want him to hurt anyone around me.

Getting dressed for the movie, I realized that I might not even make it home to see my family again. Every time I left the house I feared that I was seeing my kids for the last time. Sam and I argued all the way to the theater. I tried closing the car window but it was so hot in there. I ended up keeping the window closed so no one would hear us. Sam kept knocking me up against the window, so I got out of the car. As he wrestled me down to the ground, he sat on my stomach and kept hitting me in the face. He stood up, grabbed me by the clothes, and pushed me toward the theater. People stood around and watched, again, no one cared. He looked around at them and told them "Mind your own business!" Finally, they began to walk away as he threatened them. I was wishing that just one of them, just one would please call the police, but not one person did.

As I entered the theater, Sam asked me if I wanted popcorn. I watched the people pass by; husbands who were pushing their wives along into the theater wanted to see what we would do next, and some obviously wanted to help me. Everyone was so afraid of my situation but no one cared enough to stick his or her neck out for me. Tears ran down my battered face, as I said, "Yes," to the offer of popcorn. I knew that I would be beaten more if I said, "No." All through the movie, I cried silently to myself. Wiping the tears from my eyes, Sam would lean over and kiss my cheeks and my swollen-and-battered lips. I hated him so much! When the movie was over, we all walked out and again the people stared as Sam glared at them, daring them to call the police or say something.

We drove back home and as I entered the house, Nene dropped the silverware she was drying and accompanied by September, ran to my side. Sam pushed me back to our bedroom, "Go to your room!" I wanted to fight but I knew Nene and the kids could not take it anymore. Repeatedly, over and over he told me of his love. He told me that if I were not so stubborn, he would stop hitting me. I lay on the bed with my back to him, curled up with my knees to my chest so he would not touch me. He still got into bed and held me and began kissing me. I would not respond, hoping he would go away. We would wrestle and fight till no end. He tried to take me like a rapist would but I fought him off with all the strength I had. I was not going to make love to him. Soon he would fall asleep. I would quietly get up and try to sneak into the front room to spend some time with Nene and the kids. Soon he would awake and start telling Nene to put the kids to bed. He was starting to get very jealous of our friendship. But Nene was all I had as a friend. She was the only person I could talk to while trapped in my little dollhouse. And just like I knew he would do, he started to accuse Nene and me of sleeping together. I just looked at this ill, depraved man that I called my husband. "Not many people are as sick and twisted as you!" I told Nene not to pay any attention to him, but this infuriated her so much that she decided to quit. And in a way I was glad because she was going through too much strain. We all cried as Nene packed her clothes to leave. And even though I knew I would be alone I wanted what was best for her. After she left I lay awake all night thinking about everything that had happened and how I had to get away.

Nene returned the following week. She begged me for her position back. I was so happy to see her I didn't care what Sam had accused us of. She failed to understand Sam's jealousy and when I tried to explain that he was also jealous of my babies and me too, she still could not understand. I told her not to worry. She was too innocent to understand. I didn't even understand myself, that's why I had such difficulty explaining it. I told her that whenever Sam was around to just take the kids and go to their rooms. I knew that he did not want me to have any friends or be around anyone. Pogie was in tears he was so happy to see Nene. I told her that from now on she and I were not to talk or be around each other while Sam was inside the house, since he was so jealous. And even though Nene was like a daughter to me, we made sure that she only did her work when Sam was around.

As Pogie started to get older he wanted to be around Sam more. I tried to keep him away but it did no good. He was about one-year-old and was play fighting with Sam, while I was cooking dinner. I just felt that something was about to happen. So I went into the front room and asked Sam to stop. He said, "Don't worry. I'm just toughening up my son." I was still very nervous as I watched from the kitchen. I turned away for just a second. I heard Pogie being knocked across the living room floor. I ran to pick up my son, who was now in total shock. He accidentally hit Sam in his private parts and had paid the penalty. I screamed at Sam,

"How dare you get mad at a one-year-old that didn't know what he was hitting!" It was so difficult for me to be both a mom and a mediator. I had to always be alert and aware of where my children were and what they were doing, to make sure that they were safe, nowhere near Sam. I literally would have to drop whatever I was doing, get to my kids and find a way to get them away from Sam. They were so young, naïve and forgiving. They would forget that maybe ten minutes before they were hit for something and they would be back with Sam doing the same thing again. Things were different for me. I may have laughed and talked with him, but I never ever forgot.

The house that we were living in was still not big enough for Sam. He wanted to move into an even bigger house on base and since he had gone down for a one year extension, the Air Force eagerly allowed him. The day he told me, he took me out to dinner. I knew something was up but I didn't know why. It was as though my heart had stopped beating. I asked him if we could go home to visit my mother. At first, he said, "Yes," but when he thought about it he said that we couldn't afford it. Sam knew that I would stay there once I returned to the States.

"I spoke to Anna, she'll send us money." "You can go, but the kids would not go with you." I gave up any ideas of leaving and bought a calendar. I marked an "X" on each day, counting the days until we would leave.

I had been through rapes, abuse, sodomy, stalking, and I was still around. I was determined to keep my head high, read the Bible daily, and find a scripture that would back me up on my divorce. As the year slowly went by, Sam soon announced that he had a new assignment in Spain. I was cooking supper at the time and didn't even look up at him. I just kept cooking. I knew I was not going with him.

The next day, I went to my husband's Commander and asked him to send me back to the States. The Commander started the paperwork for me to leave. I told Sam what I had done and his response was anger. I tried to sit down and explain that we needed to separate so that he could find a woman to love who would love him in return and make him a good wife. I was no longer capable of making love to him, and all I wanted to do was kill him for everything he had done to my children and me. He needed to let me go. He needed to be in a relationship that would make him happy. I had told him this many times previously, but he told me over and over that he loved me and didn't care how I felt.

Our relationship was becoming a terrifying nightmare and he was convinced that one day I would let him run me. I knew that there was no way that this was going to happen. I told him that we needed to separate now, before we killed each other.

## PART THREE

## Chapter 29

We split up the house with my belongings going to the States and his to Spain. The day that the Transportation Mobility Organization (TMO) movers were to come to the house to pack the furniture, Sam sent me to the commissary to pick up some things. I thought it was a little odd, but I didn't think anything else of it. When I got back, I noticed that the truck had an awful lot of stuff in it. Upon entering the house, I saw that they had packed my stuff onto the truck meant for Spain. It was supposed to have been sent to the States. They informed me to speak to my husband about it since he had told them to do it. They continued their work.

I was steaming mad at Sam and asked him what he had done. He smiled at me with that sneaky look he got at times and said, "You're going to Spain." Begging to differ, I went down to the TMO to get my belongings unpacked and have them sent where I wanted them. They informed me that my husband made the decision and since he was the member of the military, everything was to be sent where he wanted. (I was reminded of when I wanted to choose my son's name and was told it was Sam's decision because he was "military.") Tears ran down my face as I sat in the chair. I put my face in my hands and bawled my eyes out. They had no idea what Sam had done to me in the past or how miserable it was for the five years we were in the Philippines. I couldn't go to Spain. I didn't want to!

I went into the Colonel's office and explained the situation to him. He told me that there was nothing that he or I could do about it at that moment. The only thing I could do was, go to Spain and turn my furniture around when it got

245

there. My only other option was to go to the States with only the clothes on my back. I cried even more in front of the Colonel, but he didn't care. All he cared about was getting Sam off the base so that he wouldn't have to deal with our personal problems. With us gone, he would no longer have to hear about my abuse. The commander at the next base would have to hear our problems and my gripes. I knew he was happy to be rid of us. My whole world was falling apart, and yet Sam never received disciplinary action against him. I felt hurt, infuriated, and just plain angry.

We soon gathered our belongings and packed our bags to return to the United States. I was going to visit my parents and Sam wanted to see his family also before we were transferred to Spain. There was one problem that we had not yet faced, and that was Pogie's love for Nene. Pogie always had looked upon Nene as a surrogate mother and when we were getting ready to leave the Philippines, Pogie was five years old. We knew that this was going to be very difficult for him. I went to the doctor and explained my situation. He told me that this was not the first time a child had fallen in love with the house girl. He gave me sleeping medicine and told me to give it to Pogie one hour before boarding the plane. Nene talked about our leaving every day and told Pogie that she was going with us to assure him that no one was going to leave him. Soon, the day came and as the doctor had prescribed, I gave Pogie the dosage of medicine. But upon our arrival at the airport, Pogie was wide-awake and gripping onto Nene's leg as he played. He would not let her go. When they announced that our plane was boarding, we all started for the plane. Pogie still would not let go. We told him that Nene was going to fly later, and still he would not let go. I could see Sam getting angry, but he was not saying a thing. People were boarding the plane and we were last to leave as Pogie still held Nene's leg tightly. Sam looked at me and reminded me that he had told me not to take Nene to the airport because it would only make things more difficult. Nene began to cry and so did Pogie.

It was a very emotional scene. Passersby were crying at the frustration on my little sons face as his sad little eyes stared in complete distress. The guard at the gate told us that it was all right for Nene to walk us out to the plane and the flight attendant' helping to board the passengers, was very understanding and had seen this before so she let Nene board the plane with us. We all sat in our seats and waited as the attendant explained to the Captain what was going on. He came up to us and invited Pogie to the front of the plane to see the controls, but Pogie would still not let Nene go. The Captain took Nene up to the front of the plane, and I tried to figure out how to do this without creating a scene or badly traumatizing my child. I told Pogie that Nene had to go to the restroom, but in actuality, Nene was leaving the plane. She sadly walked across the pavement with her head down only looking back at the plane that was taking Pogie and her family away from her. I pulled out some games for Pogie to play, but he never stopped asking me where she was. I just kept saying, "She'll be back soon." I hated lying to my child, but I had no other choice.

Soon the plane took off. We played for about two hours into the flight, when Pogie finally fell asleep. September, Sam, the baby and I also fell asleep. And when I awoke, Pogie was no longer next to me. I jumped up, handed the baby to Sam and hysterically began to search for my son. The flight attendants helped look but Pogie was nowhere to be found. I went back to the restroom and discovered my little son on the floor, curled up and crying, sucking his finger. I wept as I snatched him up into my arms and took him back to his seat. I held him, and together we cried, but he never said a word to me. The whole trip, he did not speak but continued sucking on his finger. Every now and then his tender little eyes would look up to me with one single tear running down his cheek. What was I going to do about my little boy?

As planned, Sam, the kids and I stopped at my family's house first where I took the opportunity to tell my dad what was happening. He told me that the best thing I could do was to go to Spain and get my stuff as the Colonel had suggested, otherwise I was going to have to start from scratch, which would be next to impossible with no money. Sam knew what my intentions were. I was only going to Spain to get my belongings and turn right back around. Thank God that we only stayed one day in New York.

Pogie would not eat or sleep. We soon left the United States and upon reaching Spain, we all traveled with a sponsor to a big hotel.

I still tried to feed little Pogie but he refused to eat or drink. We took him to the hospital where the doctors told us that if he didn't eat soon, they would have to hospitalize him for dehydration. He was getting very weak, but I still could not get liquids into him and he was still refusing to eat. He watched as his sister played and tried to get his attention. She would try to get him to snicker, hoping to make him laugh. He started to look like the starving children in Africa with their large, swollen bellies.

Sam had arranged for us two connecting rooms and I would go back and forth to check the children. Pogie had a fever of 102°. I bathed him in tepid water to bring it down. The next day I planned to take him to the doctor because he still was not eating. I was so tired and drained from trying to care for Pogie and the baby, staying up all night with him. I fell into bed in sheer exhaustion as soon as they were asleep. My body ached as I lay down on my pillow. I was so hungry and weak I don't even think I took one breath before I fell fast asleep. Suddenly, I heard, "Mommy!" I quickly sat up and Sam jumped out of bed. He said, "You rest I'll go to see what he wants." Soon I heard a door slam, many noises, and then the door to our room slam. I lay back down and as soon as my head hit the pillow, I fell back asleep.

The next morning, the baby started to cry. I got up and fed her and started to get her dressed. I knocked on the kids' door and told them to wake up and get dressed too. I was standing in the bathroom brushing my teeth when September came through the door and gave me a look of despair. I knew something was up, so I stepped out of the bathroom, looked at her and turned to see my little son coming through the door. Little Pogie had a handprint seemingly engraved into his entire face. I said, "My God, what happened?" I turned and raced into Sam, trying desperately to kill him. I was not going to stop till he was dead. If it took every bit of my breath, if it took every bit of life in my body, I was going to kill him for this. We fought all over the room, almost on top of the baby. September grabbed the baby and took her and her brother into their room crying hysterically. They had never seen their mother in this type of rage before. I meant to kill Sam that day and I didn't care how I did it. We fought and fought and fought. In those times I didn't have much strength, but it was as though some hunter had awakened a sleeping mother bear after killing her baby cub. That day, Sam was going to die or I was going to die trying.

I fought him so hard Sam took my head and smashed it against the metal railings on the bed to stop me. Almost semiconscious, I heard myself saying, "I'm going to kill you." I finally passed out, and when I awoke, I was hurting so badly, I couldn't move an inch of my body. Most of it, I admit, I inflicted upon myself: the knots on my head, my blackened eye and busted face all came from Sam trying to defend himself. I could not believe it when I finally crawled to the bathroom and looked into the mirror. I grabbed a towel and started to wipe away the blood. I walked into the kid's room only to find them gone. I returned to my room and tried desperately to put my clothes back on. I couldn't even lift my legs. As I looked up, the door to my room opened and Sam entered with a tray of food. The first thing out of my mouth was, "Where are my babies?" "They are fine" I tried to stand up. Again I said, "Where are they, you @#$%@#$%?" He came in and pushed me back onto the bed saying, "I told you they're fine. You stay there, Kaye and don't get up. You did this to yourself." I tried again to stand up and could hardly move. He told me that he didn't know what had gotten into me, but I had attacked him. He was only defending himself. I couldn't even talk or reply at all, because of the pounding in my head. Again I tried to get up and he told me that the children did not need to see me in such a state. I laughed at him, "I'm going to get you."

I fell unconscious and didn't wake until the next day. Sam was sitting by my side with more food. When I woke up, I began to cry as he told me he loved me and I had made him do this to me. I turned my head away from him and again fell asleep. When I awoke that evening, I begged him to let me see my kids. He brought them to me. Pogie still had the handprint on his face. It had darkened and was no longer red. I could see that he was still very sick. I begged Sam to let me take him to the hospital. Sam would not allow me to take him because when the doctors saw Pogie's face they probably would discipline Sam or kick him out of the service. I told him that Pogie needed medical care. Sam said, "No one will see Pogie until his face healed." "Sooner or later you'll have to go back to work." "I told my boss that there was a family emergency." He wanted to know what had made me so mad to beat him like I did. I just looked at him. He told me Pogie had been wandering around and he hit him to get him to go back to bed. Come to find out though, Pogie was looking for his blankie. It was a blanket he always carried around with him to give him security. He had left it on the plane. O how I wished that I had bought two blankets at the time. I never realized that this, along with Nene being gone, would almost kill my child. I tried other blankets but it did no good. Children are very wise and they know what they want. I could feel my anger returning. I calmed myself because I would never be able to get my son to the hospital if I started again. I had to heal quickly so could Sam could return to work and I could get to the hospital with my son.

A week went by and soon Sam received a phone call. Sam said he would call them back. I could see the frustration on his face and sense the disappointment in his voice as he left the room and began to dress in his uniform. "Do not leave this room or I'll do something you'll never forget! "His threats meant nothing to me. All I can remember is that he took my purse with him. Not only did I lose my identification papers but also, I had no money. I didn't know where I was, how to call the base or even how to get there. I heard him walk away but as sneaky as Sam was, I wasn't going to take any chances. I went next door to be with my children and in an hour or so Sam returned. When he got back I was straightening the room and the children were watching television. Everything seemed fine with him but I could still tell he didn't trust me. Every day I looked into the mirror to see that my bruises were healing, as were Pogie's. I knew I would have no evidence once I got on base to the hospital.

When he left the next day to go to work, I went to the lobby and asked to phone the base. No one spoke English and I didn't know any Spanish. I went outside to see if I could remember which direction we had taken and if I could walk to the base. I could see nothing that looked like a base from outside so I went back to my room. I started to get frustrated as I paced back and forth in my room, trying to figure out how to get to the base. I was going crazy. I cried. I talked to myself. And deep inside I was screaming. Another day went by and I saw no results. Pogie was still very sick. When I heard Sam leave for work the next day, I pretended to be asleep and saw him leave the building. I watched at my window till Sam had driven away. I glanced over to see another GI looking under the hood of his car. I jumped up, put on my robe, not caring how I looked. I raced down the long hallway, hoping I could catch the GI before he drove away. I ran out of the hotel and sprinted up to the enlisted stranger just as he was about to get into his car. Begging him, I yelled, "Sir, please take my sick child, my children and I to the hospital." He looked at me with compassion. He said, "Yea! Sure!"

I ran back into the hotel, and dressed the kids as fast as I could. I carried them out to the car and away we went. I could not believe that I was free at last. As we were driving to the base we passed Sam on the road. Again he had sensed my vibes and knew that I was free, but he could not stop me this time. Once we got onto the base, the kind enlisted stranger dropped us off at the hospital. I wanted to hug him but was afraid he would think that I was crazy. I said my good-byes and thank-you's. I stopped and took a deep breath and grabbed my children by the hand. We entered the building. I immediately walked up to the receptionist and asked to see a doctor. They asked me for my ID but I told them that my husband had taken it with him to work. The young man stepped into the back of the receptionist's office to ask what should be done. His boss told him he would handle the situation. He walked out. "Miss Jackson." "Yeees!" "Miss Cynthia Jackson?" "Yes!" He replied, "We have been waiting for you for weeks. Please, Ma'am, come this way!"

I followed looking very surprised that he knew me. He led the kids and me to a back office, where a black, lady officer greeted me. Right away she introduced herself as, "Mrs. Bell." That's all I remember of her rank. Her name still rings out joy in my heart to this day. Mrs. Bell went on to tell of a night several weeks ago when she witnessed a child being knocked ten feet into the hallway by his father. She said she pounded on the door but no one would answer. She wanted to come to his rescue but was afraid that I would tell her to mind her own business. I understood. I realized how hard it was to press charges. Believe me, I knew. She went on to explain that she had filed a report and waited each day to see if I would come in to complain and if I did, she would have had her report on file as a witness. She informed everyone in the office that if I came in, direct me to her desk.

I hugged her and I started to cry. "Thank you. Thank you so very much, for once I have someone on my side." I told her everything that happened and how I was there for help. I told her that I had experienced years of abuse and how the Air Force always had covered it up and never came to my aid. I explained to her the circumstances of how I had been transferred to Spain. All I wanted now was to turn my furniture around and send it back to the United States. She tried to explain to me that this was a new Air Force and though they did not know how to deal with family matters or spousal abuse before, they currently were learning how. She

253

also said, "Now that you are on a base, the base commander will not condone nor will he tolerate this type of behavior." Miss Bell continued, "Now that you have given me the OK, I'll get the ball rolling by first calling his first sergeant." "I am still afraid of what he might do." Again she assured me, "Your husband may try to threaten you, but he cannot threaten the entire United States Air Force." I wanted to believe her, but I still felt very nervous. She asked, "Is there anything else you would like us to do?" "Yes." I told her. "You can help my children and I by getting us sent back to the States."

She was the first person in the United States Air Force that actually did something to help me. They ordered Sam to go to Child and Family Services' Classes, asking my support to get him through them. They felt that I too, needed counseling for the abuse that I had suffered. September and Pogie would also start getting counseling at that time. Hopefully, the counselor would help them to understand what type of person their father was and how to cope with him. I agreed, but only until Pogie was well, then I was going to leave. We started attending the counseling sessions, yet I was quite reluctant, because I felt that I really did not have a problem. My only "problem" was that I had a kind and forgiving heart. No one could ever say that I given up easily. I really felt sorry for Sam because I knew he was a very sick man and needed help.

When we started the counseling sessions Sam was very quiet and would not share anything with the group. He felt that the more he said, the more they would hang him out to dry. Every night he would return home and tell me how everyone in the counselor's room was sicker than him. He would laugh at the people in our group stating, "They're all a bunch of crazies." More and more each day, I recognized that I was dealing with a man that could not be cured.

The kids were in another room being counseled by a lady named, Miss Connie. She was the most beautiful woman I have ever met, not only did she have an outward beauty but she also had an inner beauty that I could only dream of having. She had given up her evenings to come sit and talk with innocent children, who were abused mentally or physically by their parents. After our session was over I would go pick up my kids only to hear them begging me to stay with Miss Connie. One evening she asked if the kids could all come over to her house. She spoke of the animals she had and how my kids and hers could get together and have lots of fun. The kids begged and begged. I told them, "Sure." We were welcomed to her house with fresh-baked cinnamon rolls, hot-baked yeast bread, and a hot cup of chocolate with marshmallows, of course. She was a regular little homemaker too. We had a wonderful time and didn't want to leave. But her husband had come home and I didn't want to intrude. When I left that evening I felt compelled to ask her about her church. I was afraid that she would preach against me leaving my husband. I wouldn't be in Spain very long, so there was little reason to make any friends. Again, Miss Connie asked the kids and I over for another visit. The kids were so excited about going to see the rabbits and hamsters and eating the fresh-baked pies and cakes. I tried to avoid asking her questions about the Lord even though I was dying to find out why this lady was so kind and generous. If I called in the middle of the night, she would drive over to get the children and me. Whatever I needed for the kids and I, Miss Connie or someone from her church would come to our rescue. One evening I finally decided to pop the question. She asked me to study with her and learn about their church. I decided to join them and was glad I did. I learned a lot that night. September and I were again baptized into the True Church for the remission of our sins. But even though I did it right this time, I still was not going back to Sam.

During the next counseling session, a woman was talking about killing her cat. She said the kitten continually would jump at her and bite her, but trying to stop the animal's behavior herself did not help. One day it became too much for her to bear and she threw the kitten up against the wall. She did so, continually, until the kitten died. I couldn't understand why I reacted as I did, but I broke out into laughter. I never thought it was funny but all the tension bottled up inside of me seemed to find its way out in the form of laughter. I did everything I could to stop laughing, but I couldn't. The woman said that because she wanted to have a baby, her actions made her think about what she might do to her child. I could tell that my laughter was upsetting her terribly. But I could not stop. They sent me out of the room. Sam thought I was the worst person in the world for making fun of her actions. I certainly did not laugh on purpose, but it occurred to me that if the cat thought it would die that day, it obviously would have left her feet alone. The laughter was unstoppable and I was almost in hysterics.

The therapist followed me into the hallway and asked me if I thought it was funny when someone got hurt. I told him that I had never encountered myself doing such a thing before. I was always the one to go to the extreme to help anyone who was hurt or in any pain. He explained that because the cat was being treated cruelly, my mind would not allow me to accept it. "This type of behavior," he said, "is a typical reaction to cover up the cruelty or pain that a person is going through." He also thought it was my way of getting her to avoid taking it seriously, to help her realize that it was a cat and not her own baby. Maybe she would realize that she never would do such a thing to a child. Everyone in the room got quiet and serious. The last thing I wanted was to start to cry over this. I had been through so much in my life and experienced so much cruelty. It was hard for me to accept that someone could be so upset over a cat. I didn't remain in the class much longer.

We moved to a little cottage in the hills of Zaragoza, Spain. It was such a peaceful dwelling in an area with neighbors that were very accommodating and in general, great people. The villa was about 15 miles from the military base, at the top of a mountain that always had proven an ordeal to navigate. We lived next door to an elderly couple that the children and I learned to love. I was surprised when September would go to the fence and speak with these two people. It had been a long time since she spoke to anyone, and not knowing Spanish, she still was able to communicate with them. Sam was no longer going to classes and continued beating us. Now he was using wires that resulted in bad cuts. Since he was no longer going to the classes I decided it was now time for me to make my escape. Being an intelligent man, Sam had convinced the therapists that he understood why he abused his family and that he would no longer do it anymore. He gave them the exact response that they wanted to release him from the counseling sessions, by admitting that he was not "a good man."

As for me, I had already set up a moving date and was getting my belongings ready. I had pretty much accepted that my husband was never going to change. All the talking in the world could not sway my decision to leave him. The only thing Sam was interested in at this point was his job and his career. I had now made up my mind that I didn't need scripture for me to leave. His infidelity was all I needed in order to leave him. As soon as I made enough money I would get a divorce.

# Chapter 30

I spoke with the Colonel who in turn arranged for all of my furniture to be packed up. Sam of course went through his long, drawn-out speech of how he loved me and didn't want me to go. I told him that if he had stayed and continued the therapy I would have reconsidered, but now there was no way. There was absolutely nothing in this world that he could do to keep me in Spain.

When I arrived back in Texas, Anna Mae welcomed me with open arms, but I was told that I had to get my own place in a month and take the children with me. My father on the other hand told me he would help me get a car, so this was the second car he helped me with. My little red Mustang had been sold when we moved to the Philippines and now almost all of my savings went into the new car. Since all my money was gone, he assured me that I would not have to move out right away. He would give me time to get a job and get back on my feet. But Anna Mae meant business. I bought a Toyota, which was the best little car I ever had. I looked for a job every day, knowing that the kids could not tolerate Anna Mae's beatings and yelling for long. Although I looked for a place to live, no one was interested in renting to a woman with three children. I thought that there should be a law against this type of prejudice. Pogie and Camille were doing well at this time and September showed signs of relief at being separated from their father. Even though my mother was not all sunshine and joy, they started playing, going to school and meeting new friends. I kept them off of their grandmother's nerves as often as possible.

I soon found a church that we enjoyed attending. The church helped me out with gas money and cash to get around and find a job. Of course, I refused to tell Anna Mae because she did not like me taking charity from anyone. This highly embarrassed Miss White. She wouldn't hear of it. One day while in church the preacher approached me and asked if my husband would be joining us for church. I explained that I was separated from my husband and was seeking a divorce. My only problem was I needed Biblical proof to justify it. I knew I did, because Sam had committed adultery several times, but I still wanted to be sure I was justified. I told him about all the abuse, the infidelity and how the children were suffering the most. The preacher asked me into his office where he told me, "Let me show you the Scripture you've been looking for." I was so excited that I almost wanted to cry, especially since, at that point, I had been looking for six years. I stepped into his office and we both took out our Bibles and he gave me the Scripture, Matthews 19:6. I read it to myself then read it again out loud, "What therefore God hath joined together, let no man put asunder." I told him, "I don't get it." He asked, "Do you believe that God brought you and your husband together?" "Yes." "Think about it. Were you and your husband saved and in the Lord when you came together." "No, I was totally against God and Sam definitely was not in God." "So then it was man that put you together and man who can put you asunder."

He went on to explain that if we were put together by God, then Sam would have treated me like Jesus treated the church, and Jesus loved the church so much that he died for it. And I, of course, would have respected and given him honor. Adultery certainly gave me the right to divorce Sam. In fact, I had several grounds to stand on and I ultimately felt confident to do what I had to do for survival. I agreed with him. Leaving his office that day, I decided that I would work hard and save enough money so that I could finally get a divorce.

Miss Meany told me that I had one week to find a place to live. Finding a new job was easy. I had accepted a job at Domino's Pizza as a manager trainee, and would eventually manage my own store. I looked everywhere for a place to live and finally found a little place on the other side of town. At home, I was sweating all the way to the end. I finally found an apartment. The apartment I found was very expensive and would leave little money to live on. It was a very nice-looking place. When I went down to pay my first month's rent the people in the office warned me that there was a man that lived there that looked like death. They laughed and went on to explain that he would spread manure on his walls, and that there was nothing they could do because he had signed a lease when the buildings were first built, and in the old contract he could stay forever. No matter what he did that wasn't to their liking they remained unable to do anything. Of course, I thought they were exaggerating. But who cared? I needed a place and didn't care if King Kong stayed there, as long as my children and I had a home and were safe—away from Sam.

I also had another problem. I had so much furniture I didn't know what to do. I purchased a metal shed and put it in my back yard. It came completely unassembled. September, Pogie and I began the long process of putting it together ourselves. As we opened the box, we pulled out five bags of assembly accessories. It seemed like there were millions of screws, nuts, and bolts. Planning to put a lot of effort into this shed, we began working and continued through the entire day. September held the bolts on the inside as I screwed in nuts from the other side. By the end of the day, it looked like three-quarters of the accessories were still left and we questioned if we'd ever complete our job. It seemed to me that we would never need to use all the nuts and bolts furnished with the shed, so we started to put in every other one, thinking that it would be sturdy enough if we used less. We put on the walls and roof and when we completed our task by the end of the next day, the children were running around excitedly bringing in the yard implements, bikes, and lawn mower.

About a month went by and I noticed that the shed was sagging. I questioned the children if they had been jumping on the roof, or leaning on the shed. They agreed that it looked lopsided. The bikes were leaning against the inner wall, so we moved them but by the next day, the shed was leaning the other way. The subsequent month, I found rusted bolts on the ground around the shed. I told the children that I thought they were indeed playing around the shed or on top to make it lean and pop the bolts.

Finally, I decided to purchase another shed, so I advertised the old one for sale. A gentleman looked at it and first thing he said was, "Do you have the rest of the bolts for it?" I told him that there were additional bolts left over, but I didn't know where they were. He could probably buy more. He replied that the ones included in the kit were most likely specialized for the shed and he would not entertain thoughts of paying $100 for this leaning building. "Proper bolts may not even be available to repair the shed." He told me to trash the shed after I offered to sell it to him for $25. He told me that he would be taking a problem off my hands and he wasn't interested in my proposition. Another month went by and the shed finally collapsed. I asked the children to jump up and down on the remainder of it so I could put the pieces in the trash.

This story typifies the structure of a good marriage as well as a building lesson. The bolts represent all the pieces that are necessary to build a good marriage. If we go into marriage trying to take shortcuts or leave out all the parts, it will not stay together or be truly binding. God gave us a foundation upon which to build each and every marriage, but the firm foundation is only a beginning. The inside of the shed signifies all the things we own: our possessions, what experiences we have in our lives, the things we share and everything we do to pull a marriage together. Even our children become part of the contents of the shed. The shed protects everything. It could represent a man and a woman who have a solid foundation upon which they build to create a strong family unit. If each bolt is not in its proper place and the shed is placed incorrectly on its foundation, there is little to hold it together in times of instability.

A marriage needs to be nurtured to grow. Each spouse needs to stay within his or her means, yet do special things for each other. They share the responsibilities of the home together, and in turn take care of one another, making sure that the other is fed, cared for, and pampered in any way they can afford. Each has their own responsibilities to continue building the marriage on the foundation given them. There appears a point of no return in a marriage that starts to fall apart when some bolts have been left out. Upkeep must be done every day. Buying a new shed is like looking for another spouse, which could carry with it encumbrances from previous marriages. If the original marriage could have been salvaged before that point of no return, it would be the strongest and most fulfilling one possible. The collapse of the shed signifies a divorce. At that point, nothing can be done to rebuild.

We need the Lord in our lives to keep the firm foundation strong. Without Him, we cannot do it alone. Marriage is building together a firm foundation. We must work towards a healthy marriage every day by going to church, praying together, and letting the Lord teach us. Let us structure our lives according to His plan.

# Chapter 31

The children were very accepting of plain rice and eating the best that I could afford. My sister and her husband would baby-sit occasionally, but they soon grew tired of doing it for me. I worked delivering pizzas until I soon was promoted to manager. I was very excited about this accomplishment until I found out that the job was on the other side of town, approximately 30 miles from home. Never have I worked nor been that far from my children and I was scared. I normally tried to be no more than 5 miles away at the most, but I was given the opportunity to manage my own restaurant where I would earn $90 per day. I could not pass up the opportunity of being able to feed my children real food. The man I worked for was very prejudiced. He was so prejudice that he couldn't even face me. He would often walk into my store and tell me how I should consider myself lucky, because if it were not for the white man we would be out picking cotton in a field somewhere. He also signed our paychecks, "777," because he said he was better than the Antichrist.

I would just laugh at him because I was too intelligent to stoop to his level and argue with him. I knew that I made him a lot of money and he kept giving me bonus after bonus, with at least three pay raises in two months. He used to tell me I was the best "nigga women" that ever worked for him. I used to like how he always ended his conversations with, "…You know I like you." I would smile when he walked out the door and say, "Lord, thank you, for that poor man," for something had to go wrong in his life for him to be so ignorant. Supporting my children on this salary would surely make life simpler, giving them what I felt they needed.

Next, I required a baby-sitter because in the State of Texas it was illegal for your children under the age of 12 to be left alone. September was only eleven at the time. So my sister Renee and her husband offered to help watch the kids, but soon problems got in the way. So I found a "sit-at-home mom," who lived in the same complex. She agreed that for a nominal fee, she would care for the younger two during the day while I worked. That lasted for about two weeks. One day coming home from work, I found my children in the middle of the street playing with their toys. It seemed that I had hired a baby-sitter that was far from responsible. Upon firing her, I told my eleven-year-old daughter that she would have to be responsible for caring for two-year-old Camille and six-year-old Pogie. Even knowing the consequences, I felt there was no other choice. I could not quit my ninety-dollar-a-day job, so I had to find a way. I begged September to be careful and not let the children get into any trouble.

Things were going pretty smooth except that I would occasionally come home and find the doors unlocked or the house in a wreck. But I counted my blessings. One late night when traveling home from work I stopped to get my mail. I was walking along singing a song. I strolled around the corner of the little post office that housed the mail. Not suspecting anyone to be out that late at night, I ran into what I would consider the most hideous creature I had ever seen in my life. I screamed so loud that I'm sure I woke up the whole neighborhood! All the hair on my body stood up. I looked like Larry, Moe and Curly of "The Three Stooges" or Buckwheat from "The Little Rascals." After he saw me, I'm sure it scared him to death with my loud scream. He disappeared into the night. I'm surprised that my hair did not turn completely white.

Finally I had met the man that the ladies in the office had told me about. Only their description of him was nowhere near what he really looked like. He was Jason, Freddy Kuger, Micheal Myers and "The Night of the Living

Dead" all rolled up in one. His skin was white and all the hair on his body, including his facial hairs, was white too. He walked with a slight limp. I trembled in fear as I stood there in complete shock. I couldn't even move I was so scared. He ran off into the night somewhere that I'm sure he felt safe from me. I grabbed my heart to see if it was still in my chest. As tears ran down my face I thought about suing the landlord but I had no leg to stand on, considering that I had been warned. I'm sure that I scared the man as much as he scared me, or maybe he was used to this type of treatment? But after it was all over I must admit that I felt sorry for him. I could now see why he was hiding. He had to live in darkness and could never come out. His family had hidden him away from society and the cruel people who were inconsiderate of his monstrosity, his hunchback and disfigurement. From that night forward I would run from my car into the house if I got home late. And I only went to my post office box in the daylight.

September was doing real well as far as taking care of the children until one evening around midnight. September called me at work and in the background I heard a banging. It sounded like someone was pounding on the wall with a chair. September was hysterical and was screaming, "Help me, Mommy, and help me! Some boys are trying to break into the house and hurt me!" At the time I had a very trustworthy man working for me named Russ, I told him to put the money into a drawer and lock up for me. Knowing that he would handle what needed to be done, I entrusted him with the store and ran out to help my daughter. Speeding through town, I didn't care if the police chased me. I just needed to get to my children as fast as I could. I even thought it would be a good idea for the police to chase me so that they could help me if I needed it when I got there. I didn't even care that they found an eleven-year-old child baby-sitting. By then, all I cared about was the safety of my children who were so dear to me.

I arrived and found that the door had been beaten. There were indentations that looked like someone had beaten the door with a log. I walked in, grabbed my daughter and comforted her. My sister arrived at that same moment and we began our search for the boys, knowing that they could not be far. We found a tent and knew that they must be there. My sister found one boy crawling out the back of the tent and I entered into the front. By now we were both in the tent with the boys. I grabbed one of them by the chest and told him that if he <u>ever</u> did anything like that again, I would spank them myself and drag them both to their parents. They were pleading with us not to tell their parents and to let them go. They promised never to do anything like that again.

I continued to work and told my daughter to keep the doors locked and stay inside at all times. Neighbors would complain that they saw the children parading outside the house nude and playing with fire on the balcony. One day I arrived to find all the doors and the sliding window wide open with the curtains flying in the breeze. This time I expected to find all of my children dead. I prayed to the Lord, promising that if my children were alive, I would find them proper care while I worked. I found them sleeping, with all the lights on and the house in shambles. Finally, I realized that September was neither old enough nor responsible enough to care for my two active children. If need be, I would even go back to Sam. I was between a rock and a hard place, so I called my husband. Sam said he would come to the States to pick me up but noted that he would not take the children back to Spain. He told me that he didn't want them. Sam only wanted me, and that hurt me down to my soul. I remembered one evening in the Philippines, in one of our Bible Studies. We were all asked what we would be willing to go to hell for. Sam's reply to this was that he would only die and go to hell for his wife. There it was, right in front of me. Sam didn't want his children then, either. I certainly would never die and go to hell for him. He had a sick kind of love, being possessed by me. He worshipped and idolized me. I could not imagine wanting to die for anyone but the Lord. I preferred to live and teach my children right from wrong and the love of the Lord, rather than die for anyone.

The only other choice was to go back to my husband and the continual beatings for all of us. At least until September turned 12--by that time I would have enough money to divorce Sam without jeopardizing my children's lives. September begged me not to return to him. I told her that she had put us into a situation from which there was no escape. It took me a week to debate this issue. I went to my boss and asked him to put someone in my store to take care of it until I made a decision. He didn't like this of course, and gave me till the end of the week. O how I wished my mother only had one personality and that was Anna! Someone to help me in my time of need. I knew if I begged Sam (which is what I had to do to go back to him) that I was going to have to give up everything I had fought so hard for. I had nowhere to turn.

One night as I sat in my room crying, I slowly picked up the phone and called Sam. "Sam, will you please help me?" I hated each and every word that came out of my mouth. "You know, Kaye, if I come and get you guys...," and I knew by the tone I was in trouble, "there will be stipulations." "Like what, Sam?" "Sex. You will not deny me sex at all, any time I want it, even when I beat the kids and I will beat them. You will not do anything. "I put my hand up to my mouth as I started to cry silently. Putting my head back I said, "Oh God, please save me from this." Then he went on to say, "And you will do whatever I tell you to do. If I don't want you to be with the church or with your friends, you won't be." He continued giving me demands and I kept telling myself, it's only for six months. Six months and September will be 12. I could tell that Sam was gloating on the phone as he detailed all of his demands. His conversation faded as I thought more and more about what I would have to do. I could not believe I was begging the father of my children to help us. Suddenly he said, "I will be there this weekend." I had a week to get all my plans in order.

When Sam got off the plane I could see the smirk on his face as he approached. I had already counseled the kids and told them to smile and greet their daddy. I had also told them that from now on they would have to be on their best behavior because there was nothing I could do to help them. As Sam approached us, the children's faces went from frowns to half-smiles. Looking at them I said, "Is that the best you guys can do? You're going to have to do better. Please don't make this man mad already. Please, children?" He walked up and hugged me. We went back to my apartment where we continued to pack. September tried to avoid him completely. As soon as we finished packing Sam gathered the kids together and started yelling and telling them what they would and would not do. I walked up to the front room to watch, when Sam told me to go back into my room.

I felt so afraid. Maybe I made the wrong decision? Maybe I should have quit and went on Welfare? Maybe, I should have just taken all of our own lives. Anything would have been better then this. Inside, I felt that I was going to regret my decision. But I kept telling myself that everything was going to be all right. When we went to bed I took forever getting ready and I drank beer after beer hoping to get stoned enough that I wouldn't even notice. It worked, but for how long?

# Chapter 32

We went back to the little cottage in the hills of Zaragoza, Spain. I already had pictured how our lives were going to be. But nothing prepared me for what I would encounter. As we put our things away and got settled in, Sam returned to work. The old couple next door told me about the women Sam had up to the house, but at that time I really didn't care. "Six months, you only have six months! You can do this." After returning to Spain I went into a deep depression. I didn't come out of my room. I shut the storm shutters and stayed there, only to coming out to fix the kids something to eat. That's all I was allowed to do with my kid.

Sam wanted them nowhere near me. He just wanted me at his beck and call whenever he needed me in the bedroom. I felt like a whore, only I wasn't getting paid. When Sam would leave, the kids and I would play, but as soon as he drove up we knew to go back to our places--them to their rooms and me back to bed. I must admit though, the kids had not had a beating in a long time or so I thought, until one day while asleep I heard a scream. It was my baby girl. I ran out of the room only to find September and Pogie sitting on the couch scared to death. I asked them, "Where is Camille?" They would not answer me they were so scared. I just looked at them as they sat there trembling. I heard another scream and I ran outside. Following the sounds I heard coming from the closed garage. I lifted up the garage and there Sam was beating my child with a belt that had metal spikes. I grabbed my baby and took her into my arms. Sam kept screaming, "Kaye, go back into the house. You promised me you would not interfere."

"You are crazy," I screamed, "you're crazy!" as I took Camille back into the house with her sister and brother. Now I knew why things had been going so great for the last three months. Sam was taking the kids out into the hot garage and beating them to keep me from hearing and coming to their rescue. He warned them that if they told me

271

he would kill them. After I brought Camille into the house Sam came in and called my two oldest to go outside because he thought they woke me up and told me. I told him to leave them alone. "I heard Camille's screams, that's how I knew you were beating her. They said nothing to me." He didn't believe me. He kept yelling for them to go out into the garage.

"You're going have to kill me this day, but you're not going to touch my kids."

He yelled, "That's it, that's it!"

"Sam, what are you going to do, kill us all, because that's what you're going to have to do?"

"Get your bags packed, you're going back to the United States."

"You pack them! We aren't going anywhere!

I called Miss Connie whom I had not seen in a month and asked her to come over and get us. Sam went to the garage to smoke a joint. Thank goodness again, for the marijuana. It saved our lives. When I got home that night after visiting with Miss Connie I found Sam sitting on the couch crying. The ball was once again in my court. I demanded that he permit me to get a job, and I also wanted to return to church. He agreed. Then he went on and on about how terrible he was. I couldn't do anything but hold my sick husband and feel sorry for him. For Sam to have grabbed Camille was surprising because Camille was Sam's little "star", his "angel." She sang all the time and was a very happy baby. He always treated her very special. So for him to grab her I knew he had to be having a lot of problems. I guessed it was because we were not there because we wanted to be, but because we had nowhere else to go. He wanted us to love him and to wish to be there, and yet we were unable. He did not know how to treat us. What I didn't understand about my husband was why he refused to seek some kind of help to teach him how to be a good husband and father.

Things went well for months as Sam continued to smoke dope and we stayed out of his way. Most of the time the kids and I stayed at Miss Connie's or church. I found a job on base where I saved money.

The members of the church asked me if I could have a picnic at my home. They wanted to get to know Sam and one day get him to return to church. But knowing how Sam would react caused me some concern, and to be honest, I was scared. Connie convinced me that Sam wouldn't start anything since he would see that everyone there was a good Christian and it would prevent him from causing any trouble. I looked at her, "I don't think it will work out as you hope," but I was willing to try. The church members were bringing various dishes and I would prepare the meats.

I was extremely nervous as I prepared the food and felt I needed to drink a beer to calm myself, thinking that all hell would break loose at any moment. We had a great time, singing and having fun. We watched the children run all over our yard, which was the size of a football field. I could see Sam staring at September and Pogie. They were simply having fun, as children do, but Sam felt that September was being hardheaded and told me that the party would have to end. We were just getting ready to eat but I had to tell them that the party was over. In front of the church members, Sam grabbed September and began to beat her and he herded both her and Pogie into the house. Sometime during the day he told them to do something for him and they had ignored him while they played. His anger had started to build. He grabbed me like he was going to beat me also and Connie intervened, saying, "We're all gonna leave."

I told them, "Take all the food."

Sam said, "Take only what you brought to the picnic."

I hugged Miss Connie and they all went home, leaving behind what they had provided.

Again we were not allowed to associate with the members of the Church. Sam thought that they were influencing September and I not to listen to what he told us to do. But I was not going to agree with him. We had always felt this telepathy between us, which I had actually taught him. There were times I knew that his car had broken down on the side of the road and he told me with his mind to come and get him, even describing to me where he was. I would put the kids into the car and drive to his exact location. The children thought this was amazing. I had to learn how to stop him from reading my thoughts because one day we sneaked off to Miss Connie's house, as she was baking bread for us. We were having a wonderful time as always. Sam appeared at her door, pushing me out of her house. He knocked me into the gravel and shoved the children into his car, while all the while planning to beat us when we got home. Arriving home he began beating me all over the front room and knocking me over chairs. This was the first instance where my children jumped to my side to rescue me. My daughter screamed, "Mommy, Mommy!" My son grabbed his father's pants and began kicking Sam over and over and pounding his little fists on him. My husband picked up Pogie by his shirt and yelled, "I'm going to kill you!" As Sam threw Pogie across the room, I screamed, "Get into your room, now!" Sam continued to strike me through the night, and I could only think about my choices. I had none, having lost the ability to go home to my mom or anything else for that matter. It was impossible. I was stuck in my situation.

I must admit, there was one thing different about this beating. I took it like I had never taken a beating

before. I didn't cry. In fact I got up, went to the mirror and cleaned up my face. And once I had stopped the bleeding, I got ready for bed. Straightening my back and standing tall, I marched into my children's room to kiss them goodnight. Pogie asked, "Mommy, are you OK?"
"Yes, baby, I'm all right."

There was no sense in crying, for my tears had all dried up. I wasn't there long enough to feel sorry for myself. But I knew that our relationship was over, it was just a matter of time until I would be out of his life for good. The hits were not painful anymore. The only thing that hurt now was when he grabbed my children, because I didn't want this to scar them psychologically for life. Soon I would free them from their father. Sam went out to smoke his joint. I went to bed.

Sam and his friend had been trying to build a car from parts of three other autos. Sam had parked on our lawn. One morning September and I tried to push-start the car for him. He was late for work and hitched a ride to the base. September and I pushed the car back into the garage. Later that day I felt Sam trying to communicate through my mind for me to pick him up from work.

With rollers still in my hair, I planned to start our evening's dinner. Not only did we need fresh, bottled water for our three children, but we were also completely out of propane for cooking. Normally my husband would arrive home tired, so I decided to save him the trouble of going back to the base to replenish our supply of water and propane. I'd run to the base myself.

First on the agenda was to choose a running vehicle. I chose to drive the one parked in front of the garage and try again to start it. As always, the children had to give me a push down the hill to get me started. I took off down the mountain. This time the car started and I checked on them in the rearview mirror and waved goodbye. Once I made sure they were inside the fence surrounding the house, I was on my way.

I noticed a sign on the side of the road stating that the maximum speed was 80 km and the minimum speed was 50. I remember thinking, "Why is it so important to know the minimum speed?" but continued to sing a little tune to myself, "This Is The Day That The Lord Has Made." I had driven this road many times to take my husband to work and in the past and I had seen many wreckers pulling cars up that had gone over the cliff over thousands of feet down, from out of the ravine. Dead bodies and ambulances were common sights when cars were hauled out. Approaching a tunnel that curved into the mountain and would eventually bring me out to cliffs on both sides of the road, I began slowing down just a bit to keep control of the vehicle. As I was about to exit the tunnel, I noticed a van in front of me going very slowly. My efforts to slow down, as we were both close to exiting the tunnel, were not enough and it was too late to avoid the van. I knew in my heart that what was about to ensue was not good. Closing in on his bumper, I noticed three small children playing in the back of his van. In only a matter of seconds I had to make a choice that would affect the lives of those innocent children, their driver, and me. If I hit the van, its occupants would go over the cliff, but if I chose to avoid it, my chances of survival would be slim.

Instantaneously, I turned the car into oncoming traffic hoping to go around it, but another auto came at me head on. Turning the wheel sharply, my car began to roll over and over and over, carrying me with it down over the steep cliff with sides dropping over a mile downward. My thoughts centered on plummeting to my death when I miraculously landed safely onto a small outcropping, just large enough to hold my car. It seemed as if the Lord's hand had reached out and caught me. Unbelievably, the car was squashed flat but I had survived. I remember saying, "Why, Lord, did you not take me? Why did you place this small piece of land here to catch me as I fell?"

Moments later a man knocked on my window, yelling something in Spanish that I interpreted to be whether or not I was all right. Signaling to him that I was okay, I looked around to find that my car was smashed in half, upside down, and surrounded by propane and water bottles, yet I was fine. Thanks to forgetting to remove my hair rollers, my head was cushioned from hitting the windshield. In my hurry to leave home, I had forgotten to wear my seatbelt. If I had used it, I would have been hanging upside down. The Lord was truly watching out for me on this day. Not much later, another gentleman arrived and both worked to pry open the jammed door and extract me. Since their efforts were unsuccessful, they broke the window with a mallet someone had provided. They pulled me through the open window to safety. At that moment I realized that my leg was hurt. Limping up to the top of the hill, I was greeted by clapping. The passersby were all happy to see that I was alive! (In Spain it is against the law to pass an accident scene without helping.) I felt that I should curtsey. I thanked them, smiled, and waved to the crowd as they helped me to the ambulance that was waiting for me.

In the ambulance, the attendants were asking me all kinds of questions that I could not understand. I wished so badly that I was fluent in Spanish so that I could've thanked them for treating me so nicely. Not long after reaching the hospital, the staff contacted my husband to take me home. I was sitting on a gurney when Sam arrived, and sadness entered my heart. I said, "Lord, why didn't you take me? I don't want to return to this mean and evil man, just to be beaten again." Sam helped me down from the table and assisted me to the car. I explained to him what had happened. His only comments revolved around subjects like wrecking someone else's borrowed car, possible fines, and how we were going to get out of this situation. He didn't care what happened or if I were hurt, his thoughts were on the financial consequences of the accident. Again, I asked, "Why me?" Right now I could be sitting in my Holy Father's lap, thanking Him for taking me Home.

Pulling into the drive of the villa, my three precious children ran to the car calling, "Mommy, are you OK?" Their dad came around to my side of the car and yelled for them to get back, as I tried to climb out of the car. I leaned back on the car to gain my balance as I hugged each of them, grabbed my crutches, and headed towards the house. I realized that this and this alone was why I must stay here to endure. Entrusted with these three beloved children, I appreciated that I was the only one to raise them and free them from their father. It was then that I knew that my leaving would give me peace, but place my children in the worst possible position with their father. Seeing my children through this ordeal of everyday life was the only thing that sustained my sanity. I cried and looked up to the heavens, "Thank you, Father, for bringing me back home to my babies."

Later, I was asked if I were scared. My answer was that I knew that the Lord was going to reach down and scoop me up with the palm of his hand, where he had engraved my name (Isaiah 49:15,16), and take me straight into heaven. With a big smile on His face, He would welcome me home.

# Chapter 33

Finally the day came when Sam received orders to move to another base, which was in St. Louis, Illinois. I was very pleased to learn that Miss Connie also was to be stationed there. We stopped to visit his mom in New York. Sam continued flying on to the base in Illinois and the children and I went to visit my mother prior to moving to our new home. My dad had kept my car and used it to travel to and from work while I was gone and I was glad that it had been useful to him. He had done so much for me. I felt that finally I was returning his favors. The children and I had a great time traveling to what I thought had been our destination, Illinois. I don't know where I got the idea, but I was headed to Champagne, Illinois. The kids wrote little notes for truck drivers to read and entertained themselves getting the truckers to honk their air horns as we drove. Upon pulling over at a truck stop, a truck driver came up to us and told me how he enjoyed the notes my children had held up. He said to follow him and he would help me reach Illinois safely. Hearing that he would guide us to the base, we knew we would be safe through the night. We played little follow-the-leader games with him, and as he went off in another direction, we continued to the base where I thought we should go.

I called Miss Connie and asked her how to get to her house when she informed me I had gone to the wrong base. She then gave me the directions to the correct base. The children were so tired, they whined about my mistake. I told them they should be happy, at least we had fun. Looking at their frowns, I told them that Mother had taken the scenic route. They all said, "Sure, Mama." We all laughed and began to sing Christian songs together and finally arrived at Miss Connie's house. Sam's arrival once we got to Miss Connie's place only brought sadness to the children's faces. We gathered our bags and went to our new home on the base.

At first, things went well. We joined a church there and Sam was a good husband on occasion. Not long after, he went back to his old tricks. I started a new job on base and when I would get home my children would tell me their father had threatened to beat them if they told me what he had done that day. They shared precious little information with me. Most of the time when I arrived home, the children were in bed and the next morning things seemed fine, so I had no idea what had happened the night before. When I worked nights Sam would appear at the club, again watching me, checking to see if I were cheating on him. His jealously was growing worse. I had to work hard to save money to get away. Soon, I told myself, real soon.

Sam was spending a lot of time in New York. I thought it was rather odd, but I didn't make a big ordeal of it. The kids and I thoroughly enjoyed his absences. Sam left me a phone number of the friend's house where he was staying. I didn't have to call him except once just to make sure he was still there. The kids and I did want him to pay us a surprise visit. We were scared he would find out how much fun we were having while he was gone. I was busy seeing a lawyer and taking all the information in our file drawer to him, to make sure that I would receive my share of any monies due me from any policies that I could collect on. My lawyer was a great attorney. He helped me out tremendously with information that I needed to know to get what I deserved from my divorce. After telling him some of the stories of my past, I could see he felt sorry for me and wanted me to take Sam for everything he had, including the kitchen sink.

Once Sam returned he heard that I had seen a lawyer. Sam became very violent so I took the kids, packed up the car and went to a shelter. When we entered the shelter, the lady there told us we could stay in the shelter only three days. I told her I was planning on leaving my husband and all I needed was a place to stay long enough to get my own apartment. I told her that I had some money saved. I related to her that I had to get away from the violence once and for all because my children were starting to show signs of mental problems from all of the abuse. She told me she was sorry but there was nothing the shelter could do. I had three days to find somewhere to go. So I went back home. Sam was acting rather strange when we returned. I couldn't put my hands on it but I knew he was up to something.

One evening Miss Connie called me at my job. She told me that September was at her house and was crying hysterically. I left work and went over to Miss Connie's house only to find September very upset. Her dad had threatened to beat her so she ran out the door and down the middle of the street, screaming at the top of her lungs that she was going to kill him. After calming her down, Miss Connie sent her out to play with the other kids. I sat at the table thinking about what I was going to do next. Miss Connie walked back into the kitchen and sat down.

"Cynthia, I know how proud you are and how you won't accept someone helping you, but please allow my husband and me to help. If you walk today, Rick and I will help you with food, your rent, your utilities, anything you need, just please leave Sam today. September can't take anymore, she is about to crack. Please, Cynthia, listen to me. She can't take much more. Please think about your children."

"I can't put all my responsibilities onto you and your husband."

Connie begged, "We would not have suggested it if we were incapable of helping you and the kids."

"I don't know, Connie? I need to think about it. It's just too much to ask you both."

"OK! You think about it, and give us a call and we'll come over and pack up you and the kids. You guys can stay here until you find your own place and no matter what your needs are, we will help."

We hugged and then I left. This touched me so much I went speechless. I could not believe that for once someone reached out their hands to set the kids and I free. Miss Connie offered my children and me peace. Finally I could come out of my White Room. I knew that Jesus had sent Miss Connie into my life to set me free.

Although I would be free, I still couldn't help but think that outside of my White Room somewhere, someone else was lurking, waiting to hurt me. Should I come out? Was it safe now?

I went back to work the next day still thinking about the proposition that Miss Connie had given me. I decided that I would still wait until I saved enough money. That night when I got home from work I walked in to kiss the kids "good night" when Sam came into their room. He said that he had something important to tell me. When I got to our room he told me he was going out of town again. I found it strange that he was making a big deal of going out of town when he had never cared to tell me before. Listening to him I just got ready for bed.

The next morning after Sam left for work I woke up the kids and told them to get ready for school. I went into the kitchen to start their breakfast. Chewing on a piece of bacon

I yelled for the kids to hurry up. "I'm not taking you to school if you miss the bus!" First September walked in and looked at me as if she had something on her mind. Glancing at her, I walked over to the television and turned it on. On TV the newscasters were interviewing prisoners. Camille came in next, and hopping up into her chair, she began to eat breakfast. Shortly afterwards, Pogie followed. He walked over to the refrigerator, took out some milk and walked over to the table and sat down. I told the kids that I was going to ask my boss if I could start working days so I could be home with them at night. The kids did not reply. I asked them, "Aren't you happy that Mom is going to be home with you at night?" Still not answering me, I asked them, "What's wrong?"

Pogie got up to take his plate to the sink and when he turned his head toward me, I noticed that he had ripped out all the hair on the right side of his head. I stared, as blood stained his head. My mouth dropped open. I asked him, "What happened to your hair?" He wouldn't reply so I asked him again, "Pogie, tell Mommy what happened to your head?"

"Daddy told me last night that he was gonna beat me today. I figured if I ripped all of my hair out of my head Daddy wouldn't beat me."

Suddenly I focused on one of the prisoners on T.V. that I had noticed crying. He said that he had beaten his wife and children for ten years. He never saw his children's tears. His wife noticed the children crying one day and grabbed her children on the spot and left. It was then that she realized that the children could not take the abuse anymore. They had been crying during the entire ten years, but he never saw their tears on the outside or on the inside. He continued to say that all he ever saw was red when he would beat them. I remembered Sam telling me the same thing as I

283

focused back on Pogie. He stood in front of me with tears in his little eyes. I could tell that he, as well as September, could not take any more abuse. It was time for me to go. I stood up, went straight to the phone, and called Miss Connie. Connie and her husband, Rick, came to the house that day and we discussed what I needed to do.

While Sam was still at work we filled up Rick's truck with my belongings, and moved to a little town named New Baden. Sam did not know of our whereabouts for a while. He had moved himself. He lost his base housing privileges since his family was no longer with him. Every time a court appearance for the divorce came up, he did not appear. I pleaded with him to settle, but there were things in the house that he wanted. He didn't even care to discuss the divorce. I again felt that he was trying to run my life. But I was not going to allow him to do it this time. Finally, I decided to let him have everything he wanted in return for my freedom.

He appeared in the courtroom and told the judge that he loved me and would not agree to the divorce. My reply was the same each time: "I want a divorce." He fought to keep me from receiving alimony and won, but he had to pay child support and give up some of his retirement benefits. The lawyer insisted that I receive 34% while Sam wanted to give me 10% of his pension. I was so tired and didn't want to fight. My lawyer continually told me to keep fighting because I would regret it later if I gave up, plus there was no question that I deserved something substantial for all the abuse I had taken. When the judge granted our divorce, I was standing up in front of the bench. Finally, the judge decided that I was to receive one-third of Sam's pension. The judge hit his gavel and pronounced us, "Divorced." I will never forget the complete feeling of relief that washed over me. Sam looked at me as I left the courtroom and said, "I guess you're satisfied now." I didn't even look at him, ignoring him as I walked out of the building and to my car. I did not want to talk to anyone. I even told my lawyer that I would discuss any other remaining matters with him later. Sam followed me out to my car. He asked me if I wanted to go somewhere for a drink, distrusting him I said, "No!"

I drove off with a big smile on my face and passed by a blossoming field, filled with beautiful yellow flowers blowing in the breeze. I parked my car and jumped out. I looked out into the field and said, "Thank you, Lord Jesus, thank you for my freedom." I could tell exactly what the slaves must have felt like when they were freed, I'm sure it was exactly what I felt at that moment--feelings of joy that I would never forget as long as I live. I ran out into the field and danced and danced and danced. I was acting like a Prima Donna, as I dashed and pranced into the air. Saying over and over, "Yes, yes, yes-s-s-s-s." I had enough pollen on my own clothing to start my own field of flowers.

That night when I went home I ran up the steps and into the apartment. I couldn't wait to tell the kids. When I entered the door the children were nowhere in sight. Running down the hallway, I passed them in a small, little storeroom where they sat playing with their pet guinea pigs. They looked up at me with surprise as I bellowed out, "I'm divorced, babies, I'm divorced." Camille and my son Pogie jumped up and ran to hug me. September jumped up and ran into her room. I followed her to the bedroom, wondering what I had said wrong. There she sat on her bed, crying her eyes out. I sat on the bed next to her. Her brother and sister stood beside us. "What's wrong?" I said, looking into her sad little eyes.

"Mommy I don't know why I'm crying. I'm so happy!"

I couldn't believe it, as we all held each other and cried our eyes out. Then we all began to laugh as we thought how silly we must look. I decided to take the kids out to dinner. Afterwards I brought them home and put them to bed. I walked around the house just looking at everything and then all of a sudden, sadness swept over me as I thought about the first day Sam and I had met. I thought about how we loved each other so very much. I remembered how I used to sit and imagine Sam and me at 50-years-old, still loving each after our kids were grown and gone away from home. Tears streamed down my face as I put "Still" by Lionel Richie on the tape recorder. All the abuse started flashing in front of my face and it was then that I got a reality check. I jumped up, turned off the music, put on my raincoat, grabbed my car keys and umbrella, and ran out the door.

I drove downtown where I found an empty parking garage. I parked my car, walked up the stairs till I reached the top. At the top of the empty parking garage I took out my umbrella and started doing a rendition of "Singin' In The rain" by Gene Kelly and "I'm In Heaven" by Fred Astaire. I jumped in puddles and swung around poles, and hopped, skipped, and jumped till I completely tired myself out. Soaking wet, I started to walk away when I heard cheering, whistling and clapping coming from the building across the way. Looking up, I noticed people who apparently had been watching me from a balcony. Bashfully I smiled, not knowing what else to do, I curtsied and bowed for my audience and then ran back to the stairs. I laughed to myself and stopped on the stairs to pause for a moment, and then went back up to take a peek, to see if the spectators were still there. When I didn't see them standing outside on their balconies, I galloped down the steps, dashed into my car, and drove home.

The minute I got home, the phone began to ring. It was Sam. He said he was going to die, commit suicide if I

286

didn't return to him. He could not live a moment longer without me. I didn't want to hear it so I hung the phone up, and went to bed.

The next day only brought more trouble as he kept calling and begging me to give him another chance. He would stop by my house where he would sit outside on the step of my apartment and wait for me to drive home. He kept looking for me, following me everywhere. When he appeared at the club, I would become embarrassed. I thought he had come there to start a fight. Sometimes I would look outside the club to see him walking around my car, and when I left the building I would pretend not to notice that he was parked in the back of the parking lot. He would wait for me when I came home from a date. As I drove up, he would walk up to the car with a mean look on his face and pretend to be my mate so he could scare the crap out of my dates. These were not serious dates but friendly evenings out. The men, of course, were so scared that they would leave, not wanting to start any trouble. Sam stalked me all the time and I couldn't do anything to prevent it. The only way I could get him to stop was to drive home alone. The only thing I did differently was to say good-bye to my dates at our meeting places and then drive home. I called and had a restraining order issued against Sam to leave me alone, but it did no good. He continued to hassle me.

The children were very happy that he was gone. We had little money and they were eating plain rice, sometimes adding ketchup or gravy to the grains. French fries were a special treat. Sam would call the children and ask them what they were having for supper; only to boast that he was cooking pork chops. The harassment never ended, always causing hurt feelings. He would visit just to find a reason to yell. September asked me once if she could tell him to leave them alone and "to go to hell." I answered as truthfully as I could, explaining that he was still her father and could easily come into our home and beat her again.

## Chapter 34

Pogie was now starting to go through changes. He absolutely hated his name. I could understand the children at his school teasing him, but his own teacher laughing with another teacher about his name really hurt him a lot. Going to the hospital one day, they called "Samson Jackson." He stood up and said, "Who is Samson Jackson?" After making a scene, I had to figure out a way to get him into the doctor's office. I took Pogie by the hand and led him to the pharmacy. Then we went around the corner to find the doctor's office. The doctor told me he was about to call in the next patient. I explained that my son was embarrassed by the name. I asked him to change his records to reflect my son's name as being, "Samuel Jackson," and if he could please refer to Pogie that way from now on when we visited. The doctor asked me if I was going to change it one day. I replied that Samuel would have to do it himself, when he reached the age of 18, because his father still could fight him in court over his name.

September and Camille accepted the divorce rather well, but Pogie was still having a lot of trouble with it. He was still showing signs of rebellion. One morning I was getting the children ready for school. I had prepared breakfast, and everyone was walking out the door full and happy. All of the sudden September called her brother back into the house. Her voice was very discerning and for some reason it caught my attention. She called her brother over to her and began going through his pockets. Suddenly, she pulled out a folded wad of cash that was nearly $180. I was stunned. I stood there as she said over and over, "I knew it. I knew by the way you were acting, something was up. You stole this money out of Mama's purse, didn't you?" Pogie shook his head while looking down at the ground. I walked over and took the money from him and asked, "How could you steal from your own Mother? Did you know that this was your Christmas money?" He shook his head "no." I turned and looked at September and told her to run along.

After having a long conversation with Pogie, I told him that I would have to reflect on the situation to find some discipline that would be fitting for this type of behavior.

I took Pogie to school and dropped him off. That evening when Pogie came home I told him that for what he had done he was going to receive a spanking. The full punishment intended was to write two book reports on subjects from the encyclopedia. Usually, I would grab an encyclopedia off the bookshelf and just open it up to any page. If it were something he could do for his age, I would give it to him. I always punished my children this way because I wanted them to enrich their minds while they sat in their room. The subjects I selected were: "Charlie Chaplin" and "Hawaii." When I went to tell Pogie of his punishment I learned that he had run out the door to keep from getting a spanking. I peeked out the apartment window. Down below I spied Pogie climbing into my car. September asked if she should go get him, but I said, "No." I told her that he would come home. I told the other kids to get ready for bed. September was very upset and did not want to leave him down there, but I assured her that everything would be fine.

I told September to take her baby sister, get into the shower and go to bed. I admit I was a little nervous, but I turned off the porch light and closed the curtains anyway. I kept peaking out every now and then to check on him.

I set up my bed on the couch so I could be near the window to keep an eye on Pogie all night. I waited and watched for him to come into the house. All I could see was his tiny little body curled up in the car with his blanket that I had left on the line to dry the day before.

By morning, I had fallen asleep--only to be awakened by September screaming, "Mom, Pogie's gone!" I ran to the window and looked down. Sure enough, he was gone. I thought he was probably wandering around somewhere because it was only six in the morning. I told September to put on her clothes and shoes so we could search for him. We both quickly got dressed and ran out of the house. We walked for blocks searching for him. I told September we needed to call the police, and we headed home.

The police arrived immediately. After speaking with them I decided it would be better to get into my car and start searching. Everything was running through my mind. Truckers would drive through on the main streets. I hoped they had not picked him up. Or maybe he ran away, or was kidnapped?

I placed September and the baby into the car. I started the car, and before I could put it into drive, the whole car began to fill with smoke. We all rushed out coughing and gagging. The police walked over to the car and right away knew what was wrong. In the rear of the car, in the muffler, the policeman pulled out a bundle of socks that my little monster had put there. I said, "That little bad boy! Oh you wait till I find you!" We turned off the car and went out searching every inch of the small town. There was no sign of him anywhere.

Suddenly! An image of Pogie, popped into my mind. I could feel him in someone's house. Looking at September I told her that her little brother was safe in someone's house. She said, "But which house, Mom?" I told her to hang on, that I would know the house when I saw it. As we were driving along, I kept looking and trying to use my mind to find him. Suddenly I pulled to a stop. "This is the house." I knew he was in there. September and I got out of the car and walked up to the door.

We knocked and a woman answered. I asked her if she had seen my son and she informed me he was there. I walked into the house and grabbed my son. I hugged him and started to cry as I told him to never do that to me again. I looked him in the face and told him, "Mama loves you but you must realize that I have to do what I have to do to raise you right. No matter what the circumstances are, you must learn to deal with it."

Soon we all started for home. I thanked the lady as she told me of finding him in a ditch and bringing him home. She said she found him at four o'clock in the morning. I asked her why she had not called the police or me. She said that my son had told her he was going to be beaten, so she was afraid to call. I grew silent and felt angry. I told her, "You mean, you were going to keep my son because you thought I would beat him?" I could not believe what I was hearing. I grabbed my son and raced out of the door.

I had nothing further to discuss with her. I was steaming. Feeling guilty on my way home, I decided not to whip Pogie as of yet, but to teach him a very important lesson.

When we got home I told Pogie to go take a shower and then go to his room. I went to the phone and called the police. I asked them to pick him up and take him to jail for stealing the money out of my purse. They told me they could not do that. "Well, that is where you are going to put him one day eventually, why not give him a taste of it now?" The policeman offered to call Child and Family Services to see what they thought. The phone rang shortly thereafter, and the same policeman told me he was on his way.

I went to my son's room and told him that since he felt he needed to steal from his mother and then run away from home, he was acting like a thief. Since he was acting like a thief he would be treated like a thief. He sat on his bed and stared. I told him to get dressed because the police were coming for him. As I turned and walked out of his room, I had a smile on my face.

A policeman came to the door and rang the doorbell. I let them in. In a very stern voice, he said, "All right, where is the young man who stole from his mother and then ran away?" Suddenly, Pogie appeared from his room with tears in his big round eyes. The officer told him that he would have to go with him. "We do not allow children to steal from their parents, or anyone else." Pogie turned and looked at me. It was so hard for me to contain myself. I said, "Don't look at me, you are the one that decided to steal from your mother." The policeman sternly told Pogie, "It's time to leave." He began crying as the officer led him down the stairs and into the back of the police cruiser.

A wave of sadness washed over me as Pogie marched away scared and all alone. I had to be stern. They drove off and about ten minutes later I got a call. The police told me they would show him around and let him sit in the jail cell. They were going to keep him about twenty more minutes and then bring him home. They told me they served him lunch and had a big talk. "He is such a polite little boy," the officer said. "I don't think he will ever do anything like this again."

About twenty minutes later, they brought him home. Again the policeman sternly told him never to do anything like that again, because next time he would not be allowed to go home. In a scared voice, Pogie assured the policeman he understood. The police officer looked at me, winked, and said, "Okay, we'll leave him with you. He promises to be good from now on."

I thanked the policeman as he walked out of the door. I took Pogie to his room and made him take a nap. I told him that when he woke up it would be time for him to start on his book reports. Once the policeman arrived back at the station, he called me once again. He complimented me on what I had just done. "If more parents took the time to inform or educate their kids as you've done, there'd be a lot less stealing and running away." I thanked him for the lessons he had taught my son and for taking the time to do so.

Pogie did the two book reports for his punishment. One night he lay awake until I got home and when I arrived he met me at the door crying.

"Mom," he said, "I loved this story. Can I read it to you now?"
Being tired, I said, "Tomorrow, son."
"Please, Mom, please let me read it now."

Looking at the tears in his eyes, I said, "OK." He started to read his report, telling me of how Charlie Chaplin spent his whole life trying to make others happy but was very unhappy himself. Crying, Pogie told of how Chaplin had died alone. Pogie and I hugged as he looked at me and said, "I'm sorry, Mama." I told him that I forgave him. He went back to bed. I'm glad I gave that book report to him. It was the perfect book report to end a perfect day.

# Chapter 35

We were very content being in New Baden, especially distancing ourselves from Sam. I was working at a restaurant, and because of our lack of food, I would eat leftovers from customers' plates. I never ate at home, as I saved all the food I purchased for the children. When I served the meals to customers, I would feel pleased if they ordered something that I particularly liked. I would rush them through meals so that there might be something left for me. Some days I would not eat anything but the scraps of leftovers that children left on their plates. September was doing well at this time, as far as watching my children. September agreed to do anything she could, to keep our independence. I found a second job because I was having trouble paying the rent, and as always we had a shortage of food.

The second job was working at a convenience store. I had just gotten off my day job and had two hours in-between to arrive at my night job. When I got there at 10:00 P.M. my boss greeted me with a smile. She was so happy I was there because she was tired and wanted to go home. She introduced me to another worker, Kathy. Kathy and I politely shook hands. My boss went on to tell me how she was going to spend the evening with me while I trained Kathy on the register, gas pumps, and how to make the sandwiches. Kathy was going to work the morning shift.

Soon, my boss waved goodbye and rushed out the door. I turned to Kathy and explained that I thought she would learn better by just observing everything I did. We started talking about each other's lives, children, homes, and jobs, as I went about my nightly duties.

In the early hours of the morning, I was working the register while Kathy sat in the back room, eating soup and a sandwich she had just prepared. I was waiting on a customer when a strange man walked in and glanced at me. He strolled over to the shelves of food. He then picked up something off the shelf and walked up to the counter. I thought he was acting rather oddly. Still waiting on another customer, I saw the strange man step up to the register. After all the customers left, the gentleman told me he was going to rob the store. I laughed because I thought he was joking. He glared at me and said, "No, this is for real." I wasn't sure what to think because when working at the base I would often be put through simulated robberies. They consisted of fake robbers and a real base policeman. The robber would come in and pretend to rob me. He then would leave the store and I would call the police and describe what the robber looked like and which direction he went. Usually, I passed the tests. The establishment I worked for then would receive merit points and the boss would pat me on the back.

For some reason I thought that's what was going on. Then all of the sudden reality set in. I felt fear wash over my body, and a wave of panic. I looked into the man's face and saw complete seriousness. I immediately opened the cash drawer and began pulling the money out as fast as I could. Suddenly, Kathy walked out from the back room. I had been so involved in what was going on I had forgotten that she was even there. "Cynthia, what should I start on next?" she asked. I turned to look at her and told her, "This is a robbery." With uncertainty Kathy asked me to repeat myself. I could see the robber was beginning to get nervous. He kept glancing out the window and telling us to hurry. He ordered Kathy to go to the back and get the cash out of the safe. I turned to go with her and he yelled at me to stay. He gave Kathy a bag that I had already filled with money and directed her to put the money from the safe into it. As she rushed to the back, I could see that she was scared to death. This was her first night working and already she was involved in a robbery.

I stood behind the counter waiting for Kathy. The robber was getting very antsy. He pulled out his gun and turned it toward me. He asked if there was a phone in the back of the store. "No." He asked me to follow him to the back room. I was beginning to freak out. The robber kept yelling at me, wondering what was taking Kathy so long to get the money out of the safe. As we both moved toward the back room, Kathy burst out through the swinging door and literally threw the bag of money at him. He grabbed the bag from her and turned for the door. As he was leaving he said, "I'm sorry that I had to do this to you!" I didn't understand what he meant, until later.

I turned to see if Kathy was all right. I was surprised at how completely cool and calm I had become. I walked over to the phone and called the police after making sure the robber was nowhere around. Kathy panicked and began screaming and crying. I didn't know what to do. Then I remembered a scene in the movies, where a woman started screaming and getting hysterical until someone finally slapped her to bring her out of her panic. I turned around and slapped Kathy as hard as I could. She fell to the floor. I told her I was sorry, but I didn't know what else to do. Then I called my boss. I began pacing, waiting for the police and checking on Kathy. Finally, the police arrived. Right away the policemen began to question me. While they were questioning me, the baker showed up to deliver doughnuts. I set the doughnuts on the table and continued answering questions.

When my boss arrived the first thing she said was, "Why haven't you put the doughnuts out yet?" I looked at her as if she had gone crazy. She didn't even bother to ask if we were all right, or anything else.

Kathy sat in the booth across from me, still crying, as we continued to be questioned. When I got to the part of the story where Kathy was taking so long in the back, the police asked her why. She said she was trying to decide whether to give the robber the $1000 in bills or the $400 in small change. I got really angry. "You mean to tell me that while our lives hung in the balance, you were in the back room trying to decide how much money to give him? I should slap you again!" I was irate. This only made matters worse. Kathy began to cry even more, so the police let her leave. The police started dusting the counter for prints when again my boss approached me about the doughnuts. I told her she could shove the doughnuts up her you-know-what, and left. The police followed after me, asking if they needed more information how they could go about contacting me. "Just call me at home."

Once I was safe in my house the reality of what had happened hit me. I fell to my knees shaking all over, and thanked the Lord for saving my life.

The next day the robbery was in the newspaper. According to the police report, the items taken were $424 in bills, $46.32 in coins, $2 in food stamps, and $2 in Illinois lottery tickets. The total was $474.32. However, almost all of the money taken was found in a nearby yard. The police did not say why the robber had thrown the money away, but I heard details from another officer. He told me that all the robber wanted to do was eat. He went to the grocery store after he robbed me and bought enough groceries to have dinner, and then went home. The robber was hoping to be picked up by the police so he could go back to jail. No one would give him a job because of his criminal record. In jail he was comfortable. He had food and shelter. That is why he threw the remainder of the money into the yard, and that is also why apologized to me for doing what he did.

People seem to take for granted what God has blessed them with. As long as we stay within the boundaries of the law and serve God, we don't have to worry about hunger or a place to live. God takes care of the birds and the bees, just as he will do for us. We should never have to fret because God will take care of us. "He said to His disciples, 'Therefore I tell you, do not worry about your life and what you will eat, or about your body and what you will wear.'" (Luke 12: 22-31) Once someone breaks the law he or she has entered the place of no return. It is hard for these people to make amends to society because no one wants to trust them. That is why God plays such a very important role in my life. Now I understand why some prisoners feel prison has a revolving door. Even though Kathy and I suffered nightmares and were scared out of our wits from what happened that early morning, we realize now that the robber didn't want to harm us. He only wanted to return to prison. There is a thin line you cross when you go from good to bad, and it is hard to cross back over.

I returned to work the following day and my boss fired me. She told me that my son was in her store that day stealing candy. I went home to Pogie and asked him, "Why would you steal from the store? I've lost my job because you did that." His reply was, "Mommy, you stole." I told him that was untrue, but he reminded me of a day in the Laundromat when the soda machine had malfunctioned. Looking back, I knew he was right, but it was only on a technicality. I always had given the children a quarter to buy soda at the Laundromat. This particular day, the machine dropped can after can down the chute and into our hands. It wouldn't stop until the machine was empty. I called the emergency number on the machine to no avail. No one was in the Laundromat to report it either. I even called the Laundromat's owner, who told me to call the soda company. After being unable to reach anyone, I took the soda home. If I had left it there, someone would have taken the cans. My son saw this as stealing, even though I tried to rectify it.

I told Pogie I would not punish him that night, but I did make sure he understood that what he had done was wrong. He wasn't involved when I tried to return the sodas, so he didn't know how hard I tried correcting the malfunction. All he saw was that I had been "stealing." In his young mind I had set a bad example and if I did it, he thought he could too. I explained that there were two different matters, but I had created for him a bad impression. I warned him never to do it again and told him he would be punished if he did. He agreed with me and said, "No, Ma'am, I will never steal again." Children are so impressionable. Parents have to be completely aware of their actions at all times to keep their children from picking up the wrong ideas.

# Chapter 36

On my days off I spent wonderful times with my kids. Sometimes I'd just sleep. I was tired from working two jobs. One night the next-door neighbors had a party and as I was getting a soda from the refrigerator, I heard a thudding noise outside. It was snowing badly and I had put the kids to bed. I looked out to see all the people running out to their cars and trucks, jumping into them and driving off, whooping and hollering. Suddenly one man ran out to join the rest and slipped on the ice at the top of the stairs. Down he plummeted to the bottom. By this time everyone else had gone and he lay there badly scratched and banged-up.

I brought him into my house and put him into my bed. I put alcohol on his bareback where he had scratches from falling down the stairs. Not having a shirt on and being drunk didn't help him. I made my bed and went to sleep on the couch. And in the morning, September saw the guy in my bed. She ran into the kitchen where I was preparing breakfast. She was very angry as she accused me of lying to her. "You promised me that you would never have another man in your bed, you promised!" I told her that it was not that kind of situation and that she had misunderstood. I told her to go to her room and I'd talk to her later. I went into my bedroom and helped the gentleman. I asked if he wanted breakfast. He said, "No, thank you, I owe you my life. I'll go and get out of your hair."

I helped him to the door as he left. Then I went into September's room. "Step into my bedroom." I showed her the bed, which was covered with his blood, and explained the circumstances. I could tell that September felt bad but I couldn't help but be angry at her accusations. I also understood what it must have looked like to her. I reminded her again of the importance of not bringing a man home while I had girls in the house. I promised her that I would have to be married before she ever found another man in my bed. One day the gentleman did return, bringing me some flowers. Again, he told me, "Thank you for helping me through that night."

I started going out to relieve the tension of working two jobs. I would go out after work with my girlfriends. We would have a good time. Sam would call me at the club, telling me he was depressed and wanted to commit suicide. I left the club early one evening and found him crying at his home. I stayed with him because I wanted him to work through that low period of his life. Soon I found myself being with him every weekend. At least I didn't have to worry about AIDS or be bothered by some stranger. My girlfriends advised me to not be a fool the second time around, and to be careful. I told them that I wasn't married to him anymore. I refused to worry. If he started anything I would leave in a minute. But they still strongly advised me to stop seeing him. I found myself being lonely and wanting to be with my husband again.

Before I knew it Sam and I were talking about marriage again. I couldn't believe these words were coming out of my mouth after all I had been through. Miss Connie asked, "Cynthia, do you really believe he's changed? Sometimes we allow our hearts to get in the way of our thinking. Please, be careful because you must first consider your children." When I told September she just ran to her room. Maybe Miss Connie was right? Maybe I was letting my loneliness take over my thinking? She asked me to get away from him for a while and see what I thought. He was treating me properly and things were going well. But then how could I take him back and put the children into that abuse situation again? I decided that we should get married again, but continue to live in two different houses. I saw a documentary show on television explaining how families were trying a new thing. They would live in separate homes but would still be married. Most of the reasons were because children from two different marriages did not get along. Then there was one couple where one did not like the heat and the other disliked winter. There was also a couple that was not sure they wanted to sell their houses and leave their jobs. I thought that maybe this would work for us, especially since it was the children that Sam could not be around. But Sam wanted to get married again and live as a family. I was going crazy trying to figure out what to do.

One evening I was over Sam's, visiting. We had gone out for videos when Sam decided to go out for some wine and a few snacks. Suddenly the phone rang. Normally Sam would turn off the phone when I was over visiting with him. I heard a message coming from his phone recorder. It was from another woman. She said she missed him, loved him, and wanted to see him again. I can't say that I was shocked because I asked for it. I grabbed my purse and out the door I stormed. I had returned to this man, cared for him, and even became his lover again, and he had the audacity to have another woman on the side! This time I would be successful in my attempt to kill him. He would never be around me or enter into our lives again. With him gone I could finally get on with my life, even if it was from a jail cell. At that time I could not care less what happened to me. I had finally gone to the point of no return, just like a prisoner. If this is what would drive me over that fine line, then I finally could understand why some people stepped over it. I had everything all planed out. My girlfriend would care for my children, who always enjoyed themselves there, should I go to jail. I knew that they would be raised properly. My children loved her and her family. I knew everything would be okay.

I decided not to buy a gun this time because the waiting period would again allow me to cool off. I wanted him dead now. Again I would put on my act, pretending to want to be with him while all along scheming to stab him. I went out looking for a special knife, a Japanese suicide knife, like that I had seen during my stay in Japan. It had a long, narrow blade that was capable of doing a lot of damage. I found one in an Oriental store. I waited till nightfall and drove to his apartment. I knocked on the door and he did not answer. Figuring that he stepped out, I decided to sit in my car and wait for his arrival. I remember being very nervous and very impatience. Soon my patience wore out. I thought that it would be better to wait for him inside the apartment. I knocked and banged on the door and no one answered, so I walked to the back of the apartment trying to find a way in. I climbed the downspout running up the side of the building and soon found myself on the ground, with half the wall's pipe on the ground with me. The spout had broken off as I tried to climb the pipe. It was more embarrassing than it was funny, especially when small kids observed me doing it, got scared, and ran off to tell their parents. Going back around to the front of the apartment, I again tried everything I could to break in, even using keys and credit cards. Finally, I kicked the door with all my strength. It gave way.

I waited for about an hour for Sam to show up, but in his absence the anger overwhelmed me and I cut up everything in sight. I slit his pillows, sheets, blankets, and rugs. I went on to rip up his clothes and even his uniforms. His breakables were the next to go. On the shelves he had glass trinkets, which I knocked off. As I walked to the kitchen I began to destroy everything on his counters. We had purchased a stereo unit in Spain, which I knew he was crazy about, and I knocked it to the floor. I started to cut up his front room curtains. While doing so, I looked down the street to find two women standing below the window, watching in awe. They observed me ripping the curtains to shreds. I immediately hid behind the remaining part of the curtain because it suddenly occurred to me that they could call the police and have me arrested. I watched as they slowly walked away. This was a tough job, but it was helping me dissipate the rage that had built up inside of me. It was already starting to get dark when I began cutting up the couch. I walked back to the stereo and found a doll that I had purchased many years ago in Japan. I once had owned a similar one with a porcelain face when I was a child. I had loved it so much that I specifically had this one made for me out of cloth. That had become Sam's prize possession, which he kept in a glass case. But then, knowing Sam, it probably became his prize possession because he knew how much I loved it. We had argued about who would keep it during the divorce. I finally agreed that he could have it in the settlement, just to finalize my divorce from him. I went to grab it, thinking I would cut it up too, but not watching where I was stepping, I deeply cut my foot on a piece of glass. I hopped to the couch as blood dripped all over the floor. It was so painful that I grabbed a bottle of strong Japanese wine and began to drink it. The next thing I knew, I had passed out.

The next morning I heard a rustling at the door. Then a key turned in the door lock. Sam strolled in and found me lying on his ripped-up couch. I couldn't believe it, but he remained silent. Dropping to his knees, he asked, "Are you OK?" He saw the blood, and started to clean up my foot. Afterward he put me into his bed, lay beside me and held me. Always thinking he was crazy, I now had a grasp of just how crazy he was. He held me for a long time and then he took me home. He left and went back to clean up his apartment.

That night I decided to run away from it all. I called Miss Connie and asked if I could bring the children to her house to be watched because I was going through a bad time. I explained how I had heard the message on Sam's recorder from his girlfriend. Miss Connie said, "Ohhh,

Honey, I'm so sorry," and without ever cursing, she called him an awful person. But she never once said, "I told you so." I respected her for that. I loved her for her loyalty. She knew what I was going through and was always my best friend. She told me that if she were in that situation she probably would have gone back to her husband too. She dropped everything and came to my side. When she arrived I was still drinking, she knew I was in no frame of mind to have the children around. She took the kids home with her. I decided to call her and tell her to take good care of my children. She hesitated and told me, "Of course, I will." Then she called the police and asked them to check up on me because she was afraid I might do something I would regret.

The police officers broke down my apartment door and put me in a straitjacket. I had no idea why they had come for me. They explained that Miss Connie had informed them that I might commit suicide. I told them that I was not going to commit suicide that I only wanted to leave and never come back. Looking at the knife on my bedside, I tried to explain that I was only trying to scrape the blood from under my nails with the knife, nothing more. Informing me that they had to follow procedures, they wrapped me in a sheet and put me onto a gurney for the ride in the ambulance. They stripped my clothes upon arrival at a destination that I could not recognize. They hosed me off. I was so cold as I lay there, trying to hide my body. I begged them to let me put on some clothes, but they said this was what they do with people who want to kill themselves. They made me lay there on the cold, bare floor for an hour. Every so often they would walk back and laugh at me as I lay shivering. Finally they dressed me, put me into another ambulance, and took me to a psychiatric facility.

The patients at this facility were like zombies, walking around aimlessly, hitting their heads against the wall, screaming and slobbering. I had never seen anything

305

like that. I refused to get off the gurney. I just sat in bed watching those "crazy people." Then the attendant told me I would have to get down and join them. I told her that I didn't belong with them because I was not crazy. Respecting the woman, I answered all of her questions with, "Yes, Ma'am." I think she questioned if I really needed to be in her facility. She asked the ambulance drivers if I had been placed in the correct ward. After looking at their paperwork they admitted that I was in the wrong place and they moved me to another ward where the patients were psychotic and on drugs.

Showing me to my room, which contained a small bath and three other women patients, they administered some medication to me. I soon fell asleep and had a very difficult time waking the next morning. When I awoke, they took me to another room where a counseling session was taking place. They were asking why we thought we were there and what our thoughts were. I kept nodding off and actually fell out of the chair several times. A staff member kept yelling at me to wake up and sit up straight. I couldn't do as she asked because I was so sleepy and could not function. I finally went totally out and awoke to find myself back in my bed. More medication was administered to me at that time, and I fell back asleep. The next day I finally got myself together. When I was asked to do my laundry, I walked down a long hallway. At the end of the hallway were several people slowly moving towards me. I thought that I was in the movie, "Night of the Living Dead." I was so afraid of them that I dropped my basket and ran directly to my room. After I figured they had left, I went back to find someone had picked up my basket of clothes and put it in the laundry room. I was too scared to do laundry that night. I just pretended that I had finished, so I could go back to my room.

On my third day at the institution, my nurse told me that the following day they would put me in front of a board to decide if I were to remain a patient there or be released. Deciding that I could not be sleepy, I knew I would have to be lucid enough to explain why I wanted to kill my husband and why I was not the type of person to commit suicide. When the nurse returned to give me my medication that night, I hid it under my tongue then removed it from my mouth and placed it in my bra. I stayed up most of the night planning what I was going to say to get myself out of there. I was very alert the next morning.

Somehow, I would have to get out of this crazy house. I was taken in front of the board, and I was ready to do whatever was necessary to be released. I told them the entire story. I told them that my husband had abused me for thirteen years and all the details of those horrendous times, the divorce and how I had again become involved with him. Continuing to explain that he had been seeing another woman, I told them that I had planned on killing him. I had asked the police to keep him away, but no one helped me. My friend had feared for my safety. Not understanding that I was going away for a while and needed her to watch my children in my absence, she believed that I meant to kill myself when she called the police. I began to cry as I explained that I had no thoughts of suicide. I was simply cleaning the blood from my fingernails that had gotten there when I cut my foot on shards of glass at the apartment.

One of the ladies on the board looked at the other board members as they sat speechless. She got up from her chair, walked over to me and asked me to go out and sit in the hallway while they made their decision. Calling me back in, their warning to me was to distance myself from this man and go as far away as possible to keep from any further involvement with him. They seemed to feel sorry for me after my explanations. They were surprised that I had lasted this long but were proud that I had divorced him.

After my release, I had only a brown paper sack that they gave me to carry my belongings back home. As I walked out of the facility, Sam was there to meet me. He said that he was here to talk them into letting me go. Again, he was reading my mind. I refused to speak on the ride home. I had to close off my thoughts so that he wouldn't know how I was planning to get away once and for all.

# Chapter 37

After leaving the institution I was making plans to go to another state to live, when I received a phone call from Sam. He called to tell me that he was sure I would be happy to know that he had been given an assignment in Germany. He probably thought I was sad to hear his news. I had been hoping and praying that something would end our relationship and I would never have to see him again.

I offered him my home as a place for him to stay before he flew overseas. I thought that if he were with me in my home, when he finally packed up the furniture and left, it would be for good. I wanted to see this event take place. This time he would be physically leaving my life. While he was living in my home, a man that I was trying to get rid of decided to stop by my house to visit. Sam saw him, started an argument and decided to beat me one more time. The children tried to rescue me and it turned into a big brawl. A neighbor called the police. Sam started yelling at the police. The policemen asked me to follow them to the car. They told me of their desire to take him somewhere to beat him up, so he would never bother me again. I told them, "Please don't take this one opportunity away from me to see him finally leave my life for good. Tomorrow at 3:00 P.M. he's going to board a plane to Germany and I will never see him again. Any other time I would have gladly let you take him, but I'm tired and just want him to go. Nothing will stop him from boarding that plane, if I can help it." I assured them that he would be gone the following day.

I drove him to the airport the following day and Sam handed me a black box. As he presented the box to me, I saw it contained a large, oval diamond ring. He said, "Cynthia, marry me again." I handed the ring back, laughed, and drove away. Finally, he had handed me the ring that I had deserved many years before. When I saw that one-carat diamond ring,

I knew in my soul that I had deserved it and more. I would have been the best wife he could ever have, if only he had reciprocated and respected the person he had married. He called to inform me that since I did not want to marry him he had "no other choice but to marry someone else." Was I sure I didn't want to marry him? This was my last chance! I hung up the phone. Looking at the number on my Caller ID, I recognized the phone number. I fetched my purse to find the number of the friend that he was supposed to be staying with during our marriage, and the numbers matched. During the last month of our marriage, I realized that he had been seeing her. I laughed. At least he was consistent all the way to the end.

After 13 years of the worst marriage that I could have possibly lived through, I have concluded, with this observation:

A Christian Marriage is strong when we return to the pattern that God gave for the home. Then we will have an end to the critical rise in divorces.

The greatest book on earth that deals with our most intimate relationship is the Bible. Home consists of the husband, wife, and the children. To me, "home" is a state of mind and a created situation where two people, who love each other and are committed to each other's well being, live together in complete harmony, love, forbearance, and consideration. Their job is to rear their children with tremendous love, tenderness, and care to the glory of God.

The house you build is not just a home, but the attitude that prevails inside. God's plan was to have a leader in that home--not a dictator, monarch, or master attitude, but rather a man that loves his family as much as he loves himself. That's the way that Jesus loved the church, so much that He gave His life for it.

310

In my case Sam thought that the word, "head," meant that he made all the decisions without my input or consulting me in any way. This is not true. I cannot think of one decision Sam should have made that affected our family, in which I should not have been involved as his wife and partner. This is called: Consideration and Love.

Each day we should have shared our daily time, family lives, future goals, and ambitions with one another. And most importantly we needed to communicate, share in conversations. Soon, we didn't know anything about each other and we began to care less for each other. We didn't share common interests. We stopped talking and listening. So our lives went in two different directions. Communication is the key to a successful marriage. I actually woke up one morning, looked over at Sam and wondered who he was.

I could no longer depend on us because of the hate. We were both in our own little worlds. And when the entire universe turned against us we did not have each other to lean on. We were no longer committed to one another.

As far as our bodies, we are to share them with one another and not with just any person of the opposite sex. A sexual relationship in marriage is to be used as an expression of love. With our goals, we all should work together so we might enjoy our personnel gains. Selfishness has no place in the Christian home.

"A husband should provide for his own, and especially for those of his own house, for if not he has denied the faith and is worse than an infidel." (1 Tim. 5:8) The husband is to make the living and the wife is to make the living worthwhile.

The husband is to protect his wife, love and cherish her, and most of all continue to court and date her even after they have said their "I do's." And most of all he is to honor his wife. "A virtuous woman is a crown to her husband: but she that maketh ashamed is as rottenness in his bones." (Proverbs. 12:4) The Bible also says, "Who so findeth a wife findeth a good thing, and obtaineth favor of the Lord...." and, "Husbands are to love their wives, and be not bitter against them." (Col. 3:19) I could talk about what a husband is supposed to do for days, but I cannot forget the duties of a wife.

Honor and give respect. (Eph. 5:33) The wife's submission to her husband grows out of her submission to Christ. (Rom. 6:16-18) Women are to be industrious and frugal, not indolent and slovenly. They are to live within their husband's income. They are to avoid being a spendthrift, which might make it necessary for their husbands to moonlight to meet their obligations. A lot of women at first cannot live contentedly because they expect their husbands to give them what their fathers were able to provide after a lifetime of labor and savings. Avoid overextending your credit. In fact I say, "Get rid of your credit cards."

Most of all, maintain your femininity and your attractiveness. Take care of yourselves, don't let yourself go. Try to stay as attractive as you were the day you married him, so he will be proud of you. Keep yourself up, healthy in body and mind. Don't neglect yourself. Let someone help you with the children, for you need a break so that you don't have a nervous breakdown.

Most importantly, love one another:

For love is very patient, very kind. Love knows no jealousy, love makes no parade, love gives itself no airs, love

312

is never rude, love is never selfish. Love is never irritated nor is love resentful; Love is gladdened by goodness, Love is slow to expose, Love is eager to believe the best, love is hopeful, and Love never disappears. (1Cor. 13: 4-7)

Remember it is very important to maintain communication with one another's soul, mind, and body. And most of all help one another get to heaven. (1Cor. 7:16)

We must not allow Satan to control our lives. The divorce rate must decline. Work on your marriage every day. It's not something you can put away and work on tomorrow. But it is important that you wake up thinking about what you can do to make one another happy in some kind way, and go to bed doing the same. And don't give up if things start to get rocky, get you up, shake yourself off, and start all over again. In the long run it will be worth it!

Making up should be a very special time. Always forgive and make a pact to smooth things over before the sun goes down. If I learned anything in my 13 years of marriage, I must say that I did learn this much for sure.

# Chapter 38

The kids and I were really enjoying our freedom. We had started going back to church and were really getting our lives back in order. In church, I met a man whom I found extremely attractive. Felmen didn't seem to notice me, but we shared an interest in the Lord. When I talked about the Lord, Felmen saw a fire in me that attracted him. We began to go over the Bible together and I shared my thoughts with him. At the same time, once Sam was out of my life, the problems that he had fostered in September grew worse. September was seeing a psychologist. She was suicidal. I too, had entered counseling.

One night I invited Felmen over for dinner. September was starting to gain weight and wanted to go on a diet. I thought she should too. Trying to curb September's eating habits was hard. She was growing larger than a child her age should be and that could prove very unhealthy. She found solace in her eating, but I knew that was not where she would find comfort.

I was fixing one of her favorite meals, a Filipino egg roll dish with Lumpia and Pansit. I told her she would have to eat her salad in her room that night. She asked me why. "I'm making one of her favorite meals." "I'll be okay eating my salad."

"But it'll make us all uncomfortable, especially your brother and sister. It'll also make Felmen uncomfortable. September, no one will want to eat this big dinner in front of you, while you're only eating a salad."

September started having a hissy fit. She was being so rebellious I had to threaten her with a spanking. She still refused to eat in her room. She was making me very angry. I told her to stay in her room and not to come out until I told

314

her it was okay. She began to throw things and stomp around the room, all the while screaming at the top of her lungs.

I ran up the stairs and told her that if she didn't quit I would make her leave. I went back downstairs.

At this time, Felmen decided he should leave. Our whole meal had been ruined. I apologized as I showed him to the door. Suddenly the phone rang. It was my girlfriend, Connie. She told me that she was coming to pick up September. I agreed because by this time, I was so angry I wanted to send her away.

Later that night I received another phone call. This time September had called her grandmother and asked if she could stay there. I knew this would never work because September was disturbed and so was my mother. They would never be able to get along. What upset me the most was, what was I to do with my other two children? September was my backbone. She was the only hope for my own sanity and survival. What was I to become without her? I knew I had started to take advantage of her. During my days off she looked after the children because I was always sleeping. I was so tired from working three jobs. I never helped her and knew that being as alone as she was, it was quite a responsibility for such a young girl. Plus, September had been abused so much that she was not capable of handling this situation any longer.

I was in utter dismay. I couldn't think. I was so upset I just went to bed early. I told myself to wait until the morning. Connie came to get the younger kids and deliver each of them to school. She brought September. September instantly went up to her room to pack. When she came back down through the door she lunged at me exclaiming, "Mommy, I'm so sorry!" We hugged each other. I realized that I must let her go. She was not capable of handling the situation. I needed someone stronger and she was battling with her own depression. I loved her and only wanted her to get away.

As I helped her pack, I could see she was tired and worn-out. She didn't ask for this life, it had just been given to her, so she had every right to call out for help.

After she left I went to my boss to explain my situation. I asked for time off. The baby had to go so I called my sister and begged her to take my youngest. My sister was excited for the opportunity to take care of the baby. She had wanted a baby girl so badly but was only blessed with two boys. She jumped at this opportunity. I knew I could count on my sister because she was the only one that would ever help me.

As I watched my oldest girl get on the plane, my vision blurred with tears. Sadly, I walked toward my car. I decided to hang on to Pogie as long as I could. He stayed with Connie until I found a baby-sitter. I had called my brother and his wife to see if they could care for my son until I sent for him, and I think my brother did want to help but my sister-in-law refused. She said that she had enough on her hands trying to take care of her own boys. I was understanding, but also felt that if I were in her position, with a husband and especially since my brother was a very good father, I would have taken my child. But not everyone thinks the way I do. The only other place to send Pogie was with his father and I didn't want to put my son through that.

As I returned home to an empty house, I walked through trying to recall the sounds of my little children fussing echoing through the hallways. I walked up the stairs to their rooms and looked in each of them, thinking of the kids asleep at night as I would arrive home from work and sit by their bedsides. I stood weeping. I held my head back and cried out, "O Lord, please don't take my babies away from me! Not the babies I have fought a thirteen-year battle to defend and keep safe! Please Lord, bring them back safely into my arms again. Show me what I am doing wrong in my life so that I may keep them."

I walked down the steps to my kitchen to get a beer, tears streaming over my face. I stood in my front room and let the tears flow freely. I fell upon my knees and asked for His forgiveness. I wanted another chance.

I became extremely angry with Sam, because I knew deep down that all of this was his fault. I yelled out, "I hate you, Sam!"

The next morning I found myself asleep on the couch. Beer cans were everywhere. I stayed in bed the entire weekend. I had no motivation to do anything besides drink. The only time I got up was to go to the bathroom and get more beer. I drank case after case.

I couldn't explain why I was buying so much beer to the store clerk so I would lie and say I was having a party. I don't think she really believed me. But I needed something to self-medicate my inner being before I went completely crazy. I knew that drinking was killing me and that the Lord was displeased with me for doing so, but I had to have something to calm my nerves before I had a nervous breakdown. By the end of the week I gave up and went back to church, only to find out Felmen had to move. I thought this would be the answer to my prayers. I could bring my son home. Felmen could move in and pay part of the rent, watching my son at night while I was at work. The church didn't like that idea so they arrived at the house to talk to Felmen and me. They told us that what we were doing was wrong. I didn't think so. I asked the church to help me, if they could watch them while I was at work. They didn't have an answer so they left. When they left, Felmen and I knew that they were right, but I was too afraid of losing Pogie, too.

Soon, what I thought would be a purely Platonic relationship turned into a serious one. It happened so fast that I could not even explain the situation. My son became very jealous and began acting out his aggression. He would start fires in the basement, swallow my sleeping pills to keep from going to school, lie, and do all kinds of other bad things. I knew that this was not going to work. A school official soon called and threatened me. If Pogie did not come back to school soon I would go to jail. I didn't want Felmen to discipline him nor did Felmen have it in him. Besides, Pogie was not his son.

One day, Pogie approached me and asked if he could go stay with his father. I fussed at him because I could not understand his wanting to be with Sam. Every time he did something and I spanked him for it, he would ask me to go stay with his father. Soon, the school called complaining that Pogie was very bad and failing all his subjects. Felmen convinced me that he probably needed to be with his father to get the discipline he needed. Pogie's father was now married to a woman he loved and she had a son. Maybe things would be different?

I gathered enough courage to call Sam. He agreed that he should take him.

"If I send Pogie to you, I hope you're not going to beat him?"

"If he deserves to be whipped, then I will whip him."

I was still very scared but I did what my son wanted. No matter how much I hated to do it, I had no other choice. It was loose him, or go to jail. When he left, I cried because my last child was gone. Hopefully, he would be safe.

Felmen and I started to become close. We talked of marriage because he was the type of man that wanted everything to be right before God. I just wanted my children back. I still yearned to be close to my kids. I knew that Felmen was right, but I didn't want to marry him. I didn't really love him. Plus, I didn't want any more children and he did. I thought about it, as long as we were married and he was a good man, then maybe it would work? And maybe just one child with a good husband and father would not be so bad after all. But not now! I didn't have my own children. I couldn't consider having another child.

Felmen asked me one day to go and visit his family. His family was a very kind and loving one, and I enjoyed myself. I became ill when we returned, thinking I had appendicitis or something. I was experiencing a pain in the side of my stomach. The doctor explained that he would have to administer a pregnancy test just in case. I assured him that I had an IUD and that could not be the reason. I waited for the doctor to return to me after taking the test; I saw the doorknob turn, but it did not open. I heard him yell down the hall, "How was the test?" A woman's voice answered, "It's positive." I knew that they could not possibly be talking about me! I couldn't be pregnant! He must have meant someone else. I said, "Please, dear God, don't let him enter this room." He entered the room and told me that I was indeed pregnant, and that the IUD was what was causing the pain. The doctor said he had to remove the IUD, although the baby may come out with it. I told him to go ahead. I knew I could not afford another baby.

All the way to the hospital the next week I prayed that when the IUD was removed the baby would be removed

319

with it. After the procedure, the baby still remained in my uterus. I wanted to go to the nearest bridge, jump off and commit suicide. There was no way I could have another child. My children were sprawled all over the country and Europe, how I could not possibly bring another child into this situation. The relationship I shared with Felmen was not what I wanted. He was on an entirely different level than me. He wanted a relationship and a family, and I didn't want marriage. I couldn't even treat Felmen right because of my history of abuse. He was such a sweet person and I was so mean. I didn't want to communicate, and I was so hateful. I wanted to treat him right but I couldn't because I wanted to be free. I must have come up with one hundred excuses why I couldn't have the baby. I was not going to be able to afford it. I wouldn't be able to get proper medical care. I was too embarrassed because I was not married. I didn't want to get fat. Where would I get food? I had enough kids already. I had too many problems. I was poor. I didn't love its father. It would be another 18 years till I raised it. I would be giving up the single life that I had only had for about 7 years. I was not mentally capable. What if I could not give it shelter? Etc., Etc., Etc.... So I decided to give it away.

Felmen's eyes gleamed when I told him the news. He was so happy. He had finally found someone that he could share his life with and start a family. I sat before him and cried, telling him I wanted to die. I wanted to give the child away or abort it, yet I turned the car around on my way to the clinic because I could not destroy the tiny life inside of me. I also knew that the Bible told me that Life begins at conception. (Luke 2:21) Now I was carrying my fourth child.

When I told Felmen that I could not have the baby, it broke his heart and he left me. He needed time to think.

September started having problems with my mother, which I knew would not take her long. I had always hidden the horrible things about my mother from my kids hoping they would never find out. She left my mother's house and went to live with my younger sister only to find out that because of September's mental condition my sister could not deal with my daughter. September moved back with me while I tried to figure out what I would do next. I was feeling awful and became weak. I felt I might just lose the baby because without medical insurance I could see no doctor. I called Anna Mae and told her that I was pregnant and asked to return home. All I needed was help to find a small apartment. Felmen returned and said that he needed to talk with me. I agreed that we needed to talk. I couldn't look Felmen straight in the face and tell him that I was going home and giving away my baby. So I pretended that things were fine.

I called my father to come and get me. Then I packed up all of my belongings, which was practically everything in the house. Felmen had gone on Temporary Duty (TDY) and while he was gone I loaded the truck with everything but his stereo. When he arrived back from TDY he found the house empty except for his stereo. I can imagine what he must have felt when he found I was gone.

# Chapter 39

When I reached San Antonio my father had rented me an apartment and had hired some men to unload the truck. My welfare payments would pay the rent, but I had to find a job so that I could afford gas for my car. My mother was changing personalities constantly, and the turbulence in my life looked like it was never going to end. No one would hire me because I was pregnant. When I told my youngest sister that I was going to put the baby up for adoption, she asked if she could have it. I said, "Sure, you can have the baby. Come to the hospital and pick it up."

Since I was on welfare, I was receiving enough food stamps so I decided to send for Camille. We would now be able to live in my apartment together. Before I went on welfare, I always questioned why recipients collecting it always seemed unwashed and smelled like they hadn't bathed in a long time. The welfare program gave you plenty of food credit, but did not allow you articles for proper hygiene. They did not supply shampoo, soap, and deodorant. Now I understood why people were selling their food stamps so that they could have cash for essentials not covered by welfare. I didn't need as much as they gave me, including what the Women, Infant, Children Program (WIC) provided me in the way of dairy products. Some that sold their food stamps would spend the money on alcohol and drugs, but there were women who needed the money to buy essentials for their children. I also received cash to pay the utilities. But I didn't have cash to buy books or shoes for the kids. So I asked them to write and ask their father. He wrote them back and told them that they were no longer his family or his responsibility. He had his own family now, and that was all he cared about. This hurt Camille and September deeply.

One night I had a dream that Felmen had looked up my name and found me. He was going to pay me a surprise visit. I knew Felmen had access to information to find me. He belonged to the OSI and was able to obtain information using my social security number. Having telepathic gifts, I felt him driving up to the house. I knew exactly when his car was about to appear. So as soon as I felt him driving close I went outside and stood in the parking lot as his red car turned the corner. He climbed out of the car, hugged me, and asked, "How did you know I was coming?" I reminded him of all the times I knew in advance what he was thinking. He bought me a diamond ring and asked for my hand. He said, "Please marry me? Please let me raise my child." I don't know why I took the ring. He had such a sincere look and I didn't have the heart to turn him down. Although he left on a happy note, I was still not ready for a commitment. I felt that something was missing. I wasn't truly in love with him. I would not have made him the type of wife he deserved. One night I found an audiotape that he was going to send to his mother. On the tape he talked about how crazy my daughter was and that he didn't know if he wanted to be involved with me. It was evident that this tape was made when he first met me. How could he have been so insensitive and uncaring? He knew how much my daughter had suffered at the hands of her father.

I sent Felmen's ring back and called him to say that I could not marry him. In the argument that ensued, he told me that one of the reasons he had left was September. He couldn't handle her screams, disrespect of him, or her suicidal tendencies. He wanted me to choose between him and my daughter, but he loved me and felt that he could now handle it. I could never choose between them. September was my flesh and blood, my daughter, and God had given me the responsibility to care for her, no matter what problems that might cause. Because of the abuse caused by my ex-husband, I could never abandon her. I could never choose between her and another man. I told him we would not be getting married, but he was welcome to visit his baby. I told him to ask at the hospital, "for the Jackson baby," and he could see his son.

Mark was born on November 2, 1988. He was due on October 31, but I didn't want to have him on Halloween. I was supposed to have a Cesarean, so I could choose my baby's birthday. I didn't want to see him since I had decided to give him away. But Anna convinced me otherwise. She strolled into my room and started to describe him to me as she told me that he lay in his little bed with his little legs propped up, and one little finger on his head as though he were thinking. I had to go to the nursery to see what my mother was talking about. Once I saw him, it was all over. He was a beautiful baby and I already had decided that I never could have given him to anyone. As he lay in the bassinet, I was so proud I had never aborted him. I looked into his tiny face and could never give him away. I took on the challenge the Lord gave me. I prayed, "Lord, you gave me this child, now you give me the means to take care of him. Please give me the food and clothing I need to take care of my baby because I will never make it alone."

When my sister arrived at the hospital to claim him, I could not pass him on to her. I told her I had been kidding when she asked to have him during my pregnancy and I said she could. I never realized how badly I hurt her that day. She really thought she was to become a mother to my son. She never had been blessed with a child and she was desperate to love a baby that she could call her own.

God did provide for my new baby and me. We did have what we needed to survive. The Lord never gives you more than you are able to bear. I am a firm believer in that, because if He puts a baby into your womb, He knows that He can help you care for that child. He will make a way, no matter how poor you are, He will provide for that child. My baby and I were living proof of that. I now understood His reasoning. It was not a punishment because I had a baby out of wedlock, but He knew with this precious little life my own life would turn out better. With my little son I was given food not only to feed him but my other children as well. I was even able to bring Camille home. I had something else precious to love and he loved me back. And believe it or not, my little son saved my life because I was headed down a one-way street. He gave me something else to live for and another reason to put my life into the right perspective. I now was ready to start all over again.

When I arrived home with the baby, I told September that she would have to become a surrogate mother to Mark while I worked. September adored him more than words could say, although her knowledge was lacking when it came to taking care of a baby. She did not want me to give him to her Auntie so she said that she would do her best to care for him.

# Chapter 40

About two months later the kids and I found a house. It was the first house that we had ever lived in since the divorce. We were so excited. It was nice to have a backyard and front yard for the kids to play in. It was a small, three-bedroom house in the suburbs. One very large tree covered the front yard. We thought that we were really living now, until everything started to go wrong. Large cockroaches infested the house. They were so big that I could hear them at night scrambling about as we slept. I awoke one night to find one of them swimming around in a can of soda I had left by my bedside. As we showered they would run down the shower curtain, scaring us half to death. The sewer in the house would back up and sewer water would fill the house. We used every towel in the house to sop up the mess. While wading through filth and body waste, we begged the landlord to do something about it. And he would do nothing but accuse us of putting things down the toilet. For the roaches he told us," Set off roach bombs."

Regardless of what we went through, nothing could light a candle to the torment we encountered next. One night we were awakened by a yell of someone in pain. We opened our windows, which is something normally we never did because of the infestation of rodents. Looking over into the next-door neighbor's backyard we saw a lady beating her husband with some type of rod. We sat in horror at what was taking place. He begged and pleaded with her, "Please stop hitting me." But she would not stop. The kids and I were in a state of shock as we watched this 5' 7" man, with a medium-chubby build crying out in pain as his wife continued to beat him. She kept yelling at him, "Go take out the trash and clean the yard!" at 8:00 P.M., after he just had arrived home from work. And even though he got off at 5:00 P.M. he had to walk a mile home and then start cooking and doing his chores, which consisted of cleaning the yard, cutting the grass, and taking out the trash. Some nights we would hear him out late cutting the grass, sometimes even at 10:00 P.M. He would carry a lamp to light his way. If he left anything undone she would send him back out to finish it, even if it took him all night.

One day I picked him up on his way to work He searched around to make sure that no one, such as his wife, was looking. He hopped into the car. I drove him to his bus stop, which was a mile or so away from the house. I asked him about his bicycle that he used to take to work. He explained to me that it had been stolen from the convenience store where he would park and lock it up. It was then that I understood why one night he was being beaten very severely. The kids and I had called the police. My little daughter pleaded and begged, "Please help him, Mommy," but I didn't know what to do, except to call 911. After the police left the residence, I called the precinct to find out what happened. They told me that it was only a domestic disturbance over a bicycle, and that I was wrong. It was the wife that accused her husband of threatening her and that her only defense was to hit him back. I told them, "No way," that we had watched her beat him! But it didn't matter to the police. They believed her.

Now I understood what was going on. The pieces of the puzzle started coming together. It was because he was a man. I say, "man," but I mean a loving, gentle, and kind man that refused to hit a woman because he was taught morals. He was being penalized for not having the guts to stand up for himself. God forbid, that he act weak or show sensitivity! So each night he lived in torment. What was wrong with this picture was that I watched the world laugh at him for being what I call, "a true man." As I dropped him off at the bus stop I started to cry. How could I convince this beaten-and-tormented man to get away, when he loved his wife so much? I watched as she drove her big, fancy Cadillac out of the garage and passed him on the street. My hands were tied behind my back. There was nothing more I could do, but pray.

I found a job working at the Noncommissioned Officer's Club (NCO) on base, which paid me enough to support my children. Working as a cook, I was well liked by my boss, who was a very nice man. He felt that I was performing my duties well and that I could work in another position to make even more money. He was one of the best bosses I had ever had the opportunity to work for. Customer satisfaction was his primary goal. And his style was the best I had ever seen. He called everyone by name and went from table to table visiting with customers. He taught me a lot about pleasing the customer and what it took to make a customer happy. His secretary usually had the responsibility of hiring, but this time he interviewed and hired me on his own. She was upset because she felt left out of the decision-making process. She felt as if he went over her head by hiring me. Because of this, she hated me, making my life at the club the most miserable eight years I had ever experienced.

There was one very special person at my place of employment that I learned to love even more. Her name was Miss Shirley. If I could choose another mother, Miss Shirley would have been my second Mom. Anna, of course, was my perfect mother. Shirley became my rock. She was strong and gave me encouragement to get me through the ensuing years. She convinced me to write a book about my life. As I told her my experiences with my family and husband, along with all the other things that had occurred over the years, she told me to put it down on paper. Shirley knew that I would be able to help many people get their lives straight, if I could relate to readers what had happened to me. Shirley was the head cashier and we worked together in the cashier's cage. Miss Shirley gave me a reason to keep working each day. I know that if it were not for Miss Shirley I never would have made it through those years. I loved her so much.

One evening I went home to find police at my door. September had called the police to tell them that she wanted to commit suicide and throw herself through a plate glass window at school. They took her to a mental institution for children where I would find her later. I met my mother and father there and found my daughter falling apart. She just wasn't there in my child's body. She began yelling at me, blaming me for all the pain she had suffered and accusing me of being the reason for her poor mental state. I could not believe I was being blamed for everything, so I decided to leave the hospital.

I started running out the door and crying when my daughter's doctor ran after me. He said, "Miss Jackson, please don't take your daughter's accusations seriously. She's a very sick little girl." I explained that it was hard for me to cope with the thought that she had been blaming me for all those years of abuse her father had given her. The doctor told me that this was normal. He said that some abused and battered children hold the innocent parent to blame for all the bad things that happened to them. I could not accept September's mental condition because I was the type of person that felt that people use excuses to be sick. I felt that if I could take it and still be strong so could September. I had a perfectly normal baby the doctors had told me, no one could tell me that she was now so sick she needed to be tied up in a straitjacket and put into a little room to yell and scream all by herself. I couldn't hold her and comfort her and love my poor little baby girl. I sat in the doctor's office in total disbelief and refused to accept what was happening. The doctor grabbed a baby doll that he had in his office for children to play with while he talked to their parents. He said, "See this doll? Pretend this is your normal baby girl that you gave birth to seventeen years ago." Then he ripped off the head from the doll's neck and said, "Here, take this doll. This is your baby now. Her mind has been taken, disconnected from her body, and she is not a normal person anymore. She is a child that has gone through so much mental abuse that now she no longer is with us. It's time you accept this and now try to love her and help her make it through. Now she needs you more than ever. She needs you to be strong and to allow her finally to let go and express the pain she is encountering." He was surprised that "she had lasted this long."

It was then that I realized that September had purposely held on all those years, just for me. She knew that I needed her, so she kept everything all bottled up inside of mind to give me the support that I needed during those years. Now she could not take it anymore so she exploded. I could not believe the anger she had bottled up inside her. Her hatred for her father was so bad that almost every night she dreamed of millions of different ways that she wanted to kill him. But when she started accusing me of marrying him and allowing him to beat her, I thought I was the one that had gone crazy. To my recollection, I was the one that was taking all the beatings for her. The doctor kept telling me not to take the blame seriously.

My parents would not accept that their granddaughter had a psychological problem. Even after all the years that had gone by, my father still didn't believe that my mother had any mental problems. Anna continued to visit September, although my dad didn't after the first day. It was too much for him to watch his first grandbaby in such a state. I told them the same thing that the doctors had told me. Sam had taken a perfectly normal child and beaten her until she was now mentally incapable of handling life. We would witness September in a straitjacket or in a "quiet room" at the hospital.

Every day I drove to the hospital I tried to believe that there was a good reason for her to be there. They would tell me that she wouldn't sleep well or eat, and I would visit to find her still yelling at me and blaming me for the past. She would call and say, "Mommy, are you coming to see me?" I would reply, "You've accused me of being the abuser and I think that you've chosen to trust your doctors. You have to let them help you get better." After all I had been through to protect her, she now was accusing me. This is what hurt me the most and I had to stop visiting her. I asked her why she was blaming me. She told me that I let her dad beat her. I told her, "I intervened in every beating you received, and took the brunt from your father. How can you say this to me?" Then she would just walk away from me and say no more. I would leave hurt and in pain from seeing my daughter that way. I never wanted to return but kept telling myself, she was my child so I had to be there for her.

As I drove home I would tell myself, maybe she was right and maybe it was my fault. "Maybe if I had left him years ago and went on the street and begged and borrowed, then my child would not be in this condition today? But be reasonable, Cynthia," I'd say aloud, "you never would have survived out there in a world you knew little about." My parents had raised me in a Walt-Disney's imaginary kingdom where I always thought that no one would ever harm me. How completely false! I felt that I had done the best I could in my circumstances. The only thing I regretted was not choosing my mate more wisely, and obtaining a good education. Then I could have walked out a long time ago. This would not have been a debatable issue for me. Unlike a lot of my friends I never would have stayed because of some of the excuses that I'd heard from other women: love, sex, scared, hope their husbands would change, and "he needs help." None of those excuses are worth any man killing you and your children either mentally or physically.

The people in the hospital helped in her recovery, taking her horseback riding. They made her go through strenuous things such as mountain and wall climbing. They were always there to talk with her when she needed consolation, but no one could take the place of her own mother. My lack of visits showed her that she missed me and in time she began to realize and accept that. September began confronting the staff at the institution, asking why they went home to their families when she needed them to be there for her. She began group therapy, where families attended with the patients. The children would speak up against their parents and September called them to the carpet for it. She asked them, "How could you dare speak badly or threaten your own parents in such a manner?" After seeing this she started to understand my position--how felt I did everything I could to help her when she was a child, even if I had to give my own life. Soon she began to ask for her mother and she stopped accusing me of causing her bad life.

Through it all I would drive home to my little daughter and baby son, and they would give me the strength to keep going. Little Mark would smile and reach for me with little goo-goo noises. And it would just make my day. Again, I praised God for my little baby He sent into my life.

In a few months September was back home, but she still spent time in three more institutions because she was unable to cope with life. The mental facilities were a form of relief to her. It was her means of escaping life with a mother who worked all the time and a baby brother demanding all her attention. At the institutions, she had fun and was able to enjoy a protected life with people her own age that also had gone through bad times such as she had. There was no fun when she was home because I had little money to entertain her. Going to an institution was almost like a vacation, she was permitted to sing, dance, and have a normal life. They permitted her to throw tantrums and yell at the staff, but none of this was allowed in my home. She wanted both lives, as it turned out, so she did the best she could to get the best of both of her worlds.

Pogie had come to stay with me and was very helpful taking care of his baby brother. While Pogie was staying with me he decided that it was now time to change his name. So we went over to the courthouse, only to be told that it would cost almost $500, which was money we did not have. We asked if we could walk the paperwork through ourselves and were told that it was very simple and would only cost us around $150. We of course were elated. We immediately went to work filling out the paperwork and doing what was required for us to change his name.

First, we had to prove that he had no criminal record and wasn't a spy of some kind. Second, we had to prove that he didn't owe a lot of bills or anything bad like a person who'd change his name so he could escape being found out, which made a lot of sense to me. Pogie decided to keep the name I given him, which was, "Samuel," and he decided to give himself a middle name, "Kwame." I didn't like it at first but when he explained to me his reasons. "What kid do you know, that actually can say he had given himself his own middle name?" I laughed because he had a good point. Soon the day came for him to change it. The judge could definitely see why. After Pogie told him the reason, the judge hit the mallet and said, "If no one here objects, then your name will be 'Samuel Kwame Jackson' from now on." Of course, I cried and thought Samuel was going to cry too, but he just gave me this big, beautiful smile and said, "Mom, you ready to go home now?"

"Yes, I'm ready finally to take home my son, Samuel Kwame Jackson."

While dealing with September I seemed to neglect my younger daughter Camille, who was now old enough to start desiring to have nice things. She was being teased at school for wearing the same clothes time and time again. Camille loved dressing up and wearing different outfits. One day she told me she was "tired of being poor." I told her that she did not know what it truly was like to be poor and drove all the kids to the poor section of town. Hoping to scare them straight and show them how life could be, I gave them a tour of what it was like to be poor. I had always done my best to give them the best that I could afford. Although they thought they were poor, it was time to open their eyes to what life was like in the projects. Houses there were boarded up, children were playing in tattered clothing, drunks were standing on the corner with their alcohol, and women were sitting on porches to escape the heat of the house and the rodents and insects.

I told my kids that if they were to get pregnant or Pogie was to get a girlfriend pregnant, this is where they would end up. I also explained that this would be their fate if they did drugs or got into trouble of any kind. I refused to support them if they did not do as I had taught them. Living with teenagers, I could not take the stress of them trying to run my house or rule me. And since Camille wanted new clothes I told her that if I were to move here, then I could afford all the clothes and shoes they wanted. They agreed that it was better to have fewer possessions than move to that area. After that time they never asked for more than I was able to give them because I could only pay for rent, utilities, and food.

The Church helped me occasionally with both money and food. The Lion's Club would also help with food and gifts, always making Christmas special for the kids. At times people would come to my door asking for food. Although my refrigerator was empty save for one whole, frozen chicken or one pound of ground beef, I would always offer them a meal and feed them. The children saw that it was the end of our food supply. I told them, "The more I give to others, the more we will receive." That belief never failed me. I stepped out on faith and the Lord always provided. People would bring bags of groceries for my family when we least expected it. I knew all along that since the Lord gave me my children, He would feed them, and He did.

But no matter how hard I tried, it seemed that I could not dig myself out of a hole into which I delved deeper and deeper. I was burying myself and although I had no debt but the car, I was constantly trying to keep my head above water. September decided to move out at this time, thinking that if she had to pay me $200 per month, she might as well live on her own. Her friends had convinced her that she needed to move out and let me and her younger siblings suffer on our own. They thoroughly convinced her that she already had done her part over the years, and that it was now time for her to live her own life and not have to worry about helping me any longer. In a way I felt they were right. September and I were arguing constantly and always at each other's throats. She would not clean her room and was always hanging out with the wrong people. I would never desert her, now, when she needed me the most. I was supporting September and she was living in my house, therefore I believed that she should follow my rules even though her friends told her otherwise. I didn't care that she was in her twenties and supposedly an adult, she was going to follow my rules or move. At first it was hard to accept her being gone but then I got used to it. I would visit occasionally just to check up on her and make sure that she was fine. I still felt very nervous when I would call and she would not answer or call me back. With her mental condition I was always uncertain about her trying to commit suicide again. One day I called and called and when I finally got in touch with her, she told me, "Get a life." This hurt me so

335

badly that it was like a knife stabbing me in the heart. I must have cried for two weeks. I tried to never bother her again.

All I had now to depend on was Camille. She had become my best friend. We got along real well. I guess it was because we both thought alike. Camille always put others first and so did I. I'm glad I was able to get away before her dad also beat her to death mentally. I just wish I was able to leave before September and Pogie were beaten so badly. When I think of all the women out there that are allowing their husbands to beat them and their children, I just wish that I could take them to institutions and allow them to see the children that are suffering because of their decisions to stay with the men they love. I do admit love is blind, but not as blind as watching children turn into young adults who are unable to live normal lives because of the cruelty administered by some abuser that the mother or father sat back and condoned.

# Chapter 41

I still was working hard to keep our heads above water. Miss Shirley was always there with food and snacks for the kids. I was telling her how I wanted to get another job but I was unable to because I had no one to care for the baby. Someone interrupted my conversation. A man was knocking at my cage. I figured it was someone who wanted to cash a check or buy cigarettes. As I walked up to the window there stood a tall, dark, very handsome man. He asked me to go to dinner. I had to turn and look around to see if anyone else was working in the cage with me, because I could not believe a man with his looks would ever ask out someone like me. I thought he must have dropped down from heaven. His gray hair complemented his beard. His beautiful, hazel eyes made me melt. He was about 5'10'', strong and muscular, and probably around fifty-years-old. His name was Moe.

Moe was warm and gentle, and so very polite, as he patiently awaited my answer. I stumbled over my words, trying to appear suave, like I had not noticed that he was gorgeous. I finally spit out the word, "Yes."

"How about Saturday at seven? Will that be all right with you?"

Not even thinking about the time or the day I gazed into his hazel eyes and said, "Yes." He smiled and went back to work in the club. He was a Disc Jockey, and was one of the best I had ever heard. I stood in disbelief when Miss Shirley walked into the cage and asked me if I was all right. I wanted to scream. I went on and on and on, talking to her about him, as she smiled at me. I felt as though I were walking on clouds that night when I rushed home to tell my kids.

They laughed as I told them of how gorgeous he was and how I could not possibly wait until Saturday. That Saturday arrived and I could not for the life of me think of anything to wear. I wanted to charm him but I also wanted to look decent. I wanted him to think I was beautiful and modest as I placed out dress after dress. Nothing seemed to catch my eye. Soon my daughter Camille ran in and started to help me get dressed. It had been years since I went on a date, and never had I been on a date with someone as handsome as this man. As I scurried around perfecting my makeup and hair, my daughter laughed at me because I was so nervous. Suddenly, my daughter picked out a dress that I had forgotten was even in my closet. It was absolutely perfect for this perfect date.

Soon, the doorbell rang. I did not know how to act as I heard the kids answering the door. He stepped in and I could hear his deep voice. "Is your mother here?" I was too nervous to go to the door so I stood in my room looking in the mirror. You would have thought that this was my wedding day. Camille soon came to the room and said, "Mom, you're right, he is handsome!" Biting at my nails I told her I knew that, as I slowly walked to the front room where he awaited. I turned the corner only to see him in a suit with a single flower in his hand. He told me "how nice" I looked. I told him, "thank you," and said he looked very nice, as well. He gracefully walked me to the car and opened the door for me. I got in and away we went.

Dinner was at a very nice restaurant and we spent the entire evening talking. He finally mentioned his eight kids. Three were grown but he had five more at home. I gathered my thoughts and realized that between the two of us we had twelve children. I completely lost focus and began to think that this would never work. I started to drown him out. I was on the verge of a nervous breakdown. There was no way I could handle that many children. I tried to smile as he kept

338

talking. I nodded "yes" to whatever he had to say. Then I heard him ask me to go skating with his children and mine. I sort of said, "Yes." I had not skated in years. He walked over to help me out of my chair and we walked to the front of the restaurant to pay the bill. I could not help but think, "Now how am I going to get out of this?" I wanted to keep seeing this man but I could not handle any more children.

When he dropped me off at my front door I wandered into my house in a daze. The following Saturday arrived quickly. He drove up in a van. He brought all of his children up to the door and introduced them. I smiled to myself as we all climbed into the van.

When we reached the skating rink and rented our skates. He sat by me and put on his skates. He grabbed my hands and said, "Are you sure you want to do this?" I smiled and kept assuring myself that I could. I prayed that I would not fall. As we took off skating I was a little shaky at first, but soon I was in the swing of things. I was going along so well that I decided to let go of his hands. The next thing I remember, I was starting to fall. I tried to straighten up only to find myself standing upright but still skating and heading straight for the wall. I slammed right into the wall and fell backwards. Moe skated toward me and asked if I was all right. Blushing and laughing, I tried to pass it off. I told him I was fine, but he reached his hand out to help me. Thanking him and blushing because of how silly I must have looked, I told him, "I'm a little rusty but give me time, and I'll catch on." I struggled to get back up on my feet. My legs were going in all directions as I tried to balance myself. Once I got up, I started to skate again.

I thought I was really in the swing of things. I even tried doing a little dance, since it seemed so easy for the children, as they passed by me. As I passed Moe, I just smiled at him as I was trying to show off my skills. The next thing I knew I was slipping again. I had nothing to grab so I went skating into a row of kids, grabbing hold of all of them. We all hit the floor and several kids behind me joined us. Everyone was fussing and complaining as they all got up and left me on the floor. My body hurt so badly! I could not get up this time. When Moe skated past me, he could not help but laugh. I asked him if he was going to help me. He said, "Nope, but the way you're going at it, you're going to need a miracle." He laughed and skated off. The only way I could get off the floor was to crawl over to the carpet. No one wanted to help me, including my own children.

I crawled over to the bench and sat on it as I got myself together. All the children skated by laughing. Soon, Moe came over and teasingly asked me if I was trying to shine the floor. I laughed as he sat down beside me. He hugged me and kissed me on the cheek. He took my hand and I felt the warmth of his smile as his beautiful hazel eyes stared at me. He asked if I would like to try it again. I knew for the sake of all the children on the skating rink floor it would be safer for them if I stayed on the sidelines.

We all had a big laugh later as we drove home. I tried to distance myself. I told him we could be friends but that's all we could be because we had too many children between us. He didn't agree but he respected my wishes. From that day forward we became the best of friends. I could always depend on him and he could always depend on me. He was someone I could lean on in times of need.

He also said the most beautiful thing anyone had ever said to me at that time in my life when I was struggling so hard to stay sane. He said, "I would like to stop over every now and then and take the kids off your hands." He also said that he would like to be with them, "as they may need a father." I told him how very much I loved him and appreciated what he wanted to do. I really needed someone to take the kids so I could get some rest.

He was a man of his word. Every so often he would visit and take the children places. My kids grew fond of him and started to love him as if he were their own father. Sometimes he would just call to see if I was off and wanted to rest. Even though I could never marry this man, I loved him very much. He became my very best friend. I think what I loved about him most was that he was one of the best fathers I had ever seen. He was just one man, but he spread himself out among ten children. He was at my son's basketball games cheering him on as he also tried to attend his own son's games. He took my daughter to her social events and stood in for her as a father figure when she was crowned queen at the prom.

I have never wanted to marry a man as much as I wanted to marry Moe, but I knew it was no good. I could never be the wife he needed for I was on the verge of a nervous breakdown. I was only holding on by a thread. Sometimes he would take the kids for the weekend, but this was still not enough. I was still drinking a lot and could feel my mind leaving me. I was slowly slipping away. My mind, body, and soul were gone. Moe told me to call him nightly to make sure I was okay. He knew things in my life were getting serious by our phone conversations. As I spoke of running away and leaving my children in foster care he would tell me, "No, not you Cynthia." He told me I was a wonderful mother and to lean on him.

One night I had one of my dreams, but with this dream I woke up crying. I did not want to accept this one. In my dream Moe found out from a doctor he had cancer. The doctor told him that he could not save him because the cancer had spread throughout his body. In my dream I cried and pleaded with Moe to quit smoking, and he took the palm of his hands and pushed me away. In the next scene he was in his bedroom. He had just gone comatose for two hours and his grandchildren had crawled up onto his bed. They were lying on his chest to tell him goodbye as his sons and daughters stood near his side crying. I tried to fight my dream as I wiggled and squirmed, and suddenly I awoke in a horrible sweat.

How was I going to tell Moe? How was I going to get him to understand that he had to stop smoking and he had to do it now? How was I going to convince my best friend and the only man that I have ever truly loved that he was going to die? So what if my other dreams have come true, maybe this time my dream was wrong? But I knew deep down, that my dream was going to come true and whether I accepted it or not, soon he was going to die. I did not get a time table so it could have been a year, or ten years from that very moment. I sat down and wrote him a long letter telling him about my dream and that he was the rock that held us all together. He had to stop smoking or his children would get into drugs and his daughters would walk the streets for love." <u>Please stop before we lose you, Moe. You are my best friend! Please stop. I love you</u>."

I sent the letter to him because I was afraid to face the man I loved, my best friend, and tell him that he was dying. I was a coward. When Moe got the letter I expected him to call me, but I received no phone call. I called his house and the kids hung up on me. I called his job and he hung up on me. I could not believe that this had affected him so badly. I did not tell him in the letter the details of my dream. I only said, "He must stop now".

I had to get my mother to call him and beg him to speak with me. He asked to meet me in our park where we used to go to walk and exercise. I stepped up to the car and I could see the anger in his face as he started yelling at me. He

342

had taken my letter the wrong way and thought that I was saying that his children were drug addicts and his daughters were whores. I told him he read the letter wrong but that it might happen if he dies. He looked at me with his hazel eyes and was very sincere, "Cynthia, I do not care what you do or what you say. I will not stop smoking." I pleaded with him, asking him if his family was not worth it. He yelled at me, "Stop!", and he put his hand to my face, just like in my dream. He told me that if I honestly loved him, I would let this go. I bent my head down and started to sob as he took me in his arms. He told me he loved me and "to let it go." I never brought up the subject again for fear that I would lose my best friend. We went back to talking to each other but I knew my limitations.

# Chapter 42

One morning I woke to find myself lying in a puddle of blood. I was scared because I had never seen so much blood. I was wondering how I could have lived through the night losing that much blood. I immediately called the hospital and made an appointment to see a gynecologist. She told me that I had several tumors that would have to be removed by giving me a total hysterectomy. But first I had to stop bleeding. We tried everything to stop the bleeding but there was nothing we could do. It just got worse. One day I could not get myself out of bed I was so weak. At the hospital the doctor told me that they were going to have to operate. My only concern was how soon I could go back to work. I couldn't afford to be out of work one day. She told me that I should only be thinking of my health. But how could I, when the kids and I were falling fast into the poor house? She told me that my recovery probably would take two months or less. I told her it would have to be less. I told myself, "I'll be up in two weeks."

After the surgery I found that I was not as strong as I thought I would be. Three weeks later, I knew we were in trouble but I did not let on to the kids. Somehow, though, my youngest daughter, Camille, knew. She went out looking for a job. Finding a job as a carhop at a burger joint, she would bring home every cent she made to help. She would stay by my side and care for me as much as she could. When she saw that I was still unable to go back to work and that the money she was making was not enough, she decided that she would get another job. I tried to tell her not to worry about it but she refused to accept it. I told her that she was not capable of working two jobs at 15-years- old. Sixty hours a week was going to be too much for her, but she would not give up. She was determined to help her family and me, survive. I would watch, as she would get up after only sleeping an hour, and drag herself to the bathroom to get ready for work. I kept begging her to listen to me. She tried to explain that it was not only for me, but also for her baby brother. She did not want us to have to move into the projects. I tried to get up and return to work, but it was harder than I thought. The doctor was right. But for me, I could not accept being defeated.

After two months I was finally able to go back to work. I made Camille quit, and though I was in a lot of pain, I didn't let her see me sweat. I thanked my little daughter for trying, but we still went under. She felt like she had failed but I told her that there was nothing more she could do. I was very proud of her. I wanted the whole world to know of her heroic efforts and her attempts to keep her family afloat during our crisis.

After I went back to work I still could not catch up. I avoided telling Camille or anyone because I knew that no one could help me now. I started sinking into a deep, deep depression. I was having a hard time remembering things. One day, I passed by a stopped school bus that had its red warning flashers on and the stop sign extended. I hadn't even realized that I had done such a dangerous thing, but the police officer that stopped me cited me and I had to go to court. When the judge asked me if I knew how dangerous of a situation that I had put those innocent children in I told him, "Yes, sir, I do, and I should be hung. I would not want anyone to pass my child's school bus!" He fined me over $300, adding that he was being lenient with the punishment. I agreed with him, yet walking out of the courtroom I knew that something was wrong with me. I would never put children in jeopardy as I had done with that school bus. I tried to understand. I kept getting lost on my way home, and doing things that were not normal for me. I was drinking even more.

Asking the Church for help, I began to receive checks from them to supplement my income, but eventually those stipends were no longer written on the church's checks. They started arriving from a gentleman in the congregation. Somehow, he had learned of my plight and decided that it was his responsibility to help. He felt committed to helping me. I was working from 10:00 PM to 7:00 AM. Upon visiting, he would talk to me and try to explain that I should move out of my house and find someplace less expensive. It seemed to me that doors were closed to me at every turn.

I sought a psychiatrist because I knew I needed help. She felt that I was having a nervous breakdown and wanted to put me in a rest home. She wanted me to get away for six months to put my life together. I do not like rules and regulations or being told what to do. What I needed was to find peace to be alone with the Lord to rebuild my life. I did not have the option of sending my children to their grandmother (she had told me that repeatedly). And because of her multiple personalities, I could never leave my kids with her. I called my cousin, Cheryl, in California, who offered me a place to live and told me she would help me find a job. I decided to take her up on this offer. But Anna Mae felt it was not a good idea. Anna Mae had the ability to look at a person's character and know what kind of person he or she was, and she didn't think that living with my cousin was such a great idea. But I had to get away or I was not going to make it. Then there was the dilemma of what was I going to do with my children.

I told the Church about my situation and they told me of a brother and sister in church that could probably help me. Once I explained to the couple what was going on they wanted to give me monetary help, but that was not the help I was seeking. Once they saw my financial situation, they agreed that it was too much to handle. Finally, I had to confide in them, and tell them that I was having a nervous breakdown and was under a doctor's care. I told them the doctor wanted to put me away but I felt that all I needed was rest. I asked if they would watch my children in my absence. I gave my psychiatrist permission to speak with them about me. The wife was not as understanding as her husband and felt that I was able to handle my own problems because she could. She felt that she had overcome and I should do the same, but there was just one major difference. Whenever she felt she needed to get away to work out her feelings, she could just do that. She would visit her family with the support of her husband, who would take care of the home in her absence. They had few bills, no children in high school, or the lack of money that I had. They received two incomes, which allowed the wife to deal with expenses while she dealt with her life problems. She had no idea about what I had suffered through, and I was too tired to beg her for help or her understanding. Still, I would never forget the kindness and generosity that they both had shown me in my time of need.

I visited the couple and exchanged information with them about my children so that they could care for them in my absence. I had legal forms drawn up, granting them guardianship. The woman told me in no uncertain terms that she disagreed with this arrangement. I didn't want to leave my children with anyone that felt this way but it was too late to find someone else. Even though she did not want me to leave my children with her I felt I had no other choice. Somehow I knew that she would give them the care they needed. I didn't want to say goodbye to my kids, so the couple planned on picking them up after school the next day. I delivered my car and furniture to a storage facility. As I boarded the airplane to California, I knew that my children would be picked up at school and would be in safe hands until my return. Tears were in my eyes during the flight. I knew that I would find the peace that I was seeking and soon would be back up on my feet again, ready to return and move my children to California to live with me.

Cheryl's daughter picked me up at the airport. As I walked through the door, I had a strange feeling about their house. Originally, I would be living there with my cousin and her daughter, but since our last conversation, her teenage son, Bill, had moved back in. I wanted to find a job as quickly as possible since I would no longer be using his room and instead would be sleeping on the couch. We all got along the first few days. I was drinking every night during that time and we would share our thoughts while sitting around in the evening. Cheryl asked me what kind of men I preferred. I told her that I liked men with dark complexions and complimenting her, I said, "It would be someone that might resemble your son, only older."

She laughed and agreed that her son was very handsome. I searched for a job daily and either walked, rode the bus, or was driven to interviews by Bill. When I went out, I carried a knife in my purse to protect myself. I became close to her daughter who warned me that we were in a dangerous area and I needed protection. One day I was washing dishes to find her son standing directly behind me at the sink. Upon my asking Bill what he was doing, he smiled and walked away. Other times, I would awaken on the couch and see him walking through or standing in front of me, watching me. Taking a shower one day, I was alone in the house and neglected to lock the door. Although I didn't think the son was home at the time, Bill entered the bathroom and began to shave. I asked him to leave and he did. I felt strangely about this young man, but I could not put my finger on what it was. Another day I was getting dressed when I noticed that all my underwear were on top of my laundry bag, after I purposely had placed them in the bottom of the bag. I put them back into the bottom of the bag to see what would happen when I got home. Sure enough, I found them in the same place again, on top of the laundry. I wanted to bring this up to Cheryl, but I didn't.

# Chapter 43

Cheryl had told Bill not to drink or entertain friends at the house. I watched as he totally ignored her and continued to entertain his friends daily. After drinking her beer, he would replace it so she would not be aware of his actions in her absence. One day as I was lying on the floor watching a video of my son, Bill strolled in and lay on top of my back. I threw him off of me and wrestled with him. I told him, "Never do that again!" Knowing I needed to discuss this with him or tell his mom, I tried to avoid him while keeping things on an even keel. If I had approached her, she may not have believed me and might have told me to leave. I had nowhere to go.

I went out to buy some beer and asked him if I could drink it in his car. Soon he walked out to the car and asked me if I could give him some advice. At first he sat in the front seat of his car as I listened to him tell me about problems that he had with his girlfriend, who at the time was pregnant. He was having issues with her family. Then he asked me for a beer. I told him, "Sure," as he got out of the front seat and joined me in the back. The next thing I knew he was trying to kiss me. I yelled, "Are you crazy? I 'm old enough to be your mother! You're my second cousin. Don't you understand what you're doing?" As he got out the car I kicked him in the back. In the house I tried to explain to him that we were cousins. I asked him if he was on some kind of drugs. He said, "No," but I knew he was. I had seen him take a bunch of pills from his friends when they stopped over. He just laughed. I began to think that maybe he was just crazy. I told him that I knew he was in my dirty laundry and even though he denied it, I told him I had proof. I told him the next time he messed with me I was going to his mother. He walked away smiling.

The next day while washing clothes I heard him open the back door and let in the dog. He knew that I was afraid of the dog and that the dog would come after me. He started to laugh as I begged him to get the animal out of the house. I knew that this was payback for me kicking him and threatening to tell his mother. He knew the dog was vicious and every time I moved around the dog, it would try to crash through the screen on the backdoor to try and bite me. The next day after I came home from the store I found the entire family around the table. My cousin said that her son had told her that I had taken her knife. I told her, "Yes, I did but I put it back as soon as I got home and Bill saw me put it back." Now, I knew what he was up to. It was because I refused to sleep with him. He was doing everything he could to get back at me. I looked at him as he smirked. I wasn't sure how I was going to handle this situation now that he had his mother on his side. I asked his mom to keep him out of the front room when I was there sleeping, especially at night. She explained that he liked to go outside and lift weights late at night. I couldn't sleep at night because he would turn on the TV or sit on my bed while I was dozing. I had to do something but I didn't know what. So I went out and tried even more to find a job so I could get away from him. I was starting to worry and my condition was getting worse. I needed to get out of that house. Feeling down, I walked to the store and bought some beer. I drank it, returned to the house and sat watching a movie.

While I was watching the movie a commercial appeared about a Psychic Network. Something inside of me was very curious about what was ahead of me. I knew though, that if I called I was turning my back on God. I knew I was miserable and that nothing was going right. When was this all going to end? When was this roller coaster going to stop? When was I ever going to get back up on my feet? And when would I get my children back? With all my unanswered questions, I decided to call the psychic hotline. Knowing that calling them was like slapping God in the face, I was so drawn to finding out about what was ahead for me in the future, I denied what I knew the Lord had told me. As I waited on the phone, a woman's voice said, "A young man around 18-20 years old is about to do you harm." I told her that I didn't care about that. I wanted to know my future. She said all she could see was that, "harm is about to come to you."

At that moment, the door slammed shut. A breeze blew past me, the phone was cut and dangled in the air, the dog stood outside barking and scratching at the backdoor viciously like he was trying to bite and scratch his way through the plate glass door. The television screen kept showing a physic host talking, and the room began spinning and spinning. I knew that the Lord had just slammed the door and left my presence because I had deserted him. He left me because He could not live in me when evil was at my door. I had just let Satan in and there was no turning back. I turned to see Bill, my cousin's son, standing in the dark staring at me. I was so scared I could not move. As I lay the receiver back into its cradle, I still heard the woman repeating that, "a man will do you harm." The next morning when I awoke, I tried to figure out whom it could be that would do me harm.

That afternoon Bill walked into the room and made mention that a company downtown was hiring. I was surprised that he told me. I assumed that he was finished with his revenge. He asked if I wanted to go with him to put in an application. I felt skeptical but said, "Yes." We filled out applications and he told me he wanted to stop at a friend's house. I thought about the warning I received the night before. Maybe it will be one of his friends? I stayed in the car. I was thinking that maybe one of his friends would shoot me. Soon he strolled out to the car and we left. I buckled up just in case we got into an accident. I was so scared that I was scaring myself.

That night I went to bed early, I was afraid to watch any television. After taking my sleeping pills I quickly fell to sleep. I was dreaming that I was in a movie riding a horse and being chased as I tried to escape. The scene changed and all of a sudden I was inside another scene, in bed with a man making love to me, which made no sense to me. This forced me to wake up and when I did, there I found Bill on top of me. I knocked him to the floor. He quickly got up and ran to his room. I could not believe that my own cousin had violated me. I followed him to his room "This is what you wanted? Was it worthwhile taking it away from me? Was it worth raping me just to get this? This is how low you had to go?" He started to yell, possibly to awaken his mother. I went to Cheryl's room to awaken her myself. He watched me from the threshold of his room to see what I would say. Standing at the door of her room, I started to knock and then I suddenly stopped. I began to think, "Where am I going to live?" I just stood there, turning to look back at Bill. I saw him watching me with another one of his sly smirks as he dared me to do it. One thing is for sure! He wasn't crazy. He had already figured out, just as I had, that I had nowhere to go, and no one would believe me. So I slowly turned and walked past him. I went back to my bed. I stayed up all night, distrustful. As Cheryl got ready to go to Church the next morning, she saw me lying in my robe on the couch. She had never seen me like that before, so she asked me if I was all right. I told her I wasn't feeling well, but what I really felt was disgust. Her son taking me during the night while I was asleep! How dare he, that disgusting creature or whatever you want to call him, have done that to me? I was his blood cousin. I had never felt so filthy and betrayed in my life. I wanted to kill him. All his other offenses could not compare to what he had done to me that night. I knew that I would never be the same. I couldn't trust family again.

Immediately, I called the Church. I told them I needed someone to take me in and they said they would try to find someone that could help me. The preacher's wife gave me the number of someone to call. No one answered so I decided to wait. After trying all night I gave up and went to bed. I took no sleeping pills nor drank any beer that night. I wanted to be clear-headed. I was so sleepy from staying up all night the day before that I immediately fell asleep, only to find myself trying to get into my White Room. But I couldn't, the door was bolted shut and I could not get in. I kept running down hallways, stopping at what I thought were doors only to find those also locked and bolted shut. Crying and shivering I kept yelling, "Lord, please don't lock me out. I love you, Lord, please don't lock me out!" Falling to my knees, with my hands hiding my face, I was sobbing uncontrollably as I begged him, "Please let me in." Then I awoke to find Bill hovering over me as if he were some kind of demon. He laughed at me as he got up. I sat up the rest of the night in total fear.

The next morning could not arrive quickly enough as I sat watching the phone I had placed on my lap. I called the number given to me from the church and begged some strange women, to please come and take me to a shelter or somewhere safe. A woman with the name, "Lynn," finally drove to Cheryl's home to pick me up and take me to her home. How could I ask the Lord for help after I called the Psychic Network? (Luke 12:22-31, Isaiah 8:19, Leviticus 19:31 and Leviticus 20:6-27) I dropped to my knees and asked for forgiveness. I said, "I am your child. I do not want to be mixed up in a world of psychics, soothsayers, tarot card readers, mediums or anything dealing in the demonic world involved with Satan. Lord God, I need you in my life. Please, dear Lord, I'll never turn against you again. Please give me another chance."

I walked through the door of Lynn's home and she introduced me to her husband. He was very knowledgeable about the Bible. I told him what had happened to me. After speaking to him I decided to search the phone book for a shelter, and upon finding one that would accept me, her husband drove me there.

I called my Aunt and asked if she could gather my clothing from my cousin's house and deliver it to me at the shelter. She sent her son Robert, Cheryl's brother, who felt that no member of the family should spend time in a shelter. I wanted to tell him what had happened, but I feared that he would not believe me. He thought his sister and I had an argument, which caused me to leave. We had gotten along well. I was truly thankful for Cheryl's help and she had been very sweet to me during my stay. But it wasn't long till Robert's wife, Kim, questioned me. Since I would be staying in their home, I decided I should tell her why I left. After telling her, she immediately called Cheryl.

The whole family believed that I was lying. Bill made up some pretty good lies. He told them that I was turned on by him and that I tried to kiss him, telling him that he was "a kisser." He actually told them that we had sex because I allowed it. I looked at him, disbelieving that he could say such things about me. Why would they believe that I would leave their home for no good reason? All my cousin had to do was put two and two together and she would have figured it out. If I were so interested in her son then why did I leave the house and go to a shelter in a town where I had nowhere else to go? If I were the culprit, then why was he falsely accusing me of stealing her knife? If I said he could kiss so good then why was I not still at her home kissing him, instead of being out on the street by myself? I think that he must have told them some detailed stories to cover up what he truly was, and that he was the one who forced me to leave. Why couldn't anyone figure out why I would leave and go to a shelter? No one believed me and the entire family was now at my throat. We all began fighting. This young man was one sick individual. I called the police, but the family told the police that they were decent Christians and that I was the culprit, that I was trying to turn their family upside down. The police believed them and the officers took me in the police car back to the shelter.

I was welcomed at the shelter by a lady named Anna that seemed to want to help me. She explained to me about finding jobs and the rules and regulations of the shelter. I was to fix supper that evening. I cleaned up the dinner dishes and went to bed. Little did I know, that for revenge, Cheryl had called the shelter and told them the family's version of what had taken place. The next morning as I was dressing to start my morning duties, I was told that I had to leave. Anna in return, lied and told the owner of the shelter that when I arrived I had a bundle of money in my bra and had told them they could not have it. Anna also felt that because I was well dressed and well mannered that I didn't deserve to be there. She wanted me to go back to my fancy home where I belonged. I didn't understand why she would want to stab me in the back.

Normally when you enter a shelter you have to tell them what you have, and if you have any money. You then have to turn it in. I did not have a cent on me. I was not the only one kicked out that day. There was also another woman that was put out. Only with her, I could understand why. She was breaking all the rules. She was always stumbling in drunk. We both left the building at the same time. We didn't know where to go so we both sat on a step outside the shelter talking about what we were going to do. I was crying because I had no money and did not know where I was. As we sat on the front steps of the shelter, I asked the other woman where she was going to stay. She knew of an alley where she had stayed before that would be safe. The next thing I knew I was asking her to let me go with her. I couldn't believe I was asking her permission to go to an alley with her. The shelter agreed to hold onto my clothing for 48 hours until I found a place to stay. Soon Anna came out to tell us not to linger on their premises or she would have us arrested. Walking away, I watched as she laughed at us. With my head down, I now knew that I was truly on the streets, all alone. That is where I dreaded I would wind up. This is why I left my kids in someone's care, just in case I ended up on the street. Arriving at the alley, I sat on a small air conditioning vent. The other lady who was kicked out told me that she was going to find a drink and would return later. I would walk up and down the alley then and pray to the Lord, not to forsake me at my lowest point. I knew that I would not be staying in that alley that night. I knew that even though I turned my back on God, he was not going to forsake me.

I walked to the school where I was to take computer lessons the following week and let them know that I was on the street and would not be attending their class. I wanted them to know that I would be returning to Texas instead. The school counselor, Barbara, told me to wait before I made any big decisions. She would try to find me a place to sleep. I called the Church in the meantime because I had heard a woman there was looking for someone to stay with her as her husband had died. When I reached her, she said that she didn't want company at that time, but she told me that maybe her sister-in-law did. As I walked out dismayed, Barbara told me that I had a phone call. I wanted to call my mother, collect my clothes, and leave the school. I answered the phone and spoke to a woman named, Cora. She and her husband, Fred, had been talking about giving me a place to live. Her husband picked me up and took me to their home, providing me a small room with a couch. Cora was like a sister to me but I didn't care for Fred. She had told me that he was abusive. She was a very giving and loving woman who didn't particularly like to cook and clean. Since I enjoyed doing household chores, I kept the house and sometimes watched her little girl. We sat and talked side by side each night, and I told her about the book I would someday write. We would pray together and she would share scriptures with me. I was beginning to feel better about myself and being with her touched my life tremendously. She brought me back and made sure I went to church. I continued my computer classes.

Knowing that I missed my youngest son terribly, she suggested that I contact my children. She knew I needed them by my side. My depression got worse as I missed my children more and more each day. She told me she would help me find a job and thanked me for coming into her life. While I lived there, her husband did not beat her and she was thankful.

I flew back to pick up my son and daughter. Camille decided that it would be better to finish high school rather than possibly drop out or change schools at that time. I picked up my car from storage, and accompanied by Camille, we all drove back to California. We had a wonderful time singing Christian songs, laughing, and playing games. I praised God because I He had forgiven me and welcomed me back into His arms as His child. I saw that I was nothing without Him and that all the bad things that had happened to me in my life were because I had turned my face from Him. I had no longer trusted Him or believed Him. I did not allow Him to work every day in my life. I knew that I had to get my life straight with the Lord once again.

We soon arrived back at Cora's. After we rested I took Camille back to the airport for the return trip to my mom and dad's. Trouble started brewing as Cora's husband began mentally abusing Mark. Mark did not eat vegetables, but was stopped from eating the meat on the plate, until he ate several spoons of mixed vegetables. I asked if Mark could skip the vegetables, since he never did like them. Cora agreed that since I was the mom, her husband should indulge me in my request. Fred didn't feel the same. I knew that sooner or later we would have to leave. By now, Cora and I were like sisters. She was such an inspiration to me. I had completed my computer classes, and with my new skills Cora felt that I could easily find a job. She tried to find something in her office for me but they were not hiring. I didn't have enough experience.

One day Cora invited me to go to a wedding with her rather than stay home. They were serving cake in another room. Mark was running around and Cora's daughter was getting into the cakes. I reminded my son that he was in the House of God and there would be no running. In the car, Cora's husband overheard me getting on Mark about running in church. So Fred told both the children, who had misbehaved, that they would have no dinner. Mark said, "Mom--" I stopped him in mid-sentence, hoping he would not say anything to upset Fred. On the way home, Fred picked up two pizzas. Upon our arrival, Fred told the children to get ready for bed. I told him that he was not the one to prohibit my son from eating. I was his mother and I would be the one to punish Mark. Besides that, why was Fred in my business, it was me that saw my own child misbehaving. For him to meddle in my affairs was wrong and I did not appreciate it. So I walked to the corner and bought Mark something to eat. Cora's husband continued to carry on and my son was too upset to eat. Fred told us that night, "It's time to move." Cora stayed quiet. She was too afraid to say anything. Besides, I didn't want her to defend us. Fred figured that because I had nowhere to go that I would allow him to treat my child and me any way he wanted. I had taken about as much as I was going to take. He was not going to mistreat my child.

A man had promised me an apartment, but when I went to see about it, he said his wife didn't want to rent to anyone without a job. She didn't want to rely on my receiving welfare and child support to pay the rent. I humbled myself to Fred, asking if we could stay an additional two or three days while I found a place to live. He told me, "No, you will leave tonight." Being winter, it was cold outside, so I bundled up my son and put him into the car. I drove to my friend's house where I had stayed after my cousin raped me, and told my son to climb through the fence and knock on her door. Later, I called them to see if my son was there. They asked me to come and stay there too. I should not be out in the cold. In the meantime, Fred had already called them, filling them with lies about my child's poor behavior. They did not know at the time that Fred was an abusive man and neither did the Church. He had hidden his true colors very well. The next morning, I decided to leave because I didn't think they would believe me over Fred. I could also see that I was not wanted there because of the lies Fred had told them, so I left. Mark and I went from store to store, through malls and restaurants to stay warm. Sometimes we were asked to move along when the managers figured out that we were "squatters" or homeless and were only there to stay warm. It's funny but I was surprised to find out they knew.

Finally I remembered a friend that told me if I was ever in trouble and needed help to contact her. I told her about the events of the past few days and being poor herself, and having a tiny house, she gave us refuge. That evening after having supper, I decided to clean the dinner dishes. I opened the freezer to put in the ice trays. In her freezer, were three small bags of frozen spaghetti sauce and in her cupboards were bags of spaghetti noodles. That was all she had. Not letting on, I told her that I would be gone by morning. I knew of a shelter where Mark and I could stay. But I had already called and was told that in California "we help Californians first," and then people from other states. I was told that nothing was available for me at the time.

My friend would have asked me to stay, but they were having hard times themselves. I told her that we would be fine even though I had no idea where Mark and I were going. Again, I decided that it would be best if I moved back with my mother. I had just enough money to make it home. But my little son kept the faith and reminded me that God was going to take care of us. More and more each day I could see why God sent this now little boy into my life. And to think I came up with a hundred reasons why I wanted to kill that innocent, little baby inside my womb. He was my reason to get up in the morning. He would lie beside me at night and sometimes put his little arms around me and tell me, "Mommy, everything is going to be all right. You'll see, Mommy."

God doesn't give us babies because he wants to make our lives more miserable. He foresees our future and the troubles ahead and sends a little, tiny infant into our lives to bring laughter, happiness, and a smile to our faces. Again I praised God for my little son, Mark.

# Chapter 44

I returned to the school and explained that I would not make it to my graduation. Barbara reminded me that I had worked hard and had tried to start a new life for myself. She told me that she would try to help.

"I can not go back to my parents."

"Keep trusting God, Cynthia, and He will take care of you."

A classmate named Peggy came in asking what was going on and she told us that we could stay with her. After staying about a week, Peggy's boyfriend did not want to support her, her son, and us too. I agreed and again we were asked to leave. Peggy said, "Wait before you leave. I have an idea."

She walked down the street to her friend who was the landlord of a small apartment complex. Peggy soon returned with a lady named, Martha. The lady was very happy to help. She had four children, one of them a new baby. She knew how she would feel in my situation and offered to help me. Being a good person, she knew it was her duty as a believer in God to help us. The Lord was sending person after person into our lives to help. She took me to the buildings' owner who told me that he knew of a program where they would pay him the first and last month's rent. I went to get the money, gave it to him, and he allowed Mark and I to move into the apartment. Mark and I only had two tents and a couple of boxes of clothing. We had some dishes and necessities to survive. It seemed like a decent place to live and we were glad to have a roof over our heads. When things broke, however, the landlord did not fix them and when we had problems with the neighbors he would ignore our requests. A drunken woman above us would go out onto her balcony and sing Spanish songs all night till dawn. There were also gunshots in the night. Mark and I would practice crawling on the floor to move around the house. Mark would spend the night covering his ears and crying, because he knew he had to go to school the following day. School was always important to Mark and I wanted him to excel, but there was nothing I could do. After work I would drive around looking for another place.

A woman living in the apartment next door would go jogging each day. I got to know her and started jogging along with her. While jogging one day in an affluent area, we passed a very large, beautiful home. In the front yard of this almost mansion-like home, was a sign that read: "For Rent." We looked at it at the same time and wondered what the rent could possibly be. My guess was $3,000-$4,000 per month. Her estimate was about $2000 per month. I wrote down the number to settle a bet I made with her, and decided to call as soon as I got back home.

I asked the owner of the house about the fee and she replied, "The rent is $495." I was in shock because there was no way it could possibly be that low. Without thinking for a moment, I told her to hold it for me because I was going to live there. She agreed to meet me there. I dressed in my best outfit so that I would look befitting of a house of that grandeur. I went to the house and stood outside disbelieving that this could possibly be true. Approaching her door, I asked the Lord, "How can You bless me so richly as to put a mansion at my feet that I wouldn't have the means to actually live in?" Just residing in this neighborhood would be more wonderful than I could imagine.

Karen, the owner, drove up and getting out of her car, she asked if I had seen it and I replied, "I haven't yet been inside." She led me to the back of the house. I wondered why she was heading to the back of the house, but I followed and figured that we were going to enter from the rear for some reason. We followed a beautiful, stone pathway around to the back of the house, where we came upon a wooden gate. She opened the tall gate only to reveal the most amazing sight I had ever seen in my entire life. There sat two big, elegant stone lionesses on both sides of a stone walkway that led into a splendid garden neatly trimmed with large trees covering the yard. The path led to a small, blue cottage with a gabled roof. The yard was full of peach, apricot, and orange trees. · Grapes lined a fence, and squirrels playfully scampered on the grass. The cottage contained a small kitchenette, one bedroom and a living room, just big enough for one person to live comfortably. What a wonderful place this would be to raise Mark! "How could I be so blessed?" I asked. Even the train station was right around the corner, in case we needed to commute. Karen told me that it was very peaceful here. I told her how beautiful I thought it was. I knew I had entered my Garden of Eden.

Karen took me through the house and another woman arrived, but the potential tenet decided that it would be too small for her and her fiancé, and she didn't care for the living room closets. The owner led me around the backyard, where I had visions of Mark running and playing. I told her, "The house is absolutely perfect for me," and I begged her to rent it to me. I could feel that the Lord wanted me to live there. I promised her that she would receive my rent payments every single month and she agreed to rent to me. I hugged her and hoped she knew what that moment meant to me. I would have peace in that cottage. That cottage is where I would be able to rest and find refuge, preparing for the day my daughter would join me. I felt such joy. All that I could do was cry and try to hold in the excitement of telling Mark where we would be living. After school I told him to start packing the car for our move. He was so happy when I showed it to him. He could hardly wait to go to his new home after school.

We shared our first dinner in our new home. Later we sat together reading the Bible, singing and praising the Lord for all He had given us. We had such great joy for what He had provided for us and where He had allowed us to live. Mark always would stay as quiet as possible, so that I could rest and become whole again. This is where I belonged; this is where God had brought me. The mansion in front was larger and much grander, but nothing could compare to my little cottage. I hold in my heart the memories of the peace and tranquility that little home gave me. I didn't have to go into an institution, for God had a very special place waiting for me where I could get myself back together again.

Having the responsibility of both the rent and a car payment, I sometimes could not pay the car note. There was no way I was going to let my little cottage escape my grasp. Eventually, the car was repossessed, though we tried to cover it with blankets in the back yard to hide it. Our old neighbors told the repossession company where we lived, so it was easy to find us. The man who picked up the car was not a friendly sort. He probably thought that I was going to yell and fuss when he took it away. I was very happy in that I had a new philosophy allowing, "whatever will be, to be," in my life. I would no longer be saddled with a $385 car payment. My burdens lightened immediately. Mark cried when they took the car away. He didn't understand that it was for the best. I would now have almost $400 each month to spend on Mark, so I felt relieved and happy.

I would sit in the yard and reflect on the mama and baby squirrels, playing and running contentedly in the yard, flipping their entire bodies to make a quick turn. I tried to find a job and worked temporarily while I looked for better employment. I met a gentleman on the bus one day and we discussed my repossessed car and student loan of over $9,000. I told him that I only had attended the school for

365

about a month, but they would not return any of my student loan. It had been hanging over my head for almost seven years. I related to him that I probably should file bankruptcy. He agreed that I should not have any outstanding debts. When asked in the bankruptcy court what were my possessions, I told the judge, "I have two tents and two guinea pigs." He just smiled, brought down the gavel, and told me that my debts were cleared. Finally, I was completely debt-free and I was never going there again.

Obtaining another job with a college, I met a woman who had worked at an airline as a flight attendant. I told her of how I always had wanted to become a flight attendant.

"Follow your dream. Become a flight attendant."

"I'm 45 years old. I don't think they'll hire me."

"They're looking for employees who are settled in their lives and responsible."

Deciding to go after my dream of a full-time career, I sent Mark to live with my sister and moved out of my little cottage. That cottage meant so much to me that I hated to leave. I cried as I left, but I knew all along that I was only there to obtain all the rest I needed to go on with my life. I now was ready to face whatever obstacles might come in fulfilling life and career.

Before I left, I had one more thing to do, and that was finally to forgive my ex-husband and go on with my life. I got down on my knees and prayed, "Lord, I thank you for Sam, and that I am capable now of doing the one thing that I thought I never would or could ever do, and that is to forgive my husband. But from this day forward, I cannot excuse what he has done, but I can… forgive him. Now that I am going on with my life and You have blessed me so, I think that it is only natural that I forgive him as You have forgiven me so many times in my life. So please, Father, now that I have forgiven him, also teach me now... to love him."

I went to the airlines for an interview and was hired. They sent me to school, and although I had lived a trying childhood which affected my grades when I lived at home, I was told that I had to earn A's and B's. Since I had a C average in school, I was afraid I wouldn't make it through their classes. I got down on my knees and prayed, "Lord, I'm going to give this one to you. I'm depending on you to help me."

When I entered the school, I met my classmates and soon found that there was one student in our class that didn't like me at all. I couldn't understand why she felt that way. The others wanted to study with me and spend time with me outside of class. I believe that this woman thought I was something that I was not, like "Miss IT". I was only there to pass and get through the classes to achieve the goal I had set for myself. For some reason, she wanted to stir up trouble for me. In class one day, we were all singing and dancing, when she grabbed my hair. Thinking it was a wig, she tried to pull it off. Since I had my hair interlocked at the time, she failed to embarrass me as she had planned. She told lies about me to my teachers and the other students, trying to alienate and isolate me. Before class one day, everyone came up to me questioning the lies that they heard. I knew I would overcome because I was in Christ. Being encouraged, I would not let her win. I kept studying and stayed pretty much to myself in order to make it through the class. All of my hard work paid off and I made it through with the grades that I needed.

Graduation day was something that I had looked forward to for a long time. Both Anna and my father showed up. They were so proud of me. Also joining me was my little son, for whom I pushed myself the most, so that I could make a better life for him. But the student that had caused me so much trouble wasn't finished with me yet. Keeping me out of pictures, eliminating me from the awards, she and my teacher tried to make my day miserable. They did not succeed, because I had reached for my goal and had achieved it with the grace of God beside me. I was so happy! All that they had done, trying to attack me and destroy my spirit, all that, didn't matter to me. I felt sorry for them, that they had to lower themselves to trying to my life. Thinking back, after the classes ended, even though I knew who the perpetrators were, I never let the instructors know. I didn't have to. Because I believed that one day they would reap what they had sown. I felt sorry for them and prayed for them. I was happy in school because I had finally received the opportunity that I had been seeking for so many years.

My life and what I could accomplish for my family and myself was now totally up to me. I could achieve anything I wanted. I went to pick up my son, moved to a new locale and found an apartment.

# Chapter 45

Once I was settled in I called Moe and told him I was flying down to see him. He said, "Cynthia, before you come I must tell you something." He paused for a few moments. "I have lung cancer and I have a year to live." I became very quiet on the phone as he went on to tell me of what the doctors recommended. He added, "Please come and see me, you have to tell me what happened in the rest of your dream."

I flew down to see him. He drove to pick me up at my sister's beauty salon. He took me back to his house. We sat at the dinner table as he described the radiation treatments and how much he wanted to give them up. He wanted so badly to live to see his sons and daughters grow up. I held him as we both cried. He pleaded for me to tell him the rest of my dream. Sobbing, I tried to tell the rest of that story. It was the most difficult time I had ever been through in my life. I told him the story but I stopped at the part where his grandchildren lay on his chest.
He looked at me and said, "I died?" "Yes, baby, you died."

I tried to explain to him that it was only a dream and it may not come true. Even though it had been three years ago, maybe he would still have time since he had quit smoking. He smiled at me and again we cried, holding each other ever so tightly.

I flew back home and about a month later I received a phone call. Moe had been told that his cancer was in remission. He was ecstatic. I told him, "See, maybe this is the first time my dreams have been wrong." I was just as thrilled as Moe. I told him that I would fly back to see him in about three weeks.

"Great, then we can celebrate."

I hung up the phone, thanking and praising God that my dream had turned out to be wrong.

I called back in a week to see how the operation had gone. He was going to have a bone marrow transplant. He told me some very sad news. He did not receive the transplant because they found that the cancer had spread. It was in his liver, stomach, and kidneys. It was all through his body. He had less than a month to live. I hung up and called the airport. I needed to be by my best friend's side, just as he had stood by mine during my nervous breakdown and by children's when they needed a father.

When I arrived, all my kids joined me as we went to his house. There we found him on the couch. He had a hat covering his baldhead because he was ashamed to show how the radiation had caused his hair to fall out.

We all hugged him, and soon we began to feel more comfortable. We began to laugh and talk. Then he tenderly looked over at me and asked me to go on a walk with him. I gazed into his sad eyes, hesitated, but then said, "Sure," with a forced smile. He took my hand and as we walked out of the door he put his arms around my shoulders. I felt choked up but I kept smiling. As we walked along hand-in-hand he stopped and hugged me. "Cynthia, why didn't you ever marry me? You were the perfect woman for me." I smiled, "There were just too many kids."

He chuckled back at me with tears in his eyes. "Cynthia, why didn't I listen to you? I love my children so much and I don't want to leave them. I love them so much."

Moe took me in his arms and squeezed me closer to him. "I'll never see my boys become men. I am so proud of them. They have brought so much joy into my life. My daughters are so beautiful and they have made me so proud by giving me wonderful grandchildren. I wish to God I had listened to you three years ago. If only I could turn back time.... I wish you would have hit me with a hammer and made me realize what I had and what I was going to lose. Hold me, Cynthia. Please hold me." We stayed wrapped in each other's arms as Moe continued to speak. "I wish you didn't have to leave. You make me feel so safe. You know how you used to preach to me, to go to church and read my Bible? I haven't gone to church, but I am reading my Bible." I smiled and gently kissed him.

Slowly, we let go of our embrace and headed back toward the house. September and I were driving back to Ohio, and it was time for us to leave. As we walked out of the house he said, "Thank you, Cynthia. Thank you, for being the greatest friend I have ever known."

"You're welcome, babe."

Trying to hold back the overwhelming tears, September and I hugged everyone and said our good-byes. Away we drove.

I knew my friend was passing away and I needed to go to him and remind him again of God's love, and how He sent His only begotten son to die on the cross for our sins. I needed to take him to church to be baptized for the remission of his sins. Camille was to get married soon and I knew that this would be the best time to fly down and take him to church.

I called and made reservations and booked September, Mark, and myself on a flight. When we arrived at the airport we checked in. Soon, an agent called my name. I walked up to the podium to get our tickets and was informed that my daughter and son's tickets were not booked with mine. I said, "That's impossible. They are traveling with me, they should be with me." The airline worker apologized but said there was nothing she could do. Then, they called two other people.

I was so upset because this had never happened to me before. I went to the ticket counter to find out if there was another flight. They told me there was another that left in two hours. I called and told the ticket agent what had happened, but I kept getting cut off. The phone was hanging up on me and no one could help me. No one knew what to do. Doors were slamming left and right. I had never in the two years of flying had so much trouble getting my family onto the same flight.

After the next flight left, when I saw we couldn't get on, I gave up. I was so upset! I called and told my daughter we would not make her wedding. I tried to explain the situation, but I was also confused as to why I was having so much trouble. Then it suddenly occurred to me, I was also going over to Moe's house to take him to church. He was going to accept the Lord and be baptized. Then I knew exactly what was going on. Satan had laid claim on his soul and was slamming every possible door in my face. I could see the Devil mocking me. I had spent years trying to get Moe baptized and he had refused and rejected the word of God. Through me, God tried tenderly to call him to his side. He had Moe now and there was nothing I, or anyone else, could do. "Here I am! I stand at the door and knock. If anyone hears my voice and opens the door, I will come in and eat with him and he with me." (Revelation 3:20) "For all have sinned, and come short of the glory of God." (Romans 3:23) Moe thought that because he was a good father and had done so much good in this world that he would get into Heaven by his works. I tried to explain to him that he could not make it to Heaven solely on his good deeds. "Not of works, lest any man can boast." (Ephesians 2:8 & 9)

At two in the morning I lay in my hotel room. My daughter, Camille called. I answered the call only to hear screaming, "Mom, Dad's dead! The only man I have ever known to love me like a father, and I didn't even have the courage to go to his side." Camille sounded very remorseful. I could only sit on the phone with tears streaming down my face. "My best friend is dead." Those five words were the only words I could manage to force out of my choked-up throat. I sat on my hotel bed and silently listened to my baby girl crying on the other end of the line.

After our call ended, I decided it best to call Moe's daughter. She told me about his last days. He had been re-admitted to the hospital. The doctor said that since Moe wouldn't eat, he would have to stay. They also said he could die at any moment. He told his daughter that he wanted to be home with his family. Kim said to him, "Daddy, you are going to have to sit up and eat. Once you do that, they will let you go home." Hearing this, Moe mustered up every bit of strength he had left in his corroding body, and ate. As promised, the doctors let him go home.

During his last day on Earth he fell into a coma for two hours. With his children surrounding him in his room, and his grandchildren lying on his chest, Moe peacefully passed away.

That day I finally decided to give up the sling I still was holding on to, and that was my drinking. I said, "Here, Lord, I finally can give this up to you." I'm glad that in my walk with God he looked down on me and like David's walk with Him in the Bible, He knew I was just as human and would make a lot of mistakes. He gave me time to finally realize that drinking was killing off my brain cells and was not good for my kidneys or bladder. It took my best friend's death to finally convince me how important life, my children, and God were to me. I often think of my best friend, today, as he cried out for someone to save him because he didn't want to die. There was nothing anyone could do to help him. Were the cigarettes worth his pain and suffering? Was it worth him dying at the young age of 52?

I remembered when I asked Moe almost four years earlier to stop and his response was, "Cynthia, I could get killed tomorrow in a car accident." I told him that he was right but it's apparent that a car didn't hit him and now it's too late to take back all the smoke. Nothing would have been as long and drawn out as six months of suffering and facing the inevitable fate of being told that you are going to die. Or that looking into your family's eyes and seeing their scared faces, knowing how much they need you and you want to make it all better. Getting hit by a car is different from making a life altering choice to stop smoking.

God gave us perfect bodies to care for, not to use and abuse. When we abuse our bodies with drugs and alcohol we are not only asking to die, but to become other than what God intended for us. Again I ask, is it really worth it?

# Chapter 46

While actually beginning my autobiography in 1989, when I began my new career, I was not yet ready, it was hard to focus and recollect all the bad memories. My major stumbling block was that I wanted the book to have a happy ending.

Stopping into a restaurant one night, I found that all the tables were full, so I sat at the bar and talked with an elderly couple. I began to relate my thoughts about my life and how I planned to write a book. They asked me about my new career and how I liked it. I explained to them that I loved people a great deal and enjoyed working with the public, having a general love for all humanity. I had trouble completing my book because I did not have a happy ending. I didn't want to end the book on an unhappy note since there was so much hurt, pain, and suffering in my life story. I wanted people to know that to be in Christ would bring happiness if only you believe and trust in Him. I wanted to end my book with me finding a good Christian man whom I would spend the rest of my life with in a lovely home. With a happy ending I could express many feelings about helping women who are abused. Showing women the strength that I had developed, I wanted to affect their lives by teaching them how to better their circumstances. I wanted to survive as a winner and give my readers hope for a happy ending in their lives.

The elderly gentleman informed me that what I had told him was my happy ending. I didn't understand what he meant. He explained, "You want to help someone out there overcome life's obstacles and make it in this world, knowing and walking with Christ. Writing the book will give you the ability to communicate with those men and women and children and enrich their lives, which will be your happy ending." I choked up and a tear came to my eye. I gave the man a big grin, realizing that he was exactly right. At that moment, I told the couple, "It is indeed time to write my book." I hugged them both and left the restaurant.

If you're wondering about my mother, well Anna Mae is still around. Miss Meany surfaces every now and then but these days I know how to handle her. Mae died of a heart attack and Mrs. White died in a car accident. Anna is not able to drive anymore but she's around the most. She depends on Daddy to take her where she needs to go. You just need to know the best time to catch her at home. I think Anna finally came out to stay because of the medication that the doctors prescribed. It seems to help Anna get rid of Anna Mae and Miss Meany. I love being around her now. Anna is unable to recall everything she's done in all those years and I'm glad she cannot remember. When someone brings up what happened long ago, she just looks at us. Although I wish that only Anna were here, I have to praise God that she's here at all. Just knowing I have a Mom, still alive, is truly a blessing.

My now-grown daughter, September, has been in at least 5 mental institutions and is living as a recluse. Because of her years of abuse she has not been able to find someone that is understanding and caring enough to love her. But she does have her animals, and a cute little tea-cup Yorkie named Ariel, which is great therapy for her. She's incapable of having children of her own for fear that she might abuse them as her father abused her. She tries each day to make the best out of her mere existence.

My son, Samuel, is not capable of living outside of the boundaries that he has set up for himself. He has agoraphobia. He's deathly afraid that someone is lurking out there somewhere to kill him. Even though he is a grown man, he is afraid to search out new adventures. I feel that he too, never should have children for he would only burden their minds with the fear that exists in his life today. He has to be very near his loved ones to feel secure. There is so much out here in life for him to truly enjoy, and yet, if he had all the money in the world and all the capabilities to enjoy them, he couldn't because of the abuse he too encountered as a child.

As for me, I've decided to become a motivational speaker for abused-and-battered men, women, and children. I want the Lord to use me as a vessel to teach others of my accomplishments. And hopefully, I'll be able to share my experiences with someone out there and get them to accept that his or her situation is not going to get any better, so they need to GET OUT.

Before I can end my book, before I say, "THE END," I need to establish a few basic lessons that I have learned in my trials. Times have indeed changed since my times of abuse. There are places to go when a woman has tried to commit suicide, been raped, put out on the street, or abused. There are also numbers that you can call for help. If you have been raped or abused, you need to report it, so that the courts at least can establish a record of it. There are many support groups for men, women and children. If you are being stalked, know your surroundings at all times. If you see the same person around you all the time, but he or she does not approach you, then you should approach them in a public place and make them aware that you know they are there. Then report the culprit to the police. Some stalkers never show themselves, so it's up to you to stay safe. A woman must know how to handle such situations. Abused wives, men and children, you now have the means to get the support you need. To obtain help, there are help lines and agencies ready to rectify the situation. Do not stay and continue to be abused. Don't let any woman or man kill you, either mentally or physically.

For those women and men out there who are staying with their spouses for all the wrong reasons, today I am here to implore you, "Please leave!" Life is too short and we only go around once. Save your children and yourselves. I know some of you say, "Well, he's not beating my children." Yes, he is. Every time he or she hits you, that person is hitting your children mentally and physically as well. Don't let their lives be ruined, as were my two beautiful children's. Your children have the right to live as normal human beings. That's what God and all His magnificent Glory intended for them.

If you are a woman, man, or child out there, hiding away in your house and fearing the world, be brave and come out. Join the crusade of all the people that have been abused and battered and raped. Their determination and will to live has set them free. Don't let your lifeline be taken away from you. You have so much to live for. Let us conquer life's obstacles together. For if we just hold onto each other and give one another the support we each need, we will conquer domestic violence. Keep your heads up high. Accept the fact, that this was not your fault. Build up your self-esteem. Have confidence in yourselves. Truly believe in yourselves and just like me, you can make it through. Be that beautiful stallion that I described, the one whose spirit you can never break. You can do it, if I can. Knowing that you are not the only one fighting this battle should help you to win. Let us hug each other and encourage one another.

Thank you for giving me this opportunity to share my life's struggles with you. I only hope and pray in some way that through our Lord Jesus Christ, I have been of some help in your lives. For God is my "White Room," and has always been in that room of protection, peace, and tranquility. If I didn't have my White Room, I would have died mentally at age nine and probably would have lived my life in an institution. Find that White Room in Christ where you can go for the same peace that God has always given me. Always keep a good sense of humor and always continue to smile. Say to yourself, as I have said each day, "I can make it."

**But still! I cannot say, "The End," for this is**

## "My New Beginning!"

# EMERGENCY CONTACTS FOR TODAY

<u>Telephone Numbers</u>

Child Help USA Hotline: 800-422-4453

Domestic Violence Intervention Center, Safe house Hotline: 334-749-1515 or 800-650-6522

Ending Men's Violence Network, National Organization Against Sexism: 415-546-6627

National Center for Victims of Crime: 800-394-2255

National Clearinghouse of Marital Rape, Women's History Research Center: 415-548-1770

National Coalition Against Domestic Violence: 303-839-1852

National Coalition Against Sexual Assault: 717-232-7460

National Domestic Violence Hotline: 800-799-7233

National Organization for Victim Assistance: 800-879-6682

National Resource Center on Domestic Violence: 800-537-2238

National Victims' Center: 703-276-2880 or 800-394-2255

Rape, Abuse and Incest National Network, Hotline: 800-656-4673

Safe Horizon (New York City), Domestic Violence Hotline: 800-621-4673

Survivors of Stalking: 813-889-0767

Women's Rape Crisis Center: 800-489-7273


Domestic Violence Resources Page: www.igc.org

End Violence Against Women: www.endvaw.org/

Family Violence Awareness Page: www.famvi.com/

Family Violence Prevention fund: www.fvpf.org

National Domestic Violence Hotline Resources
List: www.feminist.org/911/crisis. html

National Child Abuse Network: www.yesican.org/

The Clothesline Project: www.cybergrrl.com/planet/dv/orgs/cp

United Nations "Womenwatch" (global status of
women): www.un.org/womenwatch/

## RESOURCE PAGES
"...Deliver us from the evil one..."
(The Lord's Prayer) NAB

If you need help now, please skip to the next pages with emergency contacts!

Any section in such a book as The White Room must by its nature present only a summary list of resources available for anyone who is abused or suffering from stalking, rape, or domestic violence. Also, each listing must be considered, perhaps each year, for a possible change in the accuracy of contact information. What follows is separated into three areas: Definitions of Violence, Master Resource Areas (where you can obtain in-depth lists of information or associations), and Emergency Contacts for Today.

## DEFINITIONS OF VIOLENCE
Rape—Forcible sexual acts without or against another person's expressed consent. Often, the intent is to hurt or degrade the victim (from infants to elderly).

Spousal & Child Abuse—Mental, physical, or emotional attacks over time with a wife or husband (by the offending husband or wife), or against any child. Usually abusive relationships only become more violent. Onlookers are damaged equally.

Stalking—The following, observing, obsessive pursuit or actual "hunting" after an individual, at home or work or school or place of recreation, with evil intent. That includes telephone, mail, and Internet stalking, repeated gifts or surveillance or vandalism.

Violence (other behavior)—Harassment or fear tactics or threats or entrapments or coercive actions or plans against a person by a separate individual (husband, wife, parent, sibling, child, guardian, or others). Aggressive acts may lead to worse violence; often threatening behavior precedes a pattern of more intense violence.

## MASTER RESOURCE AREAS

www.abackans.com -- Professional counselor's site located in Akron, Ohio, very thorough, helpful, professional. Many resources, articles, background information. Actual domestic violence experts available through site.

www.dvsheltertour.org/links.html -- Safe Horizon, "Domestic Violence Shelter Tour," and Information Site. Worldwide Domestic Violence Page.

www.feminist.com/antiviolence/ -- National resources, e-mail updates, Global Anti-Violence Resource Guide.

www.feminst.org/911/crisis.html -- Feminist Majority Foundation, Domestic Violence Hotlines and Resources, other networking connections.

www.vachss.com/help_text/domestic_violence_us.html -- The Zero, U.S. Domestic Violence Resource, very complete, thorough with articles & organizations.

(Spiritual Counseling)

www.christiancounselingconnection.com/ -- Good, faith-based counseling site with many resources, links to counseling referral networks and organizations, networking.

www.his-net.com/ -- HIS-Net Christian Network and Christian Directory, many resources for healing, prayer.

www.mski.com/ -- My Sister's Keeper International, 24-hour prayer hotline, support groups, referrals to Christian counselors, Biblical education and training. Located in Boston, MA; phone: 888-988-0988.

<u>Web Sites</u>

Domestic Violence in Military:
www.defenselink.mil/specials/domesticviolence/

Domestic Violence Resources Page: www.igc.org

End Violence Against Women: www.endvaw.org/

Family Violence Awareness Page: www.famvi.com/

Family Violence Prevention fund: www.fvpf.org

National Domestic Violence Hotline Resources
List: www.feminist.org/911/crisis. html

National Child Abuse Network: www.yesican.org/

The Clothesline Project: www.cybergrrl.com/planet/dv/orgs/cp

United Nations "Womenwatch" (global status of
women): www.un.org/womenwatch/

# RESOURCE PAGES
"...Deliver us from the evil one..."
(The Lord's Prayer) NAB

If you need help now, please skip to the next pages with emergency contacts!

Any section in such a book as The White Room must by its nature present only a summary list of resources available for anyone who is abused or suffering from stalking, rape, or domestic violence. Also, each listing must be considered, perhaps each year, for a possible change in the accuracy of contact information. What follows is separated into three areas: Definitions of Violence, Master Resource Areas (where you can obtain in-depth lists of information or associations), and Emergency Contacts for Today.

## DEFINITIONS OF VIOLENCE

Rape—Forcible sexual acts without or against another person's expressed consent. Often, the intent is to hurt or degrade the victim (from infants to elderly).

Spousal & Child Abuse—Mental, physical, or emotional attacks over time with a wife or husband (by the offending husband or wife), or against any child. Usually abusive relationships only become more violent. Onlookers are damaged equally.

Stalking—The following, observing, obsessive pursuit or actual "hunting" after an individual, at home or work or school or place of recreation, with evil intent. That includes telephone, mail, and Internet stalking, repeated gifts or surveillance or vandalism.

Violence (other behavior)—Harassment or fear tactics or threats or entrapments or coercive actions or plans against a person by a separate individual (husband, wife, parent, sibling, child, guardian, or others). Aggressive acts may lead to worse violence; often threatening behavior precedes a pattern of more intense violence.

# MASTER RESOURCE AREAS

www.abackans.com -- Professional counselor's site located in Akron, Ohio, very thorough, helpful, professional. Many resources, articles, background information. Actual domestic violence experts available through site.

www.dvsheltertour.org/links.html -- Safe Horizon, "Domestic Violence Shelter Tour," and Information Site. Worldwide Domestic Violence Page.

www.feminist.com/antiviolence/ -- National resources, e-mail updates, Global Anti-Violence Resource Guide.

www.feminst.org/911/crisis.html -- Feminist Majority Foundation, Domestic Violence Hotlines and Resources, other networking connections.

www.vachss.com/help_text/domestic_violence_us.html -- The Zero, U.S. Domestic Violence Resource, very complete, thorough with articles & organizations.

(Spiritual Counseling)

www.christiancounselingconnection.com/ -- Good, faith-based counseling site with many resources, links to counseling referral networks and organizations, networking.

www.his-net.com/ -- HIS-Net Christian Network and Christian Directory, many resources for healing, prayer.

www.mski.com/ -- My Sister's Keeper International, 24-hour prayer hotline, support groups, referrals to Christian counselors, Biblical education and training. Located in Boston, MA; phone: 888-988-0988.

**ORDER MORE COPIES OF <u>THE WHITE ROOM</u> TODAY!**

Additional copies of Cynthia K. Johnson's powerful autobiography, <u>The White Room</u>, can be ordered direct from your favorite book store or online at Atlasbook.com or call 1-800-Book Log. . Call today for one copy or one hundred copies for a group and get our group rate.

## The White Room

Autobiography by

Cynthia K. Johnson

$18.95 + $3.95

Shipping & Handling

Part of the work of Cynthia K. Johnson is public presentations, as a motivational speaker, to help battered women, abused children, and other victims (men, women and children) of rape, stalking, or domestic violence. The proceeds from all book sales go to her personal Christian Ministry of helping others. Ms. Johnson is available for book discussions and book signings and also for seminar, discussion groups, or presentations at your office, group, church, or casual gathering. Please contact Ms. Johnson personally with your requests, scheduling of speaking engagements, questions, or ordering of her starring autobiography, <u>The White Room</u>.

**Speaker Schedules, Fees, & Assistance:**

Cynthia K. Johnson

E-mail address

Cjohnson406@oh.rr.com

"My new beginning"

To the readers that are interested in the changes in my life since I wrote this book in 2002. My life has change tremendously. I met and married a wonderful man that doesn't like to fight or fuss. He's in the lord and bought me a beautiful home. I on the other hand have been suffering with fibromyalgia which I battle with daily. I torn my rotator cuff closing the main cabin door of an airplane and could not go back to work. So I was asked to quit. But I am very, very happy that I made that decision to leave my abusive X-Husband. Patiently I waited on the lord to mold me back into the women I use to be before I was beaten and abused. He made me humble and loving again. Not every man out there is abusive. For God blessed me with one of them. I adore him. What a wonderful life; and you can have wonderful life too. All you have to do is get in touch with a shelter or the police and leave. There are so many resources out there for you that I didn't have. Take advantage of them. Call today and ask for help!! Will be writing another book soon so keep in touch.